Bad Boy of Gospel Music

Bad Boy of Gospel Music

The Calvin Newton Story

Russ Cheatham

University Press of Mississippi / *Jackson*

American Made Music Series

Advisory Board

www.upress.state.ms.us

The University Press of Mississippi is a member of the
Association of American University Presses.

Copyright © 2003 by University Press of Mississippi
All rights reserved
Manufactured in the United States of America
11 10 09 08 07 06 05 04 03 4 3 2 1
∞
Library of Congress Cataloging-in-Publication Data
Cheatham, Russ.
Bad boy of gospel music: the Calvin Newton story/
Russ Cheatham.

p. cm. — (American made music series)

Includes bibliographical references (p.) and index.
Discography: p.
Videography: p.

ISBN 1-57806-552-6 (cloth : alk. paper) —
ISBN 1-57806-553-4 (pbk. : alk. paper)

1. Newton, Calvin, 1928– 2. Gospel musicians—
United States—Biography. I. Title. II. Series.
ML420.N478 C4 2003
782.25'4'092—dc21   2002154113

British Library Cataloging-in-Publication Data available

Contents

Acknowledgments

I am especially indebted to the subject of this book, Calvin Newton, and his wife, Joyce, who gracefully tolerated my seemingly endless requests for information, materials, pictures, and documents.

In addition, Don Butler, former president of the Gospel Music Association and an original member of the Sons of Song, provided a wealth of information during three extended interviews and patiently fielded numerous follow-up telephone calls from me. Don's cooperation was deeply appreciated, since his knowledge of southern gospel music is enormous and the insights he shared were astute and beneficial. Don was especially helpful regarding the dynamic years of the original Sons of Song.

I had a particularly memorable telephone interview with Sons of Song pianist and tenor Bob Robinson shortly before his death, and will never forget his pleasant comments recounting the good old days. Bob's son, Dr. Dan Robinson, also shared memories, pictures, and audio recordings after Bob passed away in December 1997.

Former Oak Ridge Quartet pianist and all-around good guy Bobby Whitfield provided a treasure trove of memories and materials about the period when he and Calvin were with the Oak Ridge Quartet in the early-to-mid-1950s, including pictures, audio recordings, humorous anecdotes, and a discography that was absolutely invaluable. This book would have had big gaps about Calvin Newton's years with the Oaks without Bobby's input and assistance.

In all, ninety-one people were interviewed between July 1997 and July 2002. Some of the interviews lasted only a few minutes, while others consumed hours. Several people were interviewed more than once. A few followed up with letters containing additional details or memorabilia. Unfortunately, six of those interviewed have since passed away.

The following people shared memories and insights regarding Calvin Newton, southern gospel music, and the American criminal justice system: Louise Abernathy, Don Aultman, Mike Binion, Jim Black, James Blackwood (deceased), Ron Blackwood, Jean Bradford, Charles Burke, Don Butler, Bob Cain (deceased), Shirley Hollis Cardwell, Peter Carlson, Ralph Carmichael, Johnny Carter, Walter Carter, Jack Clark, Carlos and Thelma Cook, Bill Cooley, John Crenshaw, Glatta Davis (deceased), Ralph Davis, Arthur Dillon, Sammy Easom, Marie Farmer, Livy Freeman, Bill Gaither, Polly Grimes, Dr. James Goff, Jr., Hilton Griswold, Jimi Hall, Jake Hess, Warren Holmes, Special Agent (retired) Ronald House, Harvey Hudson, Josephine Vickery Huffman, Richard Hyatt, Parnick Jennings, Jimmy Jones, Nora Karasik, Charles Key, Dolly Keeling (deceased), Jerry Kirksey, Lee Kitchens, Eva Mae LeFevre, Mosie Lister, Faith and Larry McCoy, Gary McSpadden, C. P. Mathews, Wallace Nelm, Ruby Nelson, Calvin Newton, Jackie Newton, Joyce Newton, Wes Newton, Rosie Newton, Ron Page, Roy Pauley, Dean Powell, Joe Price, Mary Ann Price, Tom Probasco, Jerry Redd, Marshall Roberson, Bob Robinson (deceased), Dr. Dan Robinson, Reverend Charles Riggs, Don Romine, Tilford Salyer, Cecil Scaife, James Sheets, Henry Slaughter, Bill Smith, Gordon Stoker, Sybil Graham Sutton, David Taylor, Jeanette Cheatham Taylor, Bob Terrell, Jay Thompson, Wally Varner, Mark Waits, Billy Warren, Bob Weber (deceased), Lily Fern Weatherford, Ben White, Bobby Whitfield, Rae Roberson Whitley, Debbie Williams, Earle Williams, and L. D. "Little David" Young.

I want to thank the staff, faculty, and administration at Cumberland University, where I teach, for their assistance, particularly secretary Joyce Reese and librarian Michelle Noel.

My father and stepmother, Eugene and "Boots" Cheatham, were especially supportive of me during the preparation of this book, and I profoundly regret that both died before it could be finished.

I am tremendously beholden to prize-winning music historian Dr. Charles K. Wolfe, who encouraged me to write the book and University Press of Mississippi to publish it.

I benefited from the advice and counsel of two outstanding editors. Craig Gill, editor-in-chief at the University Press of Mississippi, guided the book expertly through its various stages and patiently endured my blizzard of pesky e-mails with stoicism and equanimity. The editor of the American Made Music Series, Dr. David Evans, provided a meticulous review and critique of the manuscript, which, in my opinion, resulted in a much better book.

This book is dedicated to my wonderful wife of almost twenty years, Sherry Tidwell Cheatham, who supported me wholeheartedly throughout the project, even when it called for big sacrifices on her part.

Prologue

Alexandria, Indiana, 1994

On the video, a group of gospel music singers, many of them senior citizens, a few of them legends, have just concluded a heartfelt rendition of "The Old Rugged Cross," one of the most popular hymns of the twentieth century. The room is filled with emotion. Some have their eyes closed in prayer, while others seem lost in somber reflection. Written by a Methodist minister, this powerful song recounts a tale of suffering, shame, and lost sinners. It seems the perfect foreshadowing for the story about to be told. A handsome sandy-haired man, now standing, clutches a microphone expertly, just as he has done hundreds of times previously. As the song ends, with the words "and exchange it some day for a crown," he begins speaking softly in a smooth tenor voice: "When I was in high school, my daddy was a 'Holy Roller' preacher and I was a boy soprano. So, I got beat up every night—I did." A sprinkling of smiles and light chuckles occur in response to the mention of "Holy Roller" preachers and getting beat up every night. The speaker continues, raising the index finger of his right hand into the air. "So, I said, 'I got to stop this; this is killing me.' So I learned how to box. Suddenly, nobody bothered me." The man's eyes light up and his voice quickens. "I could sing as high as I wanted to." The audience, composed entirely of entertainers, are now listening in rapt attention, even those who know how the sad story ends. The leader of the group, who is smiling, plays soft tones on the piano as the man continues to tell what is obviously the story of his life.

"So, then, somebody said, 'Cal, you can sing. I want you to sing in my quartet.' So, I thought, 'Well, I know how to make it; all I got to do is be tough.'" (The statement is illuminating, for it reveals how at an early age a young man learned to cope with the world: through fighting and rebellion.) He adds, in a voice now quavery and uncertain, "Thought I could handle it by myself, you know. And in the process I alienated most of you people that I love." At this point, the man, although surrounded by people, feels alone and vulnerable. Yet, throughout his life, he has never been anything less than candid, and he's holding nothing back here, either; he's laying bare a soul scarred by himself and others.

The booming reassuring voice of Bill Gaither, the man seated at the piano, can be heard saying what others felt—"God bless you, brother." But there were probably a few who wanted to "amen" the part about the speaker having alienated people, for he had been good at that.

While he speaks, various photographs are shown: a happy eleven-year-old boy wearing a suit and clutching a Bible; a serious young man in boxing trunks; a proud teenager who is a member of the world-famous Blackwood Brothers Quartet; a young adult member of the Oak Ridge Quartet, the forerunner of the popular Oak Ridge Boys. The final photograph shows a young man in a Hollywood recording studio with two other young men, making an album that changed the course of southern gospel music. All are pictures of the speaker at various stages in his life; however, they capture only the highlights of that life. Other pictures, taken when there were numbers under his chin, weren't shown.

The camera returns to the speaker, who now lowers his head, knowing things are about to become unpleasant. The humor vanishes and the man's story turns poignant. He says, using a boxing metaphor, "I've wanted to get back with you guys for the last thirty years, but nobody would give me a corner. And I don't blame you, because you were afraid." He quickly adds, "You were not afraid of me physically; you were afraid I might mess up."

"Well, I did mess up," he says emphatically. "In a prison cell in Atlanta, Georgia, where not only did I have my friends alienated from me, but my family—I was helpless to help them." He doesn't say so, but being separated from his family and powerless to help them was the lowest part of his life, a life that if charted would show a zigzag of stratospheric highs and unfathomable lows.

He mentions that Jake Hess came to see him in prison, and the camera shows Jake staring warmly and intently at him. The man's friendship with Jake goes all the way back to the 1940s when the two young singers were so hungry they stole peaches. Jake stood by the speaker when most other gospel singers abandoned him. Jake's name was the first one signed on a petition to get the man out of a Tennessee prison. Jake's expression is one of pride for his headstrong but lovable friend. The man turns and says, "I love you, Jake."

"I saw a guy killed every week for thirty-two months in prison," he says, exaggerating the number of persons killed but not the time served, almost three years in perhaps the toughest prison in America, a period when the institution was totally out of control. Bodies that had been stabbed or set on fire were carried out on gurneys so regularly that it must have seemed like every week. Things were so bad there that congressional hearings were held to try and determine how organized crime had seemingly wrenched control from prison officials.

Reflecting on a lifetime of mistakes and misdeeds, he shakes his head sadly and laments, "Thirty years of my life that I could have been singing gospel music—because I messed up—is gone now. I'm almost sixty-five." Sixty-five? His youthful looks, energy, and vitality give him the appearance of someone in his mid-to-late forties. He looks great, which is amazing, considering his long history of substance abuse.

Trying to make sense of his past, he explains, "When I started out, my dreams and aspirations were as great as anybody's in the world." His voice trails off, leaving the listener to conclude that his dreams along the way evaporated into illusions and finally disillusionment. His life somehow got away from him, and he paid dearly, being imprisoned by the government and banished from gospel music. The latter may have hurt more than the former.

Yet if he was banished, why is he now being featured on a popular video? He answers by saying, "One day I wrote Bill a letter and said, 'Bill, nobody ever asks me to sing. Nobody ever asks me to come to a singing. Nothing.' That man truly forgave me." He motions with his head towards Gaither. "You know the bible says to forgive is to reinstate. That's hard to do," he says. "*That's hard to do!*" The audience nods, yes, it is hard, but yes, Gaither did, and we do, too.

He continues with a few more brief remarks, including asking the audience if they know that there are angels. The camera shows Roger McDuff nodding in agreement. "I know there's one, and I bet there's more than one," the man says. (A wag would probably say that he needed an entire angel band to look out for him, given his wildness. There would have been lots of overtime, for sure.)

Regaining his composure, he says with a flourish, "I love you all." Turning to Gaither he asks softly, "You want me to sing?" Bill Gaither's response is yes. What follows is a stunning rendition of "Hide Thou Me," which leaves the audience amazed at the man's superlative voice.

Calvin Newton's testimony and subsequent solo on the Gaither video *All Day Singin'* capture the essence of a remarkable man and his incredible story. This book presents the story again, with additional details, insights, and perspectives. It tells of a handsome, talented, charismatic entertainer who, through sheer self-destruction, squandered a golden opportunity to become a legend in gospel music. He was truly gospel music's prodigal son, mimicking the young man from the biblical parable who "wasted his substance on riotous living." And, like the prodigal son, he was ultimately welcomed back by a forgiving patriarch, and later honored by the profession from which he had been exiled.

Many who are knowledgeable about southern gospel music are aware of Calvin Newton's problems with drug abuse and crime, yet few, if any, truly understand the forces that compelled him to behave in such a dysfunctional and self-destructive manner. This book attempts to provide the reader with an understanding of why he did the things he did, and why he was the way he was.

While portions of the book relate episodes of great unhappiness, it is ultimately a story of the triumph of the human spirit, revealing how in moments of bleak despair and seemingly endless adversity, a man's unconquerable will, coupled with the support and devotion of a strong, loving wife, enabled him to conquer or at least subdue the inner demons that he had grappled with throughout his life.

Calvin Newton is best known as a talented gospel music singer, and a good portion of this story is devoted to chronicling his experiences in that profession. However, Calvin was exiled from gospel music for most of his adult life, and much of this book covers his struggles off stage and out of the spotlight. Unlike many of his colleagues whose lives were firmly embedded in gospel music, Calvin traveled in a number of realms and had significant experiences in other endeavors, including stints singing popular, country, and rock and roll music as well as extended periods having little, if anything, to do with music.

In addition to being a biography, *Bad Boy of Gospel Music* is a candid, behind-the-scenes look at southern gospel music during its heyday—the late 1940s through the mid-1960s—revealing that beneath the facade of smile-a-while/sunny side/happy faces, there was an underworld of cutthroat competition, business chicanery and threats, promiscuous sex, adultery, and rank hypocrisy. This book is by no means an indictment of the profession, but attempts to take a more balanced, objective, and critical view than previous books on the subject.

As this is written, Calvin Newton is seventy-two years old and in remarkably good health for someone his age; he is also intelligent and articulate. He has, however, suffered two mild strokes that have caused memory loss, and his long-term memory has been affected by the mere passage of time. His recall is additionally hampered by the fact that he has never been detail oriented; instead, he is a classic extrovert—someone who has spent his life participating in events rather than standing off to the side observing them.

Consequently, much of what is recounted in this book is the result of a synthesis of information from numerous sources. For that reason, the book is primarily related in the third person, although the subject—Calvin Newton—willingly participated in the project and was the main source of information. However, the author assumes complete responsibility for all statements, representations, and depictions herein, and anyone taking issue with any portion of it should do so with me, not Calvin Newton.

I wrote this book for several reasons. One is that I find Calvin Newton to be an extraordinary person who has lived an unusual and highly interesting life, worthy, in my opinion, of being memorialized. In addition, I feel that he has never been fully recognized for the contribution he made to southern gospel music, primarily through the tremendous influence he exerted on individuals and groups who later dominated the field.

Finally, my interest in Calvin Newton goes back to his appearance with the Sons of Song in my hometown when I was a teenager. Their incredible, mesmerizing concert that day—particularly Calvin's performance—remains one of my most salient and cherished childhood memories. I subsequently learned that countless others who saw Calvin during that period were similarly impressed. Seeing the Gaither video rekindled that memory, and, more than that, filled me with a resolve to share his story with others. Here it is—I hope you enjoy it.

Bad Boy of
Gospel Music

1. Ancestors

"Jails, penitentiaries and ropes are yawning for them . . ."

Newton is an English name, and a most prestigious one at that. Sir Isaac Newton is considered by many to be the greatest scientist of all time. Grade school children the world over have been taught that Sir Isaac's discovery of the law of gravitation came to him as an epiphany, when an apple fell from a tree and struck him in the head: what goes up must come down. Another Englishman, John Newton, composed one of the best-known anthems to the power of God's mercy—"Amazing Grace." Calvin Newton is related to both, according to several family members who traced their ancestry.

Calvin's cousin, the late Dolly Keeling, was the unofficial family historian. Over the years she amassed volumes of handwritten notes, letters, newspaper clippings, photographs, and official records attesting to births, marriages, and deaths in her large and unusual family. Dolly's memory was keen, too. She recalled personal experiences as well as stories handed down to her from older relatives about family saints and sinners whose behavior ran the gamut from fighting to praying, drinking to abstinence, and killings to conversions.

Consulting both her written records and her memory, Dolly Keeling recalled, "James Newton moved to Kentucky from Virginia in the early part of the 1800s, bringing his wife and fifteen kids. He bought forty thousand acres, which was almost three full counties. Some of us went down to see the area one time and it was beautiful." James Newton was Calvin's great-great-grandfather. Dolly was asked what happened to all the land.

"Well, I suppose when you parcel it out among fifteen kids, and then they divide it with their kids and so on, you'd wind up with each person getting a plot of land the size of a postage stamp," she said, laughing.

According to Dolly, James Newton settled in Hancock County, located in northwest Kentucky. Calvin's great-grandfather, Jacob Hardin Newton, was born there in 1844, and Calvin's grandfather, William Edward Newton, was born in Hancock County in 1870. Like many others in the rugged Kentucky countryside, Ed Newton engaged in farming, coal mining, and serious hell raising.

"When they laid out Ed for burial they said he had scar tissue from the top of his head to the bottom of his feet," said Dolly. Ed fought with knives and obviously so did his adversaries. "He was the devil when he was a sinner; I mean, an out-and-out devil, except to his family. Most of the trouble he got into was fighting and drinking," recalled Dolly. "Down in Kentucky it was a thing when you took a crop in or a load of lumber to town, you drank and you got drunk. Many times Ed would come back with his brother-in-law and they'd be racing on horses, beating one another with horsewhips. Ed was wild and had no fear."

The brother-in-law, Eugene Phillips, was cut from the same cloth. An area newspaper, the Owensboro *Daily Messenger*, reported that in 1903 Phillips shot Marshal John Guess in the knee with a shotgun after Guess had ordered Phillips to halt. Lying on the ground, Guess returned fire with his revolver, killing Phillips. Guess subsequently had to have his leg amputated at the knee. Guess had been trying to serve a warrant on Phillips for aggravated assault for having struck a blacksmith in the head with the blacksmith's own hammer. The newspaper account stated, "Ordinarily he [Phillips] was a peaceable man, but when drinking he was a terror."

Calvin's cousin-in-law, Rosie Newton, yet another family genealogist, reinforced the newspaper's observation: "You definitely did not want to say the wrong thing to them when they were drinking, and most of them did drink."

Following the Phillips shooting, the *Daily Messenger* later carried this account of Ed Newton: "December 13, 1905. Ed Newton of Victoria was badly carved in the face by William Shores on Tuesday evening of last week, while returning home from Cloverport. They delivered tobacco here and are said to have gotten under the influence of liquor, the cutting being one of the results. Dr. Frymere of Patenville was called in to dress Newton's wounds."

Ed Newton, Calvin Newton's paternal grandfather, had an older brother, Dora A. Newton, who was apparently the worst of the worst. A January 9, 1890, article in the Breckinridge *News* reported in headlines: "Sam Steel shoots Dora Newton in the breast and kills him instantly, the tragedy the result of a drunken spree—the homicide surrenders himself to be tried." According to the newspaper account, Dora Newton and a few others got drunk after work and began swearing and behaving in a manner that was offensive to women and children. When they refused to stop being rowdy, J. R. Steel, Dora Newton's employer, went to get his brother, Sam, to help him restore order. The men came back with guns and confronted Newton and the others. Unimpressed with the show of force, Dora Newton reached for his knife and then made for J. R. Steel. Seeing this, Sam Steel shot Newton in the chest, killing him instantly.

The Breckinridge *News* had no sympathy at all for Dora Newton or his drinking buddy, John Allen Smith, stating that both were bad men, then adding, "Newton was especially desperate and Smith is said to be a member of the family of Smiths who so foully murdered Isham Anderson a year or two ago." Warming to his task, the writer continued, "The neighborhood in which the killing occurred is a peculiarly murderous one. Many of the people seem to be no more than half-civilized, the church and the school-house and their uses being almost unknown."

On January 15, 1890, the Breckinridge *News* reported that the evidence against Samuel Steel in the examining trial or inquest was insufficient to hold him for further trial. Then the paper declared, "[W]e sound this note of warning to the lawless element of Pincheco. Their lawless conduct will be suppressed and that effectually and speedily. The surrounding law abiding communities have become tired of the lawlessness in Pincheco and intend to tolerate it no longer. There is a law in this and Hancock Counties and these fellows can no longer evade responsibility to it. The good people of the two counties of Hancock and Breckinridge propose to have no more foolishness out there. They will not be allowed at their pleasure to get drunk and 'take the country.' *Jails, penitentiaries and ropes are yawning for them* [emphasis added] and if these outbreaks continue short shrift will be made in ridding the country of those in the neighborhood who recognizes no law or society but their own evil minds."

On December 8, 1891, Ed Newton married Mary Elizabeth "Mollie" Spencer, a deeply religious young woman whose family were devout members of the Church of God. Mollie Spencer was undoubtedly instrumental in eventually bringing positive change to Ed's life. Rosie Newton remarked, "Ed got saved and became one of the best people in town. They said that the lawmen celebrated." Ed and Mary's union produced six children: four boys, Emmett, Ancel, Roscoe, and Leonard, the baby, and two girls, Mina and Bessie.

Dolly Keeling observed, "Calvin's dad and uncles were all hell raisers when they were young. They were all coal miners, too. Emmett was the oldest and he was just like the rest of them. He fought; he was the sheriff, he beat up and got beat up. Then when they got in the church, they were the best Christians you'd ever want." All four of the boys became Pentecostal preachers. Emmett dropped dead in the pulpit in the midst of a sermon.

Dolly continued, "The next brother was Ancel. He wasn't much of a brawler like the rest was, he was the sissy. That's what they called him. He was a minister, too, and got into preaching earlier than the other boys did. The next boy was Roscoe, my dad. He was a hell raiser, too. He wasn't scared of the devil himself. But he became a preacher when he was young. He worked in the mines first and he was a Church of God preacher like the rest of them. I didn't go to his services; they were before I was born, but I remember some of the old ones talking about him even today. They said the minute he walked in the room you could feel—not see—but *feel* his spirit. He was that kind of person. Calvin's dad, Leonard, was the baby and turned out to be a great guy. He worked in the mines and became a minister just like they were, but he got educated and had doctor before his name. He became the Church of God's Illinois state overseer for the YPE. Calvin's mother came from a real religious family."

Like many others living in northwest Kentucky during that period, Ed Newton moved his family to southern Illinois around 1915, to work in the coal mines that proliferated in that area. Ed's boys worked in the mines, too, including Leonard, who became known as "Boots," because of the child's fondness for walking around in his dad's oversized shoes. Leonard had been born in 1906.

In August 1926 Leonard Newton married a young woman from a highly religious family, just as his father had done. Irene Richard was the daughter of Luther Richard, a highly respected minister in the Church of God. The two commenced their life together in West Frankfort, Illinois. Soon thereafter, they began a family. A girl was born, then a boy.

2. Big Boy

He was the second of three children born to Leonard and Irene Newton. His parents named him Wesley, in honor of the prominent British theologian John Wesley. As it turned out, the Wesley he should have been named after was John Wesley's musically talented brother, Charles. The infant's father, a staunch conservative, chose Calvin for the middle name, after the tight-lipped Republican president Calvin Coolidge. Wesley Calvin Newton was subsequently called Calvin or Cal.

Hospital births were rare in those days, and he was born at home, as most babies were. The midwife, noting his size, dubbed him "Big Boy," in contrast to his older sister, Lenora, who had been delivered two years to the day earlier, and whom the midwife had nicknamed "Tiny." The names were appropriate, because, for the rest of their lives, Big Boy would overshadow Tiny, to the older sister's regret, hurt, and anger. The term "Big Boy" was somewhat fashionable in the 1920s and was typically uttered with insouciance, as in "Hey, *Big Boy*, who do you think you are?"

Another girl, Glatta, was born two years later, completing Leonard and Irene Newton's family. Lenora had been born in 1927, Calvin in 1929, and Glatta in 1931.

Calvin's birth date is easy to remember, for his entry into the world came only the day before the beginning of America's darkest period. He was born on an uneventful Monday that was followed by what historians refer to as "Black Tuesday"—October 29, 1929—the day the stock market crashed, precipitating financial ruin and sudden and enduring poverty for most of the nation for more than a decade. There is perhaps a certain irony in the timing of the two events.

While the Newtons quietly celebrated the birth of a son, others through-out America were experiencing profound despair over their instantaneous financial ruin; some of the more desperate shot themselves or jumped out of windows. The Wall Street crisis soon affected millions of Americans who lost a lifetime of savings through bank failures.

The Newtons were caught up in the tide of dark events, and, like most others, they became well acquainted with privation and hardship. The Newtons were poor but never went hungry, and they always had decent albeit inexpensive clothes. Because of Leonard Newton's fierce commit-ment to his family and his stout work ethic, they kept their heads above water. He worked in the mines, tended a garden, milked his cows, and slaughtered a hog each fall for meat.

The town where the Newtons lived, West Frankfort, Illinois, is located in the southern portion of the state, an area of eleven counties known as "Egypt" or "Little Egypt." It was given the name in the 1820s and 1830s when those who lived north of the area journeyed south to buy corn and seed, just as the sons of Jacob "went down to Egypt to buy corn," accord-ing to the forty-second chapter of Genesis. Several southern Illinois com-munities had biblical names: Cairo, Palestine, Lebanon, Mt. Carmel, Eden, Goshen, Olive Branch, and Herod.

Most of the people who lived there in the early twentieth century had come from the Carolinas, Tennessee, and Kentucky before and immedi-ately after the Civil War. Little Egypt was rich in coal deposits, which had precipitated the migration to the area. The coal from Franklin County, where West Frankfort is, had the reputation of being a high-energy fuel. West Frankfort was home of the Old Ben coal mine, one of the largest in the world, with some of its seams located three and a half miles down in the ground. Leonard Newton became familiar with the deepest recesses of Old Ben.

As word of the coal boom spread, Italians, Czechs, and Poles, West Indians, and African-Americans joined the Anglo-Saxon and Scotch-Irish southern strain that had already settled there. According to one account, West Frankfort, with piles of coal slag stacked high to the very edge of the municipal limits, resembled a town under siege. Author Darcy O'Brien stated that at night, the coal dust from the piles sometimes ignited spontaneously, lighting the air with a strange orange flicker. Ravaged by industry, much of the pockmarked landscape in Little Egypt was grim and austere.

Coal mining has always been hazardous. Toxic gas, cave-ins, explosions, and human error posed risks in which any forewarning of an accident was unlikely. Anyone surviving these perils was usually rewarded with emphysema, resulting from years of breathing coal dust. The inherent dangers made it an occupation that seemed to attract a rowdy element. Many of those who lived in Little Egypt were every bit as rough and tumble as some of the Kentucky Newtons.

Observing the behavior of those who lived in the area, humorist Will Rogers told a reporter for the Marion *Daily Republican* in 1926: "There's not a lot of murderers and cutthroats in southern Illinois. They are real people, congenial and hospitable. But instead of being a lot of committees, fussing and arguing, calling each other names, they just shoot it out if it's necessary." Rogers made light of a situation that in reality wasn't funny— lawlessness and violence permeated the area. The Ku Klux Klan was prominent, and in some quarters was actually welcomed as a source of social control. Criminal gangs openly flaunted the law, robbing banks and manufacturing bootleg liquor that was sold in roadhouses also featuring gambling and prostitution.

The best-known group of outlaws was the infamous Charlie Birger gang, fearless desperados equipped with Thompson submachine guns and Browning automatic rifles. It was said of Charlie that what he did best was rob and kill people. After years of blatant disregard for the law, Birger was hanged in 1928 for killing a state trooper and his wife. Execution day pictures revealed that Charlie was a sport about it, smiling all the way to the gallows, even remarking, "It's a great day to be alive," just before the noose was placed around his neck.

Labor strife also contributed to bloodshed in southern Illinois. The infamous Herrin Massacre of June 22, 1922, claimed the lives of twenty strikebreakers, killed by miners whom they had replaced. None of the perpetrators was convicted of any crime, despite the fact that many prominent Americans—including General John J. Pershing, former president

Theodore Roosevelt, and President Warren G. Harding—denounced the crime as "wholesale murder," "atrocious," and "butchery . . . wrought in madness."

Children growing up in southern Illinois accepted violence as the accustomed manner of resolving disputes. Calvin's childhood friend Don Romine recalled, "Me and Calvin were pretty good with our fists and used to get in fights all the time. The entire neighborhood was touchy like that."

Leonard Newton's wife, the former Irene Richard, was from Copper Hill, Tennessee, close to where the Church of God began in 1886. Irene's people belonged to the Church of God, a group who came to be called "Holy Rollers," for the spirited fervor of their religious services. Her father, Thedus Luther Richard, said to be the first traveling evangelist for the Church of God, journeyed by horseback to bring salvation to the masses. He was accompanied by a song leader, a man whose name would become extremely well known in southern gospel music—Otis McCoy.

Like most wives of that era, Irene kept busy with housekeeping and her children. In addition, she devoted an inordinate amount of time to religious activities, praying and Bible reading at home, attending church every time the doors swung open for worship. She was a petite, attractive woman with a sweet but sometimes forceful disposition.

Undoubtedly influenced by his wife and father-in-law, as well as by his own father and brothers, Leonard Newton was not only saved as an adult but also felt a call to the ministry. He discovered he had a fine baritone voice, and the people at church encouraged him to lead the singing, which he did.

During Calvin's grade school years, his father continued to labor in the mines but began preaching on weekends. In those days, untrained jackleg preachers were commonplace: they would just grab a Bible, jump behind the pulpit, and start ranting and raving. Leonard Newton knew about them; he'd seen them all his life, and that was not the way he wanted to preach. So, at night, despite being fatigued from coal mining, he pursued a correspondence-course study of the Bible. "He'd work in the mines all day and come home at night and study until he fell asleep, often snoring with a book in his hand," Calvin recalled. Nonetheless, Leonard Newton persevered in his studies. Upon completion of the course he was awarded a doctorate of theology and thereafter became known and referred to as Dr. Newton.

As a minister, Leonard Newton was required to move frequently to various churches in southern Illinois hamlets. Johnson City, Chancey, Carrier Mills, and Christopher were all stops along the way for the Newton family during Calvin's childhood. Some of the parsonages they lived in left much to be desired. In one of them, the floor was so slanted that when they went to bed, they had to be sure the logs were wedged into the fireplace and would not roll onto the floor and start a fire. In another house, the kitchen got so cold in the winter that Calvin's mother would put bread and food in the refrigerator to keep it from freezing.

The constant moving was difficult for the children, especially Calvin. Just as Lenora and Glatta were starting to make friends, Leonard would load up the family belongings and move. The two sisters would have to start all over, getting acquainted with students and teachers. But it was different for a young boy in a new environment. Before he could make any friends he had to prove himself, and that was usually done with fists. When the family moved, he'd have to fight again. But it was more than just being the new kid on the block that made frequent fights inevitable for Calvin.

First, he was a preacher's kid, and not only that, but a "Holy Roller" preacher's kid. Children growing up in Little Egypt were no different from those anywhere else—they could be cruel and insensitive. Many of them, and their parents as well, looked down on the so-called Holy Rollers. They viewed the Church of God as a nutty, hayseed religion in which people screamed and hopped around as if they'd been given a hotfoot. The perception by others of their religious beliefs became emotionally devastating for all three Newton children.

Unfortunately, Calvin and his neighborhood friend Don Romine had to walk past the Catholic school each day on their way to public school. When the two got to the front of the school, the taunts about their strange religion would begin. Sensing some fun, the young Catholic boys would quickly congregate around the hapless pair.

However, Calvin and Don didn't take the abuse lying down. They could have opted to go the long way around in another direction, thereby avoiding the Catholic school and the inevitable confrontation. Calvin knew how to get their goat, but it would end up in a fight, and there were always more of them. He would promise Don he wouldn't do it anymore, but, though he tried to restrain the impulse, he would always give in and call them the name they absolutely detested. After a few of their insults Calvin would yell, "Catlickers"—his epithet for Catholics—and the fight would be on.

In this holy war Calvin and Don always got beat up. One day when Calvin was pinned on his back, getting pounded, he rotated his head to avoid being hit in the face by an oncoming fist. As he turned, he spotted Romine sprinting to safety. He was disappointed that Don had deserted him but concluded that it had been the prudent thing to do. From that point on, fighting gave way to running.

Time and again, it was either submit to a beating or run away in humiliation and embarrassment. A farmer/philosopher might call it damned it you do, damned if you don't; an anthropologist would call it the fight or flight response; a psychologist would call it a mixed motive conflict; Calvin Newton called it his childhood.

But it wasn't just the Catholics and it wasn't always Calvin's fundamentalist religion that caused the fights. Calvin was small, his family was poor, and his younger sister, Glatta, was cross-eyed and thus subject to the cruel jibes of children. Calvin was fiercely protective of his baby sister and anybody who made fun of her affliction would have to fight him. He was her big brother and he protected her throughout her life, even purchasing a mobile home for her and putting it beside his house when she became sick and needed care as a senior citizen. When interviewed for this book, she—like an adoring schoolgirl—repeatedly referred to Calvin as "my brother."

There was a great deal of conflict in Calvin's childhood and it exacted a price. The continual ridicule, the frequent fights, the jokes about being poor and belonging to some wacky church eventually filled him with shame, humiliation, anger, and bitterness. More sensitive than most, he began to feel inferior to others. Wanting desperately to be liked and accepted, Calvin came to believe that the only way to achieve such a goal was to be better than everyone else. Consequently, he became a perfectionist.

Six decades later all three Newton siblings—Lenora, Calvin, and Glatta—confessed to a strong sense of shame and inferiority about their childhoods. They had grown up in a strict fundamentalist household where harsh, restrictive religious tenets were rigorously enforced (more by the mother than by the preacher-father), where females couldn't wear makeup or jewelry, and where participation in worldly activities such as interscholastic athletics or going to movies was strictly forbidden. Calvin sneaked off to a movie once and his father stormed the theater and literally marched him out by the ear.

But there were good times, too. Like many other gospel music singers, Calvin began singing in the church almost as soon as he could talk. Music was strongly emphasized in the Church of God, more so than in other denominations. Its members could rejoice in music if nowhere else, and they did.

"When I was about six years old," Calvin said, "I sang in a trio with my mother and dad on Saturday mornings on radio station WEBQ (We Entertain Beyond Question) in Harrisburg, Illinois, about thirty miles from West Frankfort. WEBQ was the only radio station in southern Illinois and everybody in the area listened to it. For me, going to Harrisburg was as exciting as going to the moon would be now. Afterwards, Dad would treat us to a meal at a local restaurant, and that was a really big deal—this was during the depression. When the waitress approached with the tray of food, I would begin singing 'Heaven Now Is in View,' and everyone got a kick out that."

Leonard and Irene Newton loved their children but, like most depression-era parents, weren't very affectionate. "I don't remember much touching at all," said Calvin. "The only time there was touching was reprimand. Dad was pretty stern. I tested him quite a bit. I don't ever remember Dad saying he loved me, but I know he did. I mean, he worked his tail off to keep food on the table."

While Leonard Newton may have been stern, he nonetheless seemed to be blessed with a certain tolerance and patience, which came in handy raising a headstrong, willful son. Both Calvin and Don Romine recalled an escapade from their youths that showed their derring-do and sense of adventure.

Hopping freight trains was an accepted practice during the thirties, when people couldn't afford more conventional forms of transportation. Calvin and Don decided to take Don's father's life savings, approximately five dollars in nickels, and run away from home. "We were going to go down to Compton, Illinois, which was a fruit-growing region, and pick fruit for a living," said Romine. They were in the fifth grade at the time. They hopped a freight and rode it twelve miles to Marion, where they jumped off, walked to a store and ate ice cream, then caught a cab home, draining the remainder of Romine's father's horde of nickels.

Arriving back home that night around eleven, Calvin told his worried father that he and Romine had been kidnapped but had somehow escaped. For a long moment Leonard Newton gazed intently at his son, and then, with relief and wry resignation, said quietly, "Go to bed, son." Romine got a lambasting from his dad.

As Calvin entered his teens he had acquired both an attitude and a reputation for rebellion and fighting. Even the bullies and troublemakers who were older and bigger began to steer clear of the kid with the great voice and the chip on his shoulder. Yet there was never a surliness about Calvin; his anger lay hidden beneath a sunny smile and an engaging charm. When he wasn't getting into trouble, he got all the choice parts in the school plays, especially operettas that had singing roles. He didn't apply himself in the classroom but was bright and made above-average grades. His conduct grades were somewhat mixed but generally commendable.

He dutifully and faithfully attended church twice on Sunday and once in the middle of the week. "At first, I thought it was a grown-up's game," recalled Calvin. "I thought it was a game because I would see people acting like they enjoyed it but I just went to sleep on the bench. I've slept on many a hard bench at church and have fallen off of a few of them. Somebody could be shouting and I'd go right on sleeping. But right away I got the idea that they were playing a game, and then I would see people doing things that weren't part of the game, but was sin." Calvin didn't spend all his time in church sleeping. When he was eleven, he was leading the singing. At that point he enjoyed singing and was good at it, but gave no thought to pursuing it as a career.

When Calvin was in his midteens, the family moved to Chicago, where his dad became pastor of the Lavergne Avenue Church of God, now one of the largest of the denomination's churches. It was here that he began to detect hypocrisy among the elders, beginning with his dad. "He'd come in smelling like smoke," said Calvin. "One time somebody asked him about it and he said he was around other people who did."

His dad's smoking seemed trivial compared to what he saw on State Street. "State Street was where all the nude shows were in Chicago," said Calvin. "I was over there one day when I saw a high-ranking official of the church come walking out of a burlesque show." Calvin's rebelliousness and anger became suffused with cynicism and suspicion. "I took the view that if you were gonna smoke, I'd smoke, too. If you were tough, I'd be tougher. It was all in the negative realm."

The Newtons lived in the basement of the Lavergne Avenue church, where the chief complaint was the strong odor of natural gas that permeated the living area; otherwise, the quarters were nice. Outside were the busy streets and sidewalks of one of the largest cities in the world. The environment was strikingly dissimilar to the small-town atmosphere found in the southern Illinois communities where they had lived previously, and for Calvin, it meant yet another major adjustment. In addition to all the other childhood problems he was coping with, the frequent moves were by now taking their toll on him emotionally. The latest one only made things worse.

By the 1940s the depression had been banished by World War II, and employment opportunities abounded. Calvin worked at night in the railroad yards that laced Chicago, unloading boxcars and supervising grown men, including two who had once worked on Wall Street. By day he attended Austin High School, a huge public secondary school with six thousand students.

At school, Calvin felt like an ant crawling among thousands of other anonymous, faceless insects. In a huge melting pot of humanity with Poles, Slovaks, Irish, Italians, Hispanics, Jews, and others, he felt like a nobody, and his feelings of inferiority and worthlessness grew daily until they erupted in an act of violence in the school hallway. "I'd injured one of my hands at work the night before and I had it bandaged up. I was walking down the hallway and somebody bumped it and I popped him with my good hand." He was suspended for fighting, and Leonard Newton, fearful of the developments he saw occurring in his angry young son's life, decided that a more sheltered, structured environment was needed.

Calvin's parents knew of a place where he would be surrounded by teachers and students who were committed to the church and the Lord. At the very least, he might stay out of trouble, they reasoned. Getting into fights and mischief in Carrier Mills was one thing; in Chicago you could get hurt, locked up, or even killed. The school the Newtons had in mind was a Church of God boarding school in Sevierville, Tennessee, known as Bible Training School. Both Calvin and his older sister, Lenora, would be enrolled there.

Bible Training School, or BTS, as it was called by teachers and students, was a high school, junior college, and school of religious education. Children of church officials were given financial aid, making it possible for those like the Newton children to attend. The school would ultimately relocate in Cleveland, Tennessee, and be renamed Lee University. The Newtons' decision to enroll Calvin in BTS was momentous and life altering. They saw it as an opportunity for their son to be exposed to the ministry; the rebellious young man might even become a preacher. Leonard Newton, his brothers, and his father had been rounders before they became men of the cloth; it could happen to Calvin, too.

However, his enrollment in Bible Training School had a different outcome. It turned out to be the first step on the path of a career in gospel music, for the Newtons were sending their son to one of the finest gospel music finishing schools in the world.

3. Bible Training School

"Son, you can sing."

In his book *Like a Mighty Army*, Dr. Charles Conn stated that the origins of the Church of God can be traced to the hills of east Tennessee, where, in 1886, it began as a group of holiness separatists, pre-dating what came to be known as the Pentecostal movement by a decade. Led by Baptist preacher Richard Spurling, the small group had become dissatisfied with conditions in the area's established churches. Specifically, they felt that denominations with which they were familiar were spiritually dead and that renewal and reformation were necessary. Their disenchantment was a continuation of the fundamentalism/modernism split that had occurred during the first part of the nineteenth century.

The Church of God became part of the modern Pentecostal movement, growing as a spirit-filled Los Angeles revival meeting helped spread the word in the early twentieth century. By 1918 the church had achieved sufficient size to justify the establishment of an institution to educate and train members, particularly young people contemplating a religious career, such as preaching, directing music, mission work, or church administration. The Bible Training School was established in Cleveland, Tennessee, with one teacher.

From its very inception the Church of God, as well as other Pentecostal churches, realized the power of music to inspire worship and spread the message. In fact, the church was mindful of the oft-repeated statement that Charles Wesley sang as many souls into the kingdom of God as his brother John preached in. Recognizing that a music ministry could be a tremendous gospel outreach, church officials decided to establish a strong music program at Bible Training School. To that end, in 1934 they recruited a personable and outgoing instructor who had graduated from the Vaughn Conservatory of Music to head the music department.

His name, which would later become as well known in gospel music circles as Babe Ruth's in baseball, was Otis McCoy. Under McCoy, Bible Training School students could study musical instruments and voice. The school became a hotbed for southern gospel music—in essence a finishing school for many who went on to successful careers in that field. Years earlier McCoy had been song director for T. L. Richard, Calvin's maternal grandfather, when the pair were circuit-riding evangelists for the Church of God. A strong association developed between Holiness/Pentecostal churches and gospel music. Many gospel music singers had attended Pentecostal churches and had grown up singing music that was by turns spirited and soulful.

Gospel music falls into two broad categories along racial lines—black and white. Traditional white gospel music—the type heard at the all-night singings—is more commonly known as southern gospel music. Many assume that white gospel music is simply an extension or an outgrowth of black gospel, but that isn't so, according to music historian James Goff, Jr., who maintains that, while the two types of music frequently crossed paths, they developed independently.

Southern gospel music traces its origins to the shape-note singing schools and publishing companies that appeared in the nineteenth century. Music historians give the date of the birth of southern gospel music as May 1910 when James D. Vaughn, a music publisher, formed a quartet to tour and promote his songbooks. Thus, by the 1920s southern gospel music was rapidly developing at the same time and rate as the Church of God and Pentecostalism. With Vaughn graduate Otis McCoy as Bible Training School's first music director, the ties between the Church of God and southern gospel music became even closer.

By the time Calvin Newton got to Bible Training School in the mid-forties, Alf and Urias LeFevre and Fred C. Maples had all matriculated there and benefited from McCoy's excellent instruction and fine guiding hand. The LeFevre brothers would form the legendary LeFevre Trio with Urias's wife, Eva Mae. Maples became a mainstay of the Harmoneers Quartet. Future graduates who would become southern gospel music stars included Jerry Goff and Donny Sumner.

Bible Training School's commitment to religious music is apparent from a review of the composition of the faculty. In the 1946–1947 school yearbook, the *Vindauga*, eight of the twenty-five faculty members shown are music instructors. At BTS a student could study music theory, composition, voice, keyboards, string instruments, and other subjects taught in large music departments.

In 1937 Bible Training School moved its location to Sevierville, Tennessee, which sat at the foot of the Great Smoky Mountains. Often ringed by clouds, the Smokies loomed in stately magnificent splendor, an inspiring sight of natural beauty. Fresh from the grimy steel-and-concrete jungle of Chicago, Calvin was in love with the school and its scenic beauty before he had set his luggage down. In 1946 before the glut of tourist attractions that now blight the Sevierville/Pigeon Forge/Gatlinburg area, the landscape had a rustic, pristine quality. BTS was a boarding school with students from all over the United States, but especially from nearby Georgia, North Carolina, Kentucky, West Virginia, Virginia, Ohio, South Carolina, and, of course, Tennessee. The Church of God's orphanage was later located on the Sevierville campus. Students lived in dorms, two to a room.

Bible Training School was a high school and junior college, and also had a department of religious education. The students shared a common religious heritage, and a great many had parents or relatives with professional ties to the Church of God, including Calvin and his sister, Tiny, and their cousin Deanie Newton. Since the Church of God gave scholarships to the children of ministers, music directors, overseers, and other officials, there were many preachers' kids at the school.

Tom Probasco rode the train from Lawton, Oklahoma, to attend the school and graduated in 1947. Regarding the culture of the school and the mores of the students, he said, "They had some strict rules. My parents sent me there to get me out of the worldly environment but I got into more trouble there than I did anywhere. Kids away from home are going to try their wings the best way they can, and a lot of us did." Probasco's transgressions, however, consisted only of minor mischief.

"A big majority of the kids at BTS were preachers' kids," Probasco recalled. "We lived in dorms. There were two cliques up there. There were kids whose dads were preachers with big churches, or their dads were preachers in little churches, like mine was. We all stuck together in those two groups. I told Calvin that he was in the upper group and he replied, 'That's because I was a singer,' and I guess that's right. I don't think he had the family background to be in the upper group." Actually, because of Leonard Newton's efforts, the Lavergne Avenue Church of God in Chicago rose from small, humble beginnings to lofty prominence. The church would become one of the largest in its denomination. Calvin may have been in the BTS "upper group" partly because he was a singer, but his father's status in the church hierarchy qualified him as well.

According to Probasco, Calvin always wore a white shirt and tie and hung around with the girls. He apparently made quite an impression, being voted "Most Conceited" in the school's who's who selections. Calvin scoffs at the award. "I should have won the award for 'Most Scared to Death,' because if somebody had said 'boo,' I would have jumped out of my pants, I was so insecure in those days." Calvin hid his fear and anxiety behind a big-city swagger and a confident smirk-like smile. Most of the students were from small towns and perceived the Chicago kid as more street smart and sophisticated than they. Calvin had the social skills to cloak his anxiety with apparent confidence and aloofness. He'd rather have been considered conceited than what he was: tentative and insecure.

An undersized preacher's kid, Calvin had been a target for bullies his entire childhood. He finally got his cousin Dave Whitlow to teach him how to box. Whitlow had played college football and was an all-around athlete. An eager student, Calvin applied himself diligently and learned how to put up his dukes. It came in handy at BTS.

According to Tom Probasco, the BTS girls were having a weenie roast one night when some young men from Sevierville's Frog Alley—the rough part of town—decided to intrude on the outdoor cookout and make nuisances of themselves. Word quickly got back to the dean of men that the girls were being harassed. The dean began assembling a group of male BTS students, which included a sizable contingent of World War II vets, to confront the Frog Alley boys.

"Calvin kept saying, 'Let me go, let me go, let me go,' and the dean looked at him like he was crazy cause he always wore that white shirt and tie and hung around with the girls. So, finally the dean let him go and Calvin walked up to the first guy that he saw and popped him and the guy fell like he had been shot. Calvin went on to the others doing the same thing. We later found out that Calvin had been state Golden Gloves champ in his division," said Probasco. (Actually, Calvin's Golden Gloves bouts were a couple of years in the future, but he nonetheless showed pugilistic prowess at BTS.)

In the school's rigorous religious environment, daily chapel was mandatory. At one of the assemblies Calvin was standing near the back row, singing with the others. To amuse himself, he began singing the melody in his normal range, then effortlessly jumped an octave higher. He stayed there for a verse and then came back to his usual range on the chorus. Before the tune was over, a teacher politely tapped him on the shoulder and asked to talk with him at the end of the service. It turned out to be a member of the music faculty, who told him, "Son, you can sing. You ought to get in one of the quartets here." Calvin had grown up singing in the church and usually got the top part in the school plays if singing was required. Nonetheless, he hadn't thought of himself as a singer and was both pleased and surprised that the instructor had noticed him.

Calvin liked the idea not because it would allow him to sing, but because at BTS, music was the coin of the realm, and among the students, gospel quartets enjoyed the most popularity and respect. To sing in a gospel quartet was to be a big man on campus, a status that had great appeal for a young man with an inferiority complex who desperately wanted to be liked and admired. Calvin remembered, "My main interest was I wanted to be popular."

Consequently, Calvin sought out and began singing in some of the school gospel groups. Although he could have taken private voice lessons and studied theory, harmony, and other musical subjects, he chose not to, and instead relied solely on his talent. Leroy Carver, a close friend and colleague of Otis McCoy, provided voice lessons for student quartet singers, but Calvin never took advantage of the situation. When asked how he learned to sing gospel music quartet style, he shrugged nonchalantly and replied, "We just looked at one another and knew we had to say the words at the same time." While he didn't directly avail himself of the opportunities for developing his vocal talent, he nonetheless benefited from the musical environment simply through exposure and osmosis.

Although Lee Roy Abernathy would later claim that Calvin was one of his many students, in private Abernathy declared that Calvin and Jake Hess were the only two singers who were totally resistant to his exhortations—unteachable, in fact. It could be argued that Calvin never had a formal vocal lesson in his life; he was just tremendously talented and became skilled through his performances on stage and in the recording studio.

At BTS he sang for a while in a trio with Don Aultman, who also played piano and whose father was the state overseer for the church in Kentucky. Slender and fine-featured, Aultman was more a musician than an athlete. But, he recalled, "Calvin was always wanting me to box with him. He'd promise that we'd just sort of play around and I'd put on the gloves, and he'd beat the crap out of me." After such impromptu boxing matches, Aultman got to be leery of Calvin, coming to view him as calculating and having a hidden agenda.

Calvin also sang with a group called the Victory Four, which included two World War II veterans. The top gospel quartet at BTS at the time was known as the Kingsmen Four; they sang off campus, even out of state on occasion and made money. Everyone at BTS, even the other gospel quartets, looked up to them. Like all gospel quartets, the Kingsmen Four went through personnel changes. Floridian Harvey Hudson replaced baritone

Calvin Wigley. Hudson recalled that at the end of the school year the Kingsmen Four decided to see if they could make a go of it—become a full-time gospel quartet and make a living from concerts and church appearances. Bass singer Vernon Klaudt booked the group into some church appearances in Lakeland, Florida. However, first tenor Bennie Tripplett couldn't go because he was a member of the church's orphanage, and the church was unwilling to grant him permission to travel. Jimi Hall, not only a fine singer but also an accomplished pianist, replaced Tripplett. Second tenor Lynn Smith, the group's lead singer, decided to drop out of the group, as he wanted to pursue other interests. Calvin replaced Smith.

Thus the new lineup consisted of fifteen-year-old Vernon Klaudt, two sixteen-year-olds, Calvin and Harvey Hudson, and Jimi Hall, who had just turned eighteen. In the late spring of 1947 these four left Sevierville to go to south Florida, stopping off in Jimi Hall's hometown, Rome, Georgia, for a few days. Hall's father, Elsie, was choir director for the North Rome Church of God for a number of years and at one time sang in a quartet with Wally Fowler. Elsie Hall was also a successful businessman; he owned a dry cleaners and a used car lot. Hall purchased pinstripe suits for the group so that they would have matching attire when they performed.

While in Rome the group sang at a revival with a family that would become a household name in gospel music—the Goodmans. Jimi Hall stated, "I believe Howard Goodman [Happy] was preaching at the revival and he brought Rusty and two of his sisters, Gussie Mae and Stella, to sing." From there the group proceeded to Florida. Hall recalled, "The reason we went to Florida was to sing at the Wimauma Camp Movement, which is the granddaddy of all Church of God camp meetings. After the camp meeting, we got a gig with a preacher to do a week's revival in Winterhaven. That's where Wally Varner heard about this little kiddie group singing, and he came across town to hear us."

Varner was a twenty-one-year-old World War II veteran who had just gotten out of the service. He was impressed with the Kingsmen Four and informed the group in classic understatement that he "played a little piano." The boys were impressed with Varner's flashy style and, after an audition, the curly-haired veteran was extended an invitation to join the group. Varner was considered a twofer since he also owned a new Buick. The big automobile was large enough for the quartet and their rather modest and commonplace sound equipment, which consisted of an old Shure microphone and a one-speaker sound box with a vacuum tube amplifier. According to Hudson, the group sang strictly gospel songs except for one secular tune, "Sioux City Sue," which they did because they loved the way the harmony sounded.

Calvin remembers that the group got a housesitting job. "The owner had chickens and an orange grove and told us to help ourselves to each. We drank orange juice and ate fried chicken all summer."

Within days, the group had begun making a name for themselves, and they began appearing four to five times a week at churches and in concert. They sang a few times with a local group that had become quite popular, the Sunny South Quartet.

The Kingsmen Four successfully auditioned for a morning show with a Winterhaven radio station, which gave them good exposure and the outlet they needed for bookings. A representative for Paramount pictures heard the group and approached them about a contract for singing in the movies. Cowboy movies, especially the inexpensive B-grade westerns, were quite popular at the time, and the chances for a talented group like the K4 to sing along with a Roy Rogers type were quite good. A recording contract would probably be part of the deal.

The recollections of group members vary concerning the big opportunity, but the gist of it was that the Ames Brothers were hot at the time and the talent scout wanted a group similar to them. The deal fell through when, according to Calvin, Jimi Hall's father wouldn't sign for him. Hall, however, says the deal soured when Harvey Hudson's father wouldn't allow him to go. Hudson said it was because they were all preachers' kids and none of the fathers would have signed a contract that would have resulted in their sons singing secular music in the movies. Pentecostals of that period regarded movies as worldly, not even to be watched; participating in one would be an even greater transgression.

Wally Varner's version was that the opportunity fell through because they were late mailing an acetate disk of a couple of the group's songs to

New York City. After the blown opportunity, much of the summer was gone, and, except for Calvin, the group's members decided to return to BTS. By that point, Calvin's remarkable tenor voice and Wally Varner's musicianship had been noticed by other groups in the area. The two were about to make some major moves.

4. Headed Straight to the Top

Father, give me the portion of goods that falleth to me. And he divided them his living.

—Luke 15:12

In the mid-1940s three members of the Sunny South Quartet, of Tampa, Florida, left to form their own group. The three—Lee Kitchens, Mosie Lister, and James Wetherington—were the founding members of what came to be known as the Melody Masters Quartet. Wally Varner recalled, "The Sunny South was a super, super group. When they split up the three of them got me and another guy [Alvin Tootle], and we formed the Melody Masters across town in Tampa. The Sunny South went out and got J. D. Sumner, and of course Big Chief and J. D. were both living in Lakeland, so you might say we were all one big bunch."

Soon thereafter, Mosie Lister dropped out of the Melody Masters. When he did, Wetherington called Alabama and offered the position to Jake Hess. Wetherington had met Hess previously when Hess appeared in the Lakeland area with his brothers, who called themselves simply the Hess Brothers. When Wetherington called, Hess had been singing with the popular John Daniel Quartet but had gotten into a salary dispute and been fired.

Out of work, Hess accepted Wetherington's offer, advising the tall bass singer that he would be there in a few days. Secure with Wetherington's offer of employment, Hess took a leisurely southward journey, stopping off and visiting with friends along the way. By the time he got to Florida, he learned that the impatient Wetherington had hired Calvin Newton instead. Hess had no problem finding another job. He simply went to work for the Melody Masters' chief rival, the Sunny South Quartet.

Mosie Lister recalled, "When Calvin was sixteen, he had a voice like an angel." The Melody Masters were pleased to have him join them. At that time, Calvin was a natural first tenor and that was the part he sang with the Melody Masters. Lee Kitchens, later a baritone, sang the lead; Alvin Tootle was the baritone, and James Wetherington, later to be dubbed "Chief," sang bass.

The Melody Masters and the Sunny South Quartet had a friendly but competitive relationship which was intensified by the fact that the Sunny South Quartet hawked songbooks by the Stamps Quartet Company while the Melody Masters sold the songbooks of close rival Stamps-Baxter. Varner characterized the relationship of the Sunny South and Melody Masters as one of "butting heads," while J. D. Sumner stated that the two groups "fought tooth and nail for popularity in the area."

They frequently appeared together, which heightened the competition. On one such occasion, the Sunny South Quartet waited outside until the Melody Masters had built momentum on stage, then entered the building and stopped to shake hands and chat as they made their way down the center aisle, disrupting the Melody Masters' set. Another time, Frank Stamps, head of the Stamps Music Company, was visiting with the Sunny South when the two groups were performing at the prestigious Florida State Singing Convention. Sumner recalled that the Melody Masters opened the convention. "They really turned it on. They had the crowd rocking in no time." Seeing that the Melody Masters were going to be a hard act to follow, Stamps got out of his chair, set out in the direction of the electrical outlet and "accidentally" tripped over the electric cord to the public address system, causing the sound system to go dead. The Melody Masters consequently lost their momentum for the remainder of the performance. Stamps stood offstage chuckling. These and other incidents are illustrative of the highly competitive nature of gospel singing. Both Wally Varner and Calvin recall a time in Seffner, Florida, when Frank Stamps wasn't around to rescue the Sunny South. "I remember we were on the same show with Sunny South and the crowd clearly loved us," said Varner. Calvin was more to the point: "We kicked butt that night."

Although he had been perceived by his Bible Training School classmates as a streetwise kid from Chicago, Calvin was still somewhat innocent in the ways of the world. That began to change during his early days of singing professionally. While most of the young men he had sung with up to that point were staunch Christians, he was now beginning to come into contact with others who were a bit more worldly.

One night after a performance with the Melody Masters, Calvin was led through a darkened parking lot past numerous empty cars by an older, more experienced quartet singer. The two kept walking until they came upon a four-door automobile that appeared to be unoccupied. It wasn't. The older singer jerked open the door, and there in the rear seat was a woman lying on her back with her dress up around her chest, wearing no undergarments. Calvin saw that her legs were retracted and spread. The older singer nudged Calvin and chortled, "There's your date tonight, Sport."

My God, that woman is nearly as old as my mother, thought Calvin, as he surveyed her. Although attractive, under those circumstances she didn't stir him erotically or fire any passions. In fact, the woman lying there seemed pathetic, he thought. There she was, offering herself to a complete stranger. Why would a woman do that? he wondered. Calvin looked back at the older man, who was, he discovered, scrutinizing his behavior. Calvin nervously cleared his throat and asked, "What'll I do with my coat?" "I'll hold your coat," the man firmly replied. Although stunned by the suddenness of the situation and still raw with youth, Calvin nonetheless realized that this was a rite of passage, an initiation into—of all things—southern gospel music.

On that fateful night, he found making love to a promiscuous female stranger very difficult. The next time it wasn't so hard. After that, it got to be sneaky fun. Before long, he was the one leading quartet members back to the car, although none was ever as clueless as he had been. Calvin soon realized that having casual sex with adoring women after the singing was simply part of the dynamic and regarded as a perk of the business. Although he came to enjoy the easy sexual conquests, Calvin was nonetheless confused by the moral ambivalence of singing praises to the Lord on a brightened stage followed immediately by sweaty groping in the backseat of a car with someone whose name he couldn't recall the following day, if in fact he ever knew it. He was later appalled and then became cynical regarding the hypocrisy he noted among the many married gospel singers who committed adultery under such circumstances.

In addition to gospel, the Melody Masters had a number of secular tunes they performed during this period that were real crowd pleasers. Wetherington took the lead on "The Old Lamplighter" and the popular novelty tune "Smoke, Smoke, Smoke That Cigarette." Calvin also had a repertoire of secular songs he performed including "My Blue Heaven," the 1920s multimillion-seller pop tune sung by crooner Gene Austin. Calvin remembered, "One day we were singing 'My Blue Heaven' on our radio show and Gene Austin walked in and said he'd never heard it sung better." "My Blue Heaven" allowed Calvin to showcase his lyric tenor voice, as the tune is best sung in a soft, light manner.

The Melody Masters had a radio show on the Tampa/St. Petersburg station WSUN during which they could announce their upcoming appearances. The group would sing a song or two, then announce that they would be at a school or church that evening. The Melody Masters also had an arrangement with Stamps-Baxter to sell songbooks before, during, and after their performances. Quartets would split the proceeds with the publishing company. The group had all that any gospel quartet could have hoped for—talent, a songbook deal, and a radio show.

Despite all of the prerequisites for success they were nonetheless struggling financially, and any marketing consultant could have told them why: there wasn't much money to be made in southern gospel music, because the music appealed primarily to a group that didn't have any—poor whites. A large percentage of the population of southern Florida in the 1940s was composed of poor whites who picked fruit for a living and of rich Jews in Miami and St. Petersburg who weren't aware there was such a thing as southern gospel music, and wouldn't have listened had they known.

In the 1950s the Louvin Brothers preferred singing gospel music and were marketed that way by record labels for years before they finally gave up and became a country act. The reason was simple: you could earn about four times as much singing country music as gospel. In the entertainment field, nothing paid less than gospel music.

Thus, despite their talent and popularity, both the Sunny South and the Melody Masters were barely making ends meet. Then, the Melody Masters played a date in Jacksonville, Florida, with the mighty Rangers Quartet. Hovie Lister was the Rangers' pianist at the time and he was impressed with the Melody Masters' sound; also, he liked them and wanted to help them. Varner said, "Hovie's hometown was Greenville, South Carolina, and he knew we were going hungry in Tampa, so he told us, 'Why don't you go to Greenville and talk to the people at [radio station] WFBC.' He told us that we could get on there and get a sustaining show, an early morning show, then we could advertise all of our concerts."

The group discussed the idea and decided to give it a try. Lee Kitchens, conservative in manner and perhaps keen in judgment, wanted no part of such an experiment. He dropped out of the group and remained in south Florida. His place was taken by Jake Hess, who had been singing for the Melody Masters' archrival, the Sunny South.

Lister did more than just provide ideas and encouragement. He also called back home and told friends and family to go meet the Melody Masters and make them welcome. However, the opportunistic and conniving Lister had an ulterior motive behind his encouraging the Melody Masters to relocate in Greenville, South Carolina.

In his biography, *Happy Rhythm*, he admitted, "I listened to their singing on the record transcription, and they about blew me away . . . I thought to myself, 'I don't want this group in Atlanta, especially if I'm fixing to organize one of my own somewhere down the road. We've got enough gospel groups in Atlanta. I don't want this kind of competition here.'" When Lister finally organized the group he had envisioned, he delivered the coup de grace to the Melody Masters by hiring away the group's nucleus: lead singer Jake Hess and bassist James Wetherington. Later, Lister added Melody Masters' first tenor "Cat" Freeman to his new group—the Statesmen. Apparently, the young man's duplicity knew no bounds.

Josephine Vickery Huffman was a Greenville teenager in 1947, and was good friends with Hovie Lister and Hovie's sister. She recalled, "Hovie told his sister, 'Why don't all of you go meet the boys; they're good boys and they can really sing,' and they could!" Hovie's sister told Josephine and Geneva Vickery about the group and they told their cousin Billie. The three teenagers met the group and fell in love with them—literally.

Following Hovie Lister's advice, the group secured a gig on the local Greenville station WFBC where they sang for free advertising. An advertising flier from that period displays a picture of the group, which will be appearing for "One Night Only," and is billed as "The South's Most Versatile Quartet." Admission was fifty cents for adults, a quarter for children. Wally Varner stated, "We went up there and starved to death but we got some exposure there. Greenville wasn't that far from Atlanta and a lot of the top groups—the Harmoneers, the LeFevres, and the Homeland Harmony—were in Atlanta at the time." That the group nearly starved to death has been fully documented over the years. In fact, the Melody Masters' so-called "peach stealing" incident is one of the better known southern gospel music stories.

However, according to Josephine Vickery Huffman, the entire story has never been told. In the past, the account given by Jake Hess and others was that the group, not having eaten in three days and near starvation, raided a peach orchard for food. That much is true. What was not reported was that the peaches were filched from the orchard belonging to J. I. Vickery, Josephine's father, who, along with his wife, Maude, witnessed the theft. The actual perpetrator has never been correctly identified, either. "I was the one who went over the fence and got the peaches," said Calvin. Rather than being angered, the two adults felt sorry that the young men were so desperately hungry. "After that, my momma and daddy took them in and started feeding them; in fact, my momma fed them to death 'cause they weren't making enough money," recalled Josephine Vickery Huffman. Other families also fed the struggling quartet during this financially bleak period.

Money was so scarce that all five slept in a small room. "There were two double beds and a rollaway. Every five weeks you got the rollaway," recalled Jake Hess. There was only one tube of toothpaste, and Calvin was thoroughly chastised by Jim Wetherington one morning for squeezing out more than the bare minimum. The guys also had to share the only vehicle, a Buick. Although this period was economically bleak, it was a very fertile time for the group's musical development. In fact, it might be said that the foundation for the Statesmen Quartet was being poured during the Melody Masters' stay in Greenville.

To place the talent of the Melody Masters in perspective, Wetherington and Hess would eventually be part of the greatest gospel quartet of all time: the mighty Statesmen. In addition, Calvin Newton and Wally Varner would, at different times, be members of the famous Blackwood Brothers Quartet. Calvin's replacement with the Melody Masters, Cat Freeman, enjoyed the singular distinction of being the only person ever to sing for both the Statesmen and the Blackwood Brothers, as well as the talented Oak Ridge Quartet, where he joined Calvin.

It was love, rather than money, that the group found in Greenville. Pianist Wally Varner married Josephine Vickery's sister, Geneva. Cat Freeman married Geneva's cousin, Billie. Although both marriages ended in divorce years later, they nonetheless produced wonderful children and good memories. Calvin and Jo Vickery were best friends. "Me and Calvin were about sixteen or seventeen," stated Josephine Vickery Huffman. "Calvin could sing! He had a beautiful voice and Calvin at that time was a fine boy and well thought of and respected in Greenville."

One gospel quartet that was not struggling during this period was the Blackwood Brothers, who had moved to Shenandoah, Iowa, from Shreveport, Louisiana, at the behest of Frank Stamps. In their book, *Nothin' But Fine*, Jake Hess and coauthor Richard Hyatt observed that during the period when Calvin was with the Melody Masters "he was a hot item in quartet circles and not long after that he got a better job." Word of Calvin's talent reached James Blackwood, who issued an invitation for him to join the famous Blackwood Brothers Quartet, which, at the time, was the most popular gospel quartet in the world.

Although he was headed for greener pastures, Calvin would miss the Melody Masters. He has stated that, of all the quartets he sang with, the Melody Masters had the best four-part harmony. "The Melody Masters sang softly and featured very close harmony, something very similar to the Sewanee River Boys." Calvin also recalled that when they were with the Melody Masters neither he nor Jake Hess were vocal stylists. "Jake sang it straight back then—pretty tones, great harmonizer, great range, but no hand gestures or stylistic innovations. And, as for me, I didn't begin mixing loud tones with falsetto until I went with the Sons of Song in 1957."

Calvin had been singing professionally for only a year and a half when he reached the highest rung in gospel music, singing first tenor for the Blackwood Brothers Quartet. Thus, in the short span of eighteen months, he began living what was to become Elvis Presley's biggest teenage dream— becoming a member of the Blackwood Brothers Quartet. Calvin was only eighteen years old, the youngest person not a Blackwood ever to be a member of the fabled group—a record that still stands. To this day, no other southern gospel music singer has ever risen so quickly. "I was making a hundred and twenty-five dollars a week," stated Calvin. "I spent twenty-five on expenses and saved a hundred." In year 2002 dollars, he was making over fifty thousand dollars a year.

In *The Music Men*, journalist Bob Terrell observed that, during the late 1940s, "The Blackwood Brothers were at the apex of popularity, and by this time had probably replaced the Rangers Quartet as the most popular singers." While Calvin's climb to the top was short and sweet, it had been a different story for the Blackwoods.

After struggling in their early years, the Blackwood Brothers eventually got a daily show on a Shreveport, Louisiana, station—KWKH—where they sang for sixteen months, as well as performing in its greatly expanded listening area; the station had just increased its broadcast power to fifty thousand watts. The group's finances had stabilized and they were doing well. However, V. O. Stamps asked the group to go to Shenandoah, Iowa, and replace his brother Frank Stamps and the Stamps Quartet on radio station KMA. V. O. Stamps was in declining health and wanted Frank to come back to Dallas and help him run the business. The Blackwoods agreed to go, but unfortunately V. O. Stamps died three weeks later, in August 1940.

KMA was only a five-thousand-watt station but had an extraordinary signal that on good days covered twenty-seven states as well as three Canadian provinces. Frank Stamps told the group that he would put their picture on the cover of *The Stamps-Baxter News* if they would advertise it on their radio program. They did, and ten thousand orders flowed in immediately, which led KMA management to project that over a million listeners had heard the advertisement. Although Shenandoah was a small town, it was located in a densely populated area—only sixty-five miles from Omaha and eighty miles from Lincoln, Nebraska. In addition, Kansas City, Topeka, and Des Moines were well within range of the booming KMA signal and within driving distance for the group.

Over a six-decade period, James Blackwood acquired a reputation as someone who does 340 performances a year, and he was no different then. Those singing with the Blackwood Brothers often felt as if they worked eight days a week. However, after the war, even with the daily perform-ances, the Blackwoods were missing out on lots of dates, simply because there were so many offers. In discussing their dilemma, someone sug-gested forming a second group. By 1948, the demand for the Blackwood Brothers was sufficient to keep two groups working full-time.

James Blackwood stated that from these discussions emerged the idea that the Blackwood sound was based not so much on personalities as on presentation style, voicing, and phrasing—elements that could be achieved through practice and rehearsal. This viewpoint was bolstered by the fact that by 1948 the group had already gone through several personnel changes without any significant change in its sound. As a result, the Blackwoods decided to form two groups. Quartet #1 would be the actual Blackwood Brothers Quartet, and quartet #2 would be called the Blackwood Gospel Quartet.

Hilton Griswold recalled, "James and R. W. took the Blackwood Brothers, and Roy and Doyle took the Blackwood Gospel Quartet." Perhaps as an attempt at parity, each group had two Blackwoods, but the Blackwood Brothers Quartet was clearly the "A" team. When Calvin arrived in Shenandoah, he joined quartet #1—the Blackwood Brothers—which consisted of second tenor James Blackwood, baritone R. W. Blackwood, bass singer Bill Lyles and pianist Hilton Griswold. In the Blackwood Brothers' 1968 book, *Above All*, Cat Freeman was erroneously listed as the first tenor. However, Freeman later replaced Calvin. Calvin was the first person to fill the high tenor for the Blackwood Brothers when the organization split into two groups.

Blackwood Brothers quartet #2—the Blackwood Gospel Quartet, or the "B" team—consisted of Roy and Doyle Blackwood, baritone singer Johnny Dickson, and bass singer Warren Holmes. Texan Billy Gewin played the piano for the group. Having two groups allowed the Blackwoods to travel beyond the tether placed on them by their daily radio show requirement. If the Blackwood Brothers Quartet was far away from Shenandoah, quartet #2 would appear on KMA in their place. Often the two groups appeared on radio and stage together. At one point, the quartets jointly recorded a gospel album.

Calvin quickly learned that he was no longer working with fun-loving boys who delighted in pranks and joking. Instead he found himself surrounded by serious, mature, older men who were married and had families—men who had been tempered by the depression and were both constrained and guided by their religious beliefs. The Blackwoods had a Spartan work ethic and were totally dedicated to God, family, and work.

The demanding routine wasn't a particular problem for Calvin, who throughout his career was considered a "good quartet man"—that is, someone who shows up for performances on time, willingly participates in rehearsals, is not above carrying equipment, and assists in selling records and programs. A good quartet man will take his turn at driving even though he may be tired and will engage in public relations when he'd rather be doing something else. Except for the dark days of the late fifties and early sixties, Calvin was always a good quartet man.

Warren Holmes recalled that, in 1948, "Calvin was energetic, hardworking, and easy to get along with." But his youthful energy, playful nature, and devil-may-care attitude were met with consternation by the straitlaced members of the two quartets, which had frequent interaction. His womanizing was also noticed. Hilton Griswold observed, "Calvin's actions and demeanor at that point was a little difficult for us." Griswold was similar to James, Roy, and Doyle in temperament, attitude, and lifestyle. Extremely religious, Griswold was allowed a portion of each program for delivery of his personal testimony. He later left the group to pursue a full-time ministry. Griswold noted, "Back in those days we were a little bit different than a regular southern gospel group because we were up in the Midwest with people who were not acquainted with that type music. Our entire time up there was built on a ministry. A lot of times quartets build on entertainment. We built the Blackwood quartets on the matter of ministry to people."

While the Blackwood Brothers—Roy, Doyle, and James—were serious and reserved, R. W. Blackwood was as fun loving as Calvin, and the two hit it off immediately. Had he not died in a plane crash in 1954, R. W. Blackwood might have become the most popular gospel music singer ever. R. W. was personable and enormously talented—undoubtedly one of gospel music's greatest baritones. Don Butler stated, "In the forties he was the baritone I looked up to the most. He had some of the prettiest, most resonant tones you'd ever hear."

R. W. Blackwood was also friendly and outgoing. Both on- and offstage he projected a relaxed, congenial warmth. In addition, he was considered a man's man; he loved to wrestle, especially wrist wrestle, to see who was the strongest. While en route to a singing engagement, R. W. and Calvin got into a friendly dispute over who would get a choice sleeping spot in the back of the Blackwoods' big touring De Soto and decided to settle the matter through a wrestling match. The two quickly began rolling on the floorboard and within seconds one of the back doors was kicked completely off the hinges. James ordered the car stopped and then thoroughly chastised the two young men, telling them that their pay would be docked whatever it cost to repair the door, which was lying in a ditch about a hundred yards behind them. He was good to his word.

R. W. was a married veteran with a family and was eight years older than Calvin, but still enjoyed boyish pursuits such as wrestling and clowning around. In Shenandoah, he was like an older brother to Calvin. R. W.'s oldest son, Ron, recalled, "When I was about ten or twelve, Calvin was kinda like a hero to my dad, because there were very few guys that could match my daddy's strength. My dad loved to sing, but what he really got a kick out of was arm wrestling. And Calvin Newton was the only one that ever gave him any competition, and could put him down."

Once, while traveling to a concert, as the group sped down the highway in the limousine, Bill Lyles mentioned that he needed an article from his luggage, which was harnessed outside atop the roof. However, the group was running late and James wouldn't allow the De Soto to be stopped. No problem, Calvin offered; he'd climb on top of the car and retrieve the item while the car was in motion. He nimbly crawled out the window and onto the top of the car, found the luggage, got the item, and then prepared to get back in, only to discover that Lyles had rolled up the window. Everyone inside the vehicle, including James, was laughing. Calvin had a windswept ride for the next thirty miles as the car sped on at sixty miles per hour.

During this period, the Blackwood Brothers began churning out records on the White Church label, recorded at KMA by the station engineer. Hilton Griswold recalled that later the recordings were made at the engineer's house, after he obtained some equipment. Although Calvin was with the group only seven months, he sang on at least five recordings: "Have a Little Talk with Jesus," "Lord, Build Me a Cabin in Glory," "What a Friend We Have in Jesus," "Riding the Range for Jesus," and "Just a Closer Walk with Thee."

"Have a Little Talk with Jesus" begins with Hilton Griswold's distinctive piano work. Griswold played with authority, striking the keys stoutly and expertly, giving impetus to the group. This song was basically a Bill Lyles solo that showcased his rich voice, but Calvin is featured for a verse. The vocal backup work sounds almost like the doo-wop style of black groups, pretty daring for the Blackwood Brothers.

On "Lord, Build Me a Cabin in Glory," Griswold's musicianship includes flourishes that his successors—Jackie Marshall and Wally Varner—became noted for. The quartet sang this number straight through without any solos, their voices blending in tight harmony. "What a Friend We Have in Jesus" and "Riding the Range for Jesus" both feature great solos by R. W., while "Just a Closer Walk with Thee" allows the listener to hear Calvin's pure first tenor sound.

Calvin recalled that during his days with the Blackwood Brothers he was once approached after a concert by a professor of music at New York's prestigious Juilliard School. The man introduced himself and told Calvin that he had never heard a singer so young who had such superb voice control. Over the years, voice control has been the main weapon in Calvin's musical arsenal. Like a running back in football who can start and stop on a dime or a major league pitcher who can vary his speed and place his pitches, Calvin has a singing style that is versatile, complex, and highly nuanced.

No one remembers exactly how long Calvin was with the Blackwood Brothers, and they either do not recall or they are not willing to admit the specific reason for his departure, but a best guess would be that he was there around seven or eight months and that he left because he himself realized, as did the Blackwoods, that he just didn't fit in. Calvin's stated reasons for leaving were that he was straining his voice by singing in the high ranges required of a first tenor and that he wanted to go back to school and get his high school diploma.

On the one hand, it might seem extremely irresponsible to walk away from the opportunity of a lifetime such as that given him by the Blackwood Brothers. However, at that point in his life he had other endeavors he wanted to pursue, and getting a high school diploma was important to him. His father's determination to finish his educational correspondence course had impressed him. Furthermore, the Blackwoods usually worked seven days a week, and while he wasn't lazy, the youthful Calvin needed more leisure time than he was allowed under such conditions. He was the only unmarried quartet member and lived by himself in a boardinghouse, although by that point he had frequent female company. The other members were grown, married with children, and no-nonsense, except for the personable R. W. Blackwood.

Calvin also had another interest that was beginning to peak: Golden Gloves boxing. In the late 1940s, Calvin's dad had been transferred by the Church of God from Chicago to Richmond, Kentucky, where he began pastoring a church. Calvin decided to move back in with his parents and begin training for the Golden Gloves state boxing championships in Lexington, Kentucky.

Whether he left of his own accord or was terminated, Calvin has no bitterness about his brief period in Shenandoah. "The Blackwoods treated me real nice while I was there. Not only the members of the quartet but their wives, also. I frequently ate and visited in their homes, and they were mindful of the fact that I was young, by myself, and a long way from home." Years later as he reflected on his feelings in 1948 about Calvin's brief tenure with the famed quartet, James Blackwood stated, "I readily recognized that this young man was a great talent and would really go places in the gospel music field."

5. Singing like an Angel, Fighting like a Demon

Although he was no longer working, Calvin was flush with money, having saved most of his income from the seven months with the Blackwood Brothers. He had no firm career goals at this point but his ever-active mind churned out ideas daily. Two immediate goals were to obtain a high school diploma and to become a champion Golden Gloves boxer. He returned to high school and began taking classes, and he also started training to get in shape for the Kentucky State Golden Gloves championship to be held in January 1949 in Lexington.

The high school classes were a struggle, particularly math. His study skills were rusty from a year's layoff, and he might have pitched in the towel had it not been for an elderly teacher who took a special interest in him and stayed after school each day to help him with his math problems. Although he can no longer recall her name, her kindness remains fresh in his memory.

However, Calvin took to boxing just as he had to singing. At eighteen, he had a wiry yet muscular body. Hundreds of sit-ups and abdominal exercises had given him a rock-ribbed belly. Hours of pounding a heavy bag produced athletic shoulders, and he practiced rapidly tapping a speed bag to increase his hand-eye coordination. He acquired such good muscle definition that his torso looked chiseled. Calvin was also blessed with athletic skill. He was quick, could punch, and had good reflexes. In addition, he had the Newton family's charge-Hell-with-a-bucket-of-water fearlessness, which came in handy in a boxing ring where someone was trying to hurt you.

Since he was new to boxing, the Golden Gloves officials placed him in the novice category in the middleweight division—he topped the scales around 158. In Lexington he joined a cadre of other Kentucky youths of various sizes and abilities to compete for the prestigious Golden Gloves awards. Boxing was much more popular in those days, particularly with youngsters. The Lexington *Herald-Leader* sent its boxing beat writer to cover the bouts.

Calvin won his first two matches by decisions, earning more points than his opponents with jabs, fancy footwork and some tough counter-punching. From there he advanced to the Golden Gloves finals. If he won again he would be state Golden Gloves middleweight novice champ. Excited, he arrived at the auditorium a couple of hours before the event and was simply trying to get focused on his fight when a young man came striding purposefully towards him. "Are you Newton?" he asked. "Yes," Calvin replied, looking up. The stranger identified himself as Calvin's opponent for the championship event. Calvin observed that the young man was agitated and breathing rapidly. The youngster stared intently at Calvin for a few moments, saying nothing. Then he edged closer until Calvin could feel his breath. Looking Calvin directly in the eye, he asked, "Newton, what round are you gonna take me out in?" Calvin had expected his opponent to taunt him or make some sort of intimidating remark and was startled by the question. After an awkward silence the best response he could give was, "Uh . . . I haven't really decided yet." The vagueness of Calvin's reply apparently caused his fearful opponent to think that Calvin intended on toying with him but hadn't really worked out the details. The opponent, by now wide-eyed and trembling, simply shook his head knowingly and vanished into the crowd.

Calvin didn't know what to make of the strange conversation, but he surmised that his opponent was experiencing a good bit of anxiety. As the moment approached, he dressed and made his way to the ring. A good crowd was on hand, animated and eager for action. Calvin shadowboxed a moment in his corner until the referee called him and his opponent to the center for the ground rules—let's have a good clean fight, no rabbit punching, and all that. After the referee wished both sides good luck, Calvin went back to his corner and waited on the bell, which sounded immediately.

Needless to say, as the fight began, the opponent behaved rather timidly, making no effort to engage Calvin. Calvin also started out rather tentatively, and the lack of action produced catcalls and boos from the audience. As they say in the country, it appeared that one was scared and the other was proud of it. However, the booing galvanized Calvin into action. He bolted across the ring and hit his opponent with a one-two to the head and body. The opponent swung back futilely, doing no damage.

Calvin feinted and came back with another combination, a jab to the ribs followed by a right to the cheekbone; both blows connected, and his opponent began retreating until he was near the ropes. Smelling victory, Calvin pursued the hurt, frightened young man. Then, with his opponent at bay, Calvin rocked back on his right foot and came forward with all his weight behind a hard right, which landed on his opponent's forehead. The force of the blow knocked the fighter through the ropes, where he landed on his back on the apron of the ring. The crowd exploded in response. Who was this Newton kid, anyway? He can punch, I'll tell you that.

The *Herald-Leader* photographer captured the young man's plight. The next day in the sports section, viewers saw a picture of sports fans in the front row either coaxing or pushing the obviously reluctant young man to get back in the ring and continue fighting. However, their efforts were to no avail; the referee declared Calvin the winner by a technical knockout. The fight had lasted twenty-three seconds. Calvin was the Kentucky State Golden Gloves Novice Middleweight champ.

Richmond was just a few miles north of Renfro Valley, home of the famous *Renfro Valley Barn Dance*, an extremely popular show that was broadcast to the entire nation on network radio. Calvin hadn't been in Richmond long before he hooked up with the Crusaders Quartet, a group that was featured each week on the show. The *Renfro Valley Barn Dance* was the brainchild of an imaginative Kentuckian named John Lair.

John Lair had moved to Chicago in the 1920s but was a native of Rockcastle County, Kentucky, where Renfro Valley was located. While living in Chicago, he became a talent scout for the *National Barn Dance*. Both sentimental and nostalgic, Lair decided to return to his home in Rockcastle County and develop a live radio program that would feature mountain music by mountain people. Lair took much of the talent he recruited for the *National Barn Dance* with him, and the new program, called *Renfro Valley Folks*, which aired on October 9, 1937, was an instant hit. In fact the show was so popular that portions were beamed all over the United States on NBC's Blue Network. The programs were hosted by Lair himself, who possessed what Calvin described as a "booming, hypnotic voice," that captured the imagination of the listeners with his spellbinding description of the quaint, idyllic life and times in Renfro Valley. Its off-the-beaten-path location was a place, according to Lair, "where time stood still."

Lair was undoubtedly a visionary and was described by music historian Charles Wolfe as "a promoter, music scholar, writer, and founder of the still-thriving Renfro Valley Barn Dance." Lair was also stubborn, rigid, self-serving, and highly autocratic. His authoritative management style was in essence "my way or the highway." Paramount among Lair's ironclad dogmas was that there were to be no individual stars. Long-time Renfro Valley comedian Pete Stamper noted that at Renfro Valley, "You could have fun and frolic but you couldn't have fame and fortune."

One of Lair's biggest discoveries was Lily May Ledford, a talented, attractive, statuesque brunette, who was about as country as they come— she hailed from Pinch Em Tite Holler, Kentucky. She and her sisters had the first all-female band in country music, and Lair dubbed them "the Coon Creek Girls." Through their nationwide exposure on the weekly broadcasts of NBC, the sisters came to the attention of the president of the United States and his wife, Franklin and Eleanor Roosevelt; in fact, the Roosevelts were so captivated by the talent and personality of the group that in 1939 they invited Lily May and the Coon Creek Girls to perform at a White House dinner party for King George VI and Queen Elizabeth of England.

The *Renfro Valley Barn Dance* bore similarities to many of the other barn dances that proliferated on the nation's radio airways in the 1930s and 1940s, the chief differences being the rural location and the reliance on homegrown talent. The Crusaders Quartet was one of those groups.

Calvin joined the Crusaders in 1949. At that time the group consisted of Glen Pennington, who sang bass, baritone singer and acoustic guitarist Mose Eteker, and lead singer Rudy Shelton. Pennington was one of the most prominent performers on the *Renfro Valley Barn Dance* and served as emcee for much of the program. In addition, he was married to Lily Mae Ledford, the original Coon Creek Girl. Their son, J. P. Pennington, became lead singer for the country rock group Exile, which charted a number of hits in the late 1970s and early 1980s. At one point Glen Pennington had a financial interest in the *Renfro Valley Barn Dance*.

Calvin described the sound achieved by the Crusaders during this period as one of tight, smooth harmonies, somewhat like the singing of the Mills Brothers. "We only had the guitar backing us so we had to sound good," said Calvin. In recalling his brief period with the *Renfro Valley Barn Dance*, he stated, "It was a big old barn with benches like in the old churches. There were bales of hay all over the stage and we sat on bales of hay waiting our turn while someone else was performing. It was fun!" Audiences particularly enjoyed hearing the group perform "Dem Bones."

Glen Pennington and Lily May Ledford Pennington befriended Calvin when he first joined the Crusaders, taking him in and furnishing him with room and board and some interesting experiences. "Lily May was totally uninhibited," Calvin recalled. "When she was at home, she would walk around the house almost completely naked. There was nothing sexual about it; she just wasn't a self-conscious person. Martha Carson was just like her. I was at a show in Knoxville one time and Martha invited me into her dressing room, and she didn't have a stitch of clothes on. She just wanted to talk." (As a point of interest, both Lily Mae Ledford and Martha Carson, whose real name was Irene Amburgey, were both from the same area in Kentucky. Apparently, women in that region were a bit more unreserved than those elsewhere.)

Not long after he began singing with the Crusaders, Calvin, Shelton, and Eteker got a gig singing at a Cedar Rapids, Iowa, radio station. Glen Pennington, being a businessman and an announcer for the *Renfro Valley Barn Dance*, stayed behind. Calvin noted that Eteker had emphysema and was too weak to walk the flight of stairs to get to the station's studio, so he carried Eteker in his arms each morning when the group arrived to perform their program.

A Columbus, Georgia, automobile dealer heard the Crusaders during this period and was so impressed by their talent that he offered the group a job representing his dealership at grand openings and special events. The group would also appear on a radio show sponsored by the automobile agency. Calvin, Eteker, and Shelton eagerly accepted, pulling up stakes and moving to Columbus. Pennington couldn't go with them, as he had strong business and personal ties in Renfro Valley. He began singing with another gospel group at Renfro Valley, the Rusty Gate Quartet.

The Columbus dealership sold two types of automobiles that are no longer around today—the Kaiser and the Frazier. "The Kaiser was the cheapo and the Frazier was the luxury car," Calvin explained. For a brief period things went well, but before long the deal fell through and the Crusaders disbanded. Eteker and Shelton headed back north to Kentucky. Calvin, however, remained in Columbus and embarked on a lifestyle that few people would have either the energy or talent to pursue.

He enrolled in high school and earned his diploma, got two nightclub singing gigs, hosted a popular radio program, and began boxing again. His workday began with road conditioning exercise at 5 A.M., after which he would go to high school classes until mid-afternoon. He would then go to the gym to box and from there either to the Bamboo Club to perform or to radio station WRBL, where he sang and hosted a show known as *Dinner Interlude*. In addition, Calvin created quite a stir and attracted a lot of publicity when he chose an older woman to be his boxing manager.

The local newspaper devoted a huge section of its December 21, 1949, sports page to Calvin's incredible life. There were five large photographs: four of Calvin in boxing trunks and one of his female manager examining publicity shots of him. The article was entitled "Columbus Songbird also Good Fighter," with a subheading that read "Woman Manager Sees Golden Gloves Victory for Ex-Jordan High Pug." Written by *Columbus Enquirer* reporter Tom Kinney, it read in part: "The boy with the silver voice will enter the Golden Gloves tournament. He is, of course, Columbus' Calvin Newton—the nightclub singer and boxer. Young Newton, a graduate of Jordan High School and at present singing nightly at the Bamboo Club and on the radio, will enter the Golden Gloves tournament in Atlanta Jan. 3–5 as a welterweight in the 'open' class, it was announced today by his manager—a lady!"

The article then quoted his female manager, who said she discovered Calvin at his high school graduation when he made a speech and sang a couple of songs. She said of Calvin, "He sings like an angel and fights like a demon."

Continuing in a breezy style, Kinney observed: "Singing—shucks, that's nothing for Calvin. He wows 'em nightly at the Bamboo Club on the Opelika Highway and over radio station WRBL . . . Gym work? He works out nightly (before club hours) at the local YMCA and early in the morning he does road work. He loves boxing and singing and thinks the two mix fine. And women—he has one as a manager!"

According to Calvin, the woman's duties consisted largely of getting Calvin publicity and providing him with room, board, and the female amenities that usually accompany such a living arrangement.

Columbus was and is the location of Fort Benning, a huge army basic training facility and the home of the Eighty-second Airborne Rangers, rugged army paratroopers. The thousands of soldiers living and passing through Fort Benning pumped millions of dollars annually into the area economy, including Phenix City, Alabama, separated from Columbus by the Chattahoochee River. In the 1940s and early 1950s corrupt politicians, crooked law enforcement officials, and organized crime merged to turn Phenix City into a cesspool of gambling, prostitution, illegal liquor, and other vices. During this period, Phenix City was, many felt, the most wicked, sinful city in the United States.

Not only were the vices in violation of the law, but the gambling was rigged, the drinks were watered down, and many of the prostitutes were actual sex slaves—innocent girls who had wandered into the area looking for work and were forced to become prostitutes or be locked up in jail for vagrancy. The soldiers, even the tough paratroopers, were no match for the violent thugs who used knives, guns, brass knuckles, and knockout drops to handle disputes with those who objected to being fleeced at card games. Soldiers were beaten so regularly and their lifeless bodies fished from the Chattahoochee River so often that General George Patton, while training his troops at Fort Benning before embarking to Europe, publicly threatened to take his tanks across the river and mash Phenix City flat.

In her book *The Tragedy and the Triumph of Phenix City, Alabama,* author Margaret Barnes wrote, "By 1940 the traffic in murder, manslaughter, gambling, illegal liquor, and white slavery was such that Secretary of War Henry L. Stimson, after inspecting the Army's classified record of Fort Benning Soldiers who had been beaten, robbed, maimed, and murdered in this Alabama outlaw town declared, 'Phenix City, Alabama, is the wickedest city in America.' " Phenix City was no different when Calvin Newton was crossing the Chattahoochee bridge each night to perform at the Bamboo Club. It should be pointed out that despite the small city's sordid reputation, the overwhelming majority of its residents were both law abiding and God fearing. However, it had a sizable underbelly of lawless thugs who thrived through corruption and intimidation of public officials.

Calvin recalled, "When the Crusaders broke up, I went across the river to Phenix City and got a job there in a nightclub. It was a tough place and I was still young." The Bamboo Club, out on the Opelika highway, was a combination supper club/gambling joint that offered food, drinks, and musical entertainment in front and card and dice games in the back. Prostitutes were everywhere and could be escorted to a nearby motel, although many of the nightclubs maintained a private room for paid sexual activities. Calvin knew about the liquor and gambling but was unaware of other aspects of how the club made its money. He explained, "I didn't know anything about the prostitution, but I'm sure it was there." Calvin later sang at Chad's Rose Room, another notorious Phenix City club.

Margaret Barnes noted that the Phenix City nightclubs employed flirty barflies, known as "B" girls, who would hustle soldiers to buy them expensive mixed drinks that consisted of tea topped off with a teaspoon of liquor. In the back, according to Barnes, the house dealers wore infrared croupier shades that enabled them to see what cards the customers held. In addition, roulette wheels were mechanically adjusted to pay off in favor of the house, dice were rigged, and slot machines were calibrated to return five cents on the dollar. Prostitutes peddled their wares at the rate of a dollar per minute.

Calvin was backed by a house band that accompanied him as he sang pop and country hits. His singing went over well with the club's patrons and with Bud Thurman, the owner. However, hecklers are inevitable in such a setting, and on one particular occasion, the heckler was loud, insulting, and unrelenting. Calvin could handle himself in a ring, but local custom decreed that if you fought in or near a nightclub it had to be with guns, knives, or brass knuckles, and with heavy emphasis on eye gouging and testicle crushing. Calvin wanted no part of such an encounter, so he endured the heckler's taunts until burly Chuck Olson, the club's bouncer, came to his rescue. Olson literally gave the loudmouth the bum's rush, grabbing him by the seat of his pants and the nape of his neck, and then marched him out on his tiptoes to the parking lot where Olson administered a sound thrashing. Olson came back inside moments later massaging his hands. He gave Calvin a wink and a smile.

Calvin recalled that on another occasion a gambler, unhappy about his financial losses, pulled out a huge knife and slashed the house dealer in the abdomen. Although seriously injured, the wounded dealer chased after his attacker and caught him outside, where he pounded the man with one hand while clutching his exposed intestines with the other. Some of Calvin's relatives, particularly his granddaddy Ed Newton and his great-uncle Dora Newton, would have reveled in this violent and hedonistic environment. Assaults happened nightly and murders were frequent. Complaints of violence or cheating made to the police were not only futile, but self-defeating: the complainant was himself often charged with public intoxication, disorderly conduct, or some other trumped-up charge.

The story of Phenix City's Sodom and Gomorrah sordidness attracted national headlines when Alabama attorney general Albert Patterson was assassinated mere hours after his election in 1953. Patterson was a Phenix City attorney who campaigned on a promise to drive the criminal element out of the east Alabama city. The murder of the state's top law enforcement officer was so shockingly blatant that Alabama's governor, Gordon Persons, declared martial law. The gambling emporiums, whorehouses, and other dens of iniquity were shut down, and many of the criminals, police, and dirty politicians were either locked up or run out of town.

Calvin's nightly radio show on Columbus, Georgia, station WRBL was more refreshing and catered to the family. Backed by a blind piano player, Calvin sang the hits of the day, including the catchy Frankie Laine hit "Mule Train." The station engineer would use special effects to achieve the whip-snapping sound so that Calvin's version matched that of the Laine record. He usually arrived breathlessly at the radio station straight from the gym, where he was preparing for a return to Golden Gloves competition.

As a Georgia Golden Gloves boxer, Calvin stepped up to the more competitive "open" class, whereas in Kentucky as a newcomer he had fought as a novice. However, he shucked 13 pounds so that he could fight as a 147-pound welterweight. In Kentucky he had fought as a 160-pound middleweight. Calvin entered the Golden Gloves competition in Atlanta in January 1950 but was defeated on a technical knockout. Whatever disappointment Calvin felt over losing the bout quickly evaporated when he learned that he would soon be fighting on the same ticket as the most popular boxer in the history of the sport.

6. Advice from Two Sources

Joe Louis was arguably the finest heavyweight boxer of all time, and some insist that he was the greatest fighter ever. His fight in 1938 with German Max Schmeling in New York is considered by many to be "the fight of the century." Schmeling had given Louis his only defeat two years earlier, surprising the Brown Bomber in the first fight. The only surprise in the second was how fast it ended. Louis came out, fists smoking, and pummeled the proud German to the canvas in a few seconds over two minutes. At one point Louis struck Schmeling so hard that the German emitted a scream that referee Art Donovan said was the most terrifying noise he ever heard in a ring. "Sounded like a stuck pig" was how another ringside observer described it.

After the war, Louis dominated the heavyweight division, taking on and defeating all legitimate contenders until there were simply none left. With no one else to fight and certainly nothing left to prove, Louis officially retired from boxing on March 1, 1949. Unfortunately, he couldn't afford to quit boxing because of his debts and profligate spending habits. Louis owed huge sums in back taxes and alimony, and he also lost thousands of dollars in ill-advised business ventures and gambling. In addition, while he might have been a bomber when boxing, outside the ring he was considered the world's softest touch. Generous and guileless, he spent a fortune on girlfriends, hangers-on, and anyone with a hard-luck story.

He discovered that, even though officially retired, he could generate a lot of money simply by touring America and Europe fighting exhibition matches. An exhibition fight is what brought him to Columbus, Georgia, on the night of February 28, 1950. By that point, however, he had decided to come out of retirement and attempt a comeback against new heavyweight champion Ezzard Charles in September 1950. In fact, he made his official announcement the day after his Columbus exhibition.

Louis's Columbus fight would be preceded by a host of other preliminary matches that began at the welterweight level and worked up to the heavyweight category. The opening bout would feature two local welterweights: Don McMillan and the "Columbus Songbird," Calvin Newton. The McMillan-Newton fight was billed as a "grudge match," which Calvin and McMillan found amusing; they were best friends and sparring partners in the gym. Calvin was excited about the event, not only about fighting in front of a large crowd but also the opportunity to see Joe Louis, at that point the most popular athlete in America.

The boxing matches were held at Memorial Stadium, a football field, where the Auburn-Georgia football game was held during the 1940s. The ring was erected in the vicinity of the fifty-yard line, and folding chairs held the eighteen hundred people who attended, a good crowd for no-stakes boxing. Since all the fighters shared the same dressing room, Calvin intended to go up and introduce himself to the former champ. Although not aloof, Louis was laconic in the extreme—he simply didn't talk very much. However, while he limited his comments, what he said was often powerfully pithy—his verbal reserve masked a subtle wit mixed with street-corner wisdom. His most famous utterance occurred when middleweight fighter Billy Conn said he would fight Louis by staying on the run. Louis responded, "He can run, but he can't hide."

As soon as Calvin got to the stadium that night, he went to the dressing room and found Louis. Although he was a man of few words and a granite impassiveness, Louis not only shook Calvin's hand but was courteous enough to engage in conversation. "What do you do besides box?" asked Louis. Calvin replied that he was a singer. Louis gazed at Calvin silently, giving him the once-over but looking particularly at Calvin's face and hands.

His assessment complete, Louis advised him, "You're a good-looking kid, and young—just starting your life. I've never seen you box, but I'd advise you to stick to your singing." Calvin smiled and responded, "Why? You never heard me sing, either." "Sing me something," said Louis. Calvin thought for a second and then broke into the chorus of "Cabdriver," an old Mills Brothers song. His face still expressionless, Louis nodded his head and said, "I'd sure stick to the singing if I was you."

Calvin's bout with McMillan that evening reinforced Louis's counsel. He and McMillan skirmished vigorously in the first round. Neither's blows connected solidly, but Calvin gave a good account of himself. However, the judges gave the round to McMillan. As Calvin slumped in his stool at the end of the round, he was attended by his female manager, who wiped the sweat from his face, gave him a swig of water to rinse his mouth, and then held the spit bucket so that he could expectorate. The feminine fragrance of her Chanel No. Five was in bold contrast to the masculine odors of liniment, perspiration, and leather.

In the opening moments of the second round of their scheduled four-rounder, Calvin and McMillan had a sharp exchange of blows. Calvin loosed a right jab that McMillan ducked. When McMillan rose up quickly, the top of his head struck Calvin's eyebrow hard, breaking the skin in a vascular area. The result was a nasty cut and profuse bleeding. Head butting is illegal in boxing but is inevitable and often inadvertent, as was the case in this instance.

At the end of the round, as Calvin sat bloody-faced in his corner, with his manager nearly hysterical, the referee walked over and examined the gash and the amount of bright red fluid pouring from it. He then stepped back and said decisively, "That's it for you, bud." McMillan was declared the winner by technical knockout—a hollow victory, as he could just as easily have been disqualified. If a championship had been on the line and Calvin had had a good cut man in his corner, the referee might have allowed the fight to continue. But this was just an exhibition. Louis's fight with his opponent, Dan Bolston, a Milledgeville, Georgia, African-American, was almost comical. Louis knocked Bolston down five times. On one occasion Bolston, fearing reprisal, sought the refuge of the canvas—actually lay down on the ring floor—after "he clipped Louis on the jaw with a stinging right," according to *Columbus Enquirer* sportswriter Tom Kinney.

Although he lost his bout and was injured in the process, February 28, 1950, was a night Calvin would never forget. Not many people get to fight on the same card as Joe Louis. Moreover, he had gotten paid for the bout; now he was a professional boxer. Yet, having reached another plateau, he stretched his daily tasks even more, leaving Columbus to continue his education and to begin singing with a well-known quartet in the area.

After the McMillen fight, Calvin moved to Macon, about forty miles due east of Columbus, to enroll at Mercer University. His pursuit of a college degree would carry the added benefit of giving him a student deferment from the rapidly escalating Korean War, provided he enrolled in the school's ROTC program. He gave up his nightclub and radio gigs and began singing gospel music once more, this time with Deacon Utley's Smile-A-While quartet.

Clifford Thompson was a member of the quartet, which was one of several quartets in the Stamps-Baxter publishing stable. Thompson remembered, "We needed a lead singer and we could get Calvin, so Deacon Utley, who managed the group, got hold of him and had him come down and try out with us." The Smile-A-While Quartet had a long-running show heard weekdays on local radio station WMAZ at 6:30 A.M. and 1:15 P.M. The radio program was, in fact, the reason the Smile-A-While Quartet was in Macon. Thompson stated, "Deacon Utley—we called him Uncle Deacon—took a bunch of us single boys and came to Macon from Dallas, the headquarters of Stamps-Baxter. We started to stay in Dothan, Alabama, but Macon had a clear-channel ten-thousand-watt radio station, and that's why we stopped here in Macon. He kept the boys with him at all times in a house, and fed us and paid us a salary. We got free advertising from the radio show and every now and then one of the sponsors would buy us new suits."

Deacon Utley's son, Lynn, was the group's pianist. He later became renowned for his talented keyboard work. Lynn Utley had gone to school in Oklahoma with Doy Ott, who played piano for several quartets before he became the Statesmen's baritone singer. Thompson recalled, "When I came with them, Stamps-Baxter was paying Deacon a salary and furnishing us with songbooks. We got them for so much and sold them for a higher price and made a profit." Thompson noted that the Smile-A-While Quartet performed at churches or schools almost every night, but stayed within driving distance of WMAZ through the week, to be able to do their twice-daily show. On weekends, however, the group would often perform in Alabama, Florida, and Tennessee. Thompson stated that Calvin only stayed with the group for about a month, but did a good job while he was there. "Calvin was a good lead singer and a good salesman," said Thompson.

"I was with Smile-A-While until this guy named Dempsey Rainwater, who had a group called the Dixie Rhythm Boys, offered me more money, and I went with them," recalled Calvin. Carlos Cook was the Dixie Rhythm Boys' baritone singer, and would sing again with Calvin in another group in the future. Calvin's tenure with both Smile-A-While and the Dixie Rhythm Boys was extremely brief; in fact, his time with the former group was a matter of weeks and his period with the latter group only days. Calvin liked the avuncular Utley, a rumpled, heavyset man who always had a cigar in his mouth and cigar ashes on his suits. Although he can't remember exactly when, at one point after he left the Blackwood Brothers Calvin sang briefly with Carl Raines and the All-American Quartet. "All I can remember is Carl and the manager—some guy named Melvin," said Calvin. It didn't last long.

Calvin's lifestyle in Macon was every bit as frenzied as it had been in Columbus. He was still trying to box, which meant rising at dawn every morning for five miles of roadwork. Later in the day he would try to squeeze in some gym time. His quartet jobs required a lot of time and energy, and he was singing occasionally in nightclubs, in one instance doing a one-nighter in Dothan, Alabama. He was also enrolled as a full-time college student with an ROTC obligation. As part of those duties, he was required to march in the ROTC band beating a bass drum, a chore he found "stupid," so he simply quit going to the drill field.

He discovered that not attending ROTC during wartime carried grave consequences when he opened a letter from the U.S. Army that began "Greetings." It went on to inform him that he had been drafted into the army and that it would be a good idea if he made immediate plans to report to Fort Jackson, South Carolina, for induction. His draft notice marked the end of a truly remarkable three-year period during which he had sung with the top gospel quartet in the world, performed on the tremendously popular *Renfro Valley Barn Dance*, won a Golden Gloves championship, and fought on the same boxing card as Joe Louis, while being managed by a woman. In addition, he obtained a high school diploma, hosted a radio show, and sang in some of the world's most notorious gin mills. And his adult life was just beginning.

7. In the Army

Calvin was drafted out of Richmond, Kentucky, where his parents were living when he registered, as required by law. He reported to Fort Jackson, South Carolina, on March 30, 1951, and was assigned to Fort Bliss, Texas, for basic training. There, he spent eight weeks learning how to use a rifle, performing calisthenics, marching in full gear, getting yelled at by sergeants, and carrying out all the other duties facing a new soldier. Then he spent eight more weeks in specialized training, learning to become a medic. Calvin made the transition to the army rather effortlessly. He was in good physical condition from his boxing, and the strict regimentation he suddenly faced was in many respects no different from his stern, structured upbringing.

"I saw something on the firing range at Fort Bliss that I'll never forget," recalled Calvin. "I was watching some of the artillerymen firing these ultrahuge 120-millimeter antiaircraft guns. This one soldier that was part of a team loading and firing the large weapon was decapitated when he was struck by an ejected shell casing. As a medic, I helped others load the headless body onto the ambulance, and then I drove it to the morgue. I know this—war and its consequences were no longer abstract to me after that."

He may have been a lowly GI, but his singing career didn't miss a beat. In fact, he began performing at the officers' club at Fort Bliss, singing the same songs he had entertained Fort Benning soldiers with months earlier. "I sang at Fort Bliss with a guy named Lou Barton and his orchestra. Lou's vocalist up to that point had been his wife, who was known as 'Lorna Doone.' After I started singing with him, she just mostly sat on stage," said Calvin. Barton was regionally popular and was considered to have one of the best bands in the Southwest. Calvin sang in mufti, shedding his uniform each night in favor of fashionable civilian clothing. "Some of the young officers objected to my not wearing a uniform. A lot of the females at the club were flirting with me and the officers wanted them to know I was just a grunt—a buck private," said Calvin. He mentioned the matter to Barton, who advised him to keep singing in his civvies.

After he finished his medic's training he was ordered to report to Tokorozawa, Japan, about twelve miles from Tokyo, where he joined the Forty-third Engineer and Construction Battalion of the Third Army. Calvin wasted no time in securing a singing gig in two posh Tokyo nightclubs that were under one roof. He recalled, "They had two clubs in Tokyo, both reserved for royalty, when Japan was Japan. When the GIs took over, one of them—the Rocker Four—became a noncommissioned officers' club, which anyone could go to, and the other was an officers' club known as the Crystal Ballroom. At that time, the Japanese were famous for copying everything. The officers' club had a thirty-piece orchestra that sounded just like Stan Kenton's. The man who ran the club was a medal of honor winner. I auditioned for him and he gave me a job. I told him I didn't want to perform in my uniform, so he took me upstairs to a room where there was this closet the size of a bedroom. He pressed a button and this door slid back and he said, 'What size clothes do you wear?'

"The club was absolutely beautiful. I stood on a riser that was all lit up and sang into a big RCA mike." Calvin stated that he never rehearsed with the orchestra, so the songs he performed, which included "Have I Told You Lately that I Love You," "Maybe It's Because the Kiss You Gave Me," "Deep Purple," and "Stardust," were obviously part of the huge band's repertoire. Corporal Bill Cooley was stationed in Korea at the time but would wrangle passes to Japan on the weekend where he saw Calvin perform. "I was sort of a con artist and could manage to get weekend passes. I saw Calvin at the Rocker Four Club in Tokyo. The place was incredible; it looked like one of these nightclubs you see in the movies." Cooley had met Calvin earlier in Tennessee and the two renewed their friendship during the Korean conflict.

One night Private Eddie Fisher walked in when Calvin was on stage at the Crystal Ballroom. At the time, Fisher was rapidly becoming one of the most popular singers in America, and would soon go on to even greater fame, before eventually crashing and burning on amphetamines years later. Thinking he would attract Fisher's attention, Calvin immediately began singing "Anytime," a tune that was still popular and was Fisher's first million-seller. "He made no response at all to the song. He just ignored me," remembered Calvin. Fisher also sang at the Rocker Four and Crystal Ballroom during this period.

Calvin Newton and Eddie Fisher had much in common. Fisher had been born in 1928 and began singing in the synagogue at an early age. Calvin had been born in 1929 and had sung in his church before he began school. Fisher was a lyric baritone and a crooner. Calvin was a lyric tenor who often crooned, but could belt out tunes, too. Fisher began singing professionally at twelve, Calvin at sixteen. Fisher was drafted by the army on March 11, 1951, and assigned to the Sixteenth Armored Engineer Battalion. Calvin had been drafted about two weeks earlier and was part of the Forty-third Engineer and Construction Battalion. Although Fisher was best known for "Oh, My Papa," one of his favorite songs was "My Yiddshe Momma." One of Calvin's signature songs was "Sweetest Mother," always a favorite of disc jockeys on Mother's Day. Both singers were natural talents who never had a voice lesson in their lives. Fisher's explanation—"I just opened my mouth and let her out"—resembles Calvin's—"I just opened my mouth and let her fly."

Calvin never approached Eddie Fisher's status in wealth or popularity but was probably more vocally talented, having greater range, control, and versatility. In addition, he was a much better showman than the bland Fisher. However, at the height of his profession in the 1950s, the most Calvin ever earned was about two hundred dollars a week. Fisher was making forty thousand dollars a week in Las Vegas alone during that period and had his own television show. Fisher's big break came when singer Eddie Cantor helped him secure a recording contract with a subsidiary label of RCA, which Fisher parlayed into a recording contract with the large company. Fisher also had a good manager, and he sang pop. Calvin never had a manager, and, despite singing pop and country in nightclubs, spent most of his career in gospel music. Both were self-destructive, and a statement

Fisher once made sounds eerily similar to remarks made by Calvin. Said Fisher, "There were no rules for me. I could get away with anything so long as that sound came out of my throat."

Calvin fulfilled his military obligation without incident. After basic training he spent the remainder of his time in Japan as a medic, with such duties as giving shots, changing dressings, and dispensing pills. Unlike many other times in his life, his army duty was uneventful, and he was given an honorable discharge at the end of his two-year hitch. He returned to the states eager to get back into gospel music, unaware that he was about to embark on an amazing period of excitement, glamour, fun, and relative fame with two different groups—a phase that would be the high point of his career.

8. Wild and Crazy

And not many days after his younger son gathered all together and took his journey into a far country, and there wasted his substance upon riotous living.

—Luke 15:13

After receiving his honorable discharge in 1953, Calvin soon began a period in his life that reads like cheap fiction: nightly romantic liaisons with adoring female fans, fast and expensive cars, outrageous stage performances, wild practical jokes, and the beginnings of drug abuse and criminal behavior, including a brush with the death penalty. All of this would occur in a three-year span with a southern gospel group known as the Oak Ridge Quartet.

The group's wild-and-crazy behavior was documented by authors Walter Carter and Ellis Widner in their 1987 book *The Oak Ridge Boys: Our Story.* They wrote, "In 1953, Calvin Newton joined the Oak Ridge Quartet and their show progressed from exciting to outrageous. Bob Weber was already jumping pianos. Now they had a guy who jumped off the stage into an audience."

The gospel-singing Oak Ridge Quartet would later evolve into the Oak Ridge Boys, a country music group known for their high-energy stage and vocal performances in the 1970s, 1980s and 1990s. However, for all their animation and theatrics, the Oak Ridge Boys never approached the dynamic antics of their predecessors—the Oak Ridge Quartet of the early-to-mid-1950s.

The founder of the Oak Ridge Quartet was Wallace Fowler, a beefy baritone from a small community outside Rome, Georgia. Fowler, who was called Wally, had sung for a period in the 1930s with the prestigious John Daniel Quartet, said to be the first full-time gospel quartet; they had an early morning show on WSM radio for a number of years and also appeared on the Grand Ole Opry.

Fowler left them, however, and moved to Knoxville to start his own group, the Georgia Clodhoppers, who began appearing on WNOX. This group sang both secular and religious numbers and its members played instruments, including the accordion. Their specialty was close harmony spirituals. While in Knoxville the group began making frequent appearances at nearby Oak Ridge. There are different versions given for why he did it, but Fowler changed the name of the Georgia Clodhoppers to the Oak Ridge Quartet during this period.

Fowler and the quartet got into a dispute in the late 1940s and the three other group members—Curley Kinsey, Johnny New, and Deacon Freeman—resigned en masse. Fowler responded by hiring a group out of North Carolina—the Calvary Quartet—and they continued as Wally Fowler and the Oak Ridge Quartet. The new group included Bob Weber, Joe Allred, Pat Patterson, and Bob Prather. Pianist Bobby Whitfield was playing in Gallatin, Tennessee, at the time with a group called the Gospelaires Quartet. He left them and joined the Oaks, too.

Along the way, Fowler began promoting gospel music. When he staged the first all-night singing at the Ryman Auditorium in Nashville on a cold, rainy night in November 1948, he dramatically altered the course of gospel music. The all-night singing became for gospel music what the Grand Ole Opry was for country music—the hub, center, nexus, and focal point. Following the auspicious beginning of the first all-nighter, Fowler soon established once-a-month all-night singings in Atlanta and Birmingham, always held on the first Friday of the month. Gospel music exploded in popularity, moving from one-room schoolhouses to cavernous auditoriums.

Calvin moved to Atlanta after he got out of the army and was living with pianist Wally Varner and his wife, Ginnie, until he could get something going. Calvin had introduced Wally to Ginnie Vickery when he and Wally were with the Melody Masters in Greenville, South Carolina, in 1947. The couple was fond of Calvin and enjoyed having him as a temporary guest. Atlanta was the hotbed of gospel music during the forties and fifties, and Calvin was hopeful of getting a gig with a group. Varner was then playing piano for the Homeland Harmony Quartet.

At the time, Carlos Cook was the Oak Ridge Quartet's second tenor and emcee. Calvin and Cook knew one another from their brief period together in Macon with the Dixie Rhythm Boys. Cook tipped Calvin that the Oaks' baritone singer, Walt Cornell, had just quit, and that Weber was looking for a replacement. In addition, Wally Fowler, also a baritone, wouldn't be appearing with the group as frequently as in the past. Calvin was a natural tenor but had the range to sing baritone.

Bob Weber stated that he loaned Wally Fowler ten thousand dollars in 1953 and took ownership of the Oak Ridge Quartet as collateral. Weber, a North Carolinian, was the group's bass singer. Weber assumed that Fowler wouldn't repay the loan and that he was, in essence, buying the group. Fowler, on the other hand, may have viewed the transaction solely as a loan, thinking that the group was technically still his.

Whatever the case, Fowler planned to continue to appear with the group, particularly at his all-night singings, but not to travel as extensively because of his growing business empire, which included the all-night singings, publishing and record companies, and bookings and promotions. He would also continue to book the group, which would record on his Gospeltone label. Moreover, the group would still be referred to as Wally Fowler and the Oak Ridge Quartet.

Calvin contacted Weber and arranged an audition, which was given in an Atlanta hotel room. Weber was impressed with Calvin's voice and at the end of the audition number said enthusiastically, "You're hired." Calvin was told by Weber to meet the group in the morning in the lobby, from which they would leave for a tour. That night, however, Fowler called Calvin and proceeded to grill him about his personal habits and mannerisms. Fowler obviously felt he still had some say in the group's business, especially since they would continue to be billed as Wally Fowler and the

Oak Ridge Quartet, and because he could reclaim ownership by repaying the loan.

Fowler asked Calvin, "Do you smoke?" "Yes," said Calvin, reaching for a Chesterfield. "How about your language? Do you ever cuss?" Calvin replied that, yes, he'd been known to cuss. "He asked me a few other questions and I didn't cater to him or say what he wanted me to say, and he said, 'Well, we're gonna keep looking for somebody else,'" said Calvin. "I called Bob Weber at the hotel and told him what happened and he said, 'You be down here at 8 A.M. in the morning; you're in the Oak Ridge Quartet.' So Bob hired me, Wally fired me, and Bob rehired me before I ever sang a song."

In 1953, the Oaks were both talented and successful. The quartet made frequent recordings and toured constantly, sometimes making a two-week swing through Texas. The Oaks at that time consisted of bass singer/owner Bob Weber, second tenor Carlos Cook, first tenor Joe Allred, and pianist extraordinaire Livy Freeman, filling in for Bobby Whitfield, who was in the army. Whitfield was discharged from active duty in 1953 shortly after Calvin joined the group and was able to reclaim his spot as pianist.

When he joined the Oaks, Calvin rose to superstardom in southern gospel music, and his ascension was nothing less than meteoric. Within three weeks he moved to second tenor and became the Oaks' lead singer. Cook went to baritone. Six months later he replaced Cook as emcee. Before long, he became the group's franchise. He was a great soloist, a charismatic master of ceremonies, and a consummate and outrageous showman. Calvin's contribution to the Oaks encompassed more than just his singing and emceeing. He was also innovative, creating the arrangements for two of the quartet's most popular numbers—"Go Out to the Program," and "Tearing Down the Kingdom." Moreover, with his pop vocal stylings, he completely changed the musical direction of the group, taking them from singing pure gospel and old-timey spirituals to covering some of the top popular songs of the day, many of which during that period were inspirational or religiously oriented.

By 1955 he had a marquee name and had become something of a matinee idol. Jack Clark was pianist for the Harvesters Quartet in the mid-fifties.

Later, as a gospel music historian, he recalled, "The first time I ever saw Calvin Newton, he blew into an outdoor sing somewhere in south Georgia in a brand new 1955 Thunderbird and all of the teen-aged girls went absolutely wild." He tooled around in the T-bird convertible, his face adorned by a crooked smile and sunglasses, a cigarette dangling from the side of his mouth—gospel music's answer to James Dean. The sleek automobile, destined to become a classic, only enhanced his Hollywood image. One time when he roared through a small Florida town, the lone police officer, who was on foot, yelled at him to stop; Calvin merely waved and kept going. Slack-jawed, the police officer forlornly waved back.

Despite his being somewhat shoved into the background, Carlos Cook was never resentful or jealous. Cook recognized Calvin's enormous capability as a singer and entertainer, stating, "Calvin had the most talent of anybody I ever sang with. He could spellbind an audience; in fact, he was a master at having an audience in his hand. He also had a beautiful voice with almost unimaginable range." Cook gave an additional reason why he never had any hard feelings about being relegated to a less important role with the Oaks. "Calvin's always been like a brother to me. The Oaks were kinda like family." Cook's wife, Thelma, remarked that when the Oaks moved to Statesville, North Carolina, Calvin would stay at their house until bedtime and play with the three Cook kids, who idolized him.

Carlos Cook's warm comments about Calvin are similar to those made by Bob Weber, who remarked, "I don't think I ever had an argument with Calvin. Calvin and me had something that probably not many other people had: we had a friendship, and I mean it was a deep friendship. We'd do anything we could for the other one."

If the Oaks were a family, they were a fun-loving family: energetic, high-spirited, and full of impish mischief that usually took the form of practical jokes. Pianist Bobby Whitfield, the group's straight man, remembered standing behind the sometimes intimidating Joe Allred in a Howard Johnson's restaurant as they were settling their tabs. Allred stepped up to the cashier, narrowed his eyes, and pointed in the direction of a dishwasher wearing a dirty T-shirt and about three days' worth of whiskers. He asked loudly, "Is that Howard Johnson?" The startled cashier looked and quickly shook her head, "No, it certainly isn't." "Well, where is he?" Allred thundered. "I . . . I don't know," the frightened cashier stammered. Allred then turned to Whitfield and remarked incredulously, "What kind of place is this, anyway? This is Howard Johnson's restaurant and nobody knows where Howard is." The group had a good giggle when they got back to the Cadillac.

Another time, Bobby Whitfield recalled, the group traveled to Galax, Virginia, for a singing. "We went to a diner to eat and four of us were sitting at the counter. Joe had stopped at a drugstore, and he came in a short time after we did. When he came in he took a seat at the counter next to Calvin. After looking us over he asked, 'Are you fellows new in town?' Calvin replied, 'What's it to you, Mac?' A heated exchange went on between the four of us and Joe for a few minutes, making the waitress and customers quite uneasy. I'm sure they were glad to see us go."

Once when they were standing near the ocean in Myrtle Beach, South Carolina, in the dead of winter, Bob Weber offered Calvin a hundred dollars if he would walk out into the surf up to his neck. Calvin didn't even take off his Jarmans. By the time the water was lapping at Calvin's waist, Weber cried out desperately, "Twenty! I won't give you but twenty dollars."

When it came to practical jokes, nobody could touch the clown prince of gospel music—Cat Freeman, of Sand Mountain, Alabama, who replaced Joe Allred with the Oaks after throat problems forced Allred to quit. When Cat entered a restaurant, if he saw somebody he knew having a meal, he would immediately proceed to their table and begin eating off their plate. A frequent victim was the Blackwood Brothers' bass singer, J. D. Sumner. After numerous instances of Cat's grazing on his chow, J. D. decided to get even. Shortly thereafter, J. D. entered a restaurant and spotted Cat eating. J. D. hastily made his way to Cat's table; he was going to sit down and eat some of Cat's meal to teach him a lesson. However, as J. D. reached out to pilfer a morsel, Cat quickly spat on his food, effectively deterring the attempted theft.

Not long after that, at another restaurant, J. D. ordered up one of his favorites: a huge bowl of ripe, red strawberries doused in cream. As he dug in, J. D. observed Cat making his way to the table. J. D. had been waiting for a moment such as this. Just as Cat reached his hand out to get a strawberry,

J. D. hawked and spat on them. Cat just grinned broadly, grabbed one anyway, and started munching, giving credence to a remark Calvin made about him. "You couldn't get one over on the Cat."

But that didn't keep a group of grown-up juveniles from trying.

"One time the Oaks were way out west and stopped somewhere to eat," Calvin recalled. "It was in the summer and blazing hot, so we had all the windows rolled down. Cat was asleep. We rolled the windows up and turned the heater on full blast, and then went inside and had a leisurely meal. We came back out and Cat was either still asleep or pretending to be. It must have been over a hundred and ten degrees inside that limo and Cat was absolutely drenched in sweat. There was no way Cat would have admitted someone had gotten the best of him. He was a boy in a man's body. He joked a lot but he never, ever hurt a soul—not a one."

For singers, forgetting the words to songs is an occupational hazard. Members of a group, however, expect the others to prompt them—that is, unless it was the Oak Ridge Quartet. Nothing brought more fiendish glee among the Oaks than for one of the group to forget the lyrics during a solo. Among the Oaks, Weber was by far the worst. "Bob was notorious for not remembering words," said Calvin. "I used to have to 'feed' him his lines on solos."

One time Weber's forgetfulness sparked creativity. Bobby Whitfield recalled, "One time Bob had a solo on a song entitled 'I Need No Mansion Here Below.' C. J. Grogan, the guy that wrote the song, was in the audience. Bob forgot the words and just made up some lines. Joe Allred was real embarrassed about it." According to Carlos Cook, the audience didn't realize what Weber was doing, but the Oaks were in stitches. Grogan probably went home in search of a lead sheet, to see what he had actually written.

The Oaks even got Wally on one occasion. Wally often did a number entitled "The Funeral," a recitation made popular by Hank Williams. The tune was a tearjerker about a little black boy at a funeral, and almost always moved somebody in the audience to tears. However, at an all-night singing he couldn't recall what line came next, so he put a hand behind his back and began snapping his fingers, to let the Oaks know he needed prompting. Instead of assisting him, the Oaks just stood there and giggled while Wally died on stage. Afterwards, he reamed them out for not help-ing him.

The Oaks frequently appeared with the Chuck Wagon Gang, probably because Wally booked both groups. The two organizations got along well, but the Chucks, being somewhat dour and taciturn, were natural targets for jokesters. One weekend at a large auditorium as the Chucks were singing, their bass singer, Roy Carter, glanced offstage and saw Bob Weber stand-ing in the wings and grinning broadly, a clue to Carter that something was up. In an instant, Weber pulled a huge firecracker from one pocket and a pack of matches from another. When Carter shook his head for him to stop, Weber struck a match. By then, other members noticed Weber and they, too, shook their heads for Weber to cut it out. He responded by light-ing the fuse. The Chucks froze in horror until Weber nonchalantly tossed it on stage, at which point they forgot about the song and the audience and took cover behind the piano. Weber laughed uproariously, then walked out and picked the firecracker up and pulled the fuse from it. "It's a dummy," he explained to the startled audience. He then sauntered off stage, leaving the frightened Texans to attempt to resume singing. The practical jokes played on the Chuck Wagon Gang by the Oaks were never malicious. Bobby Whitfield noted, "The Chucks were our traveling buddies. We loved them a lot."

Weber and Calvin were the group's two Romeos. The baby-faced Weber had picture-perfect teeth, to the extent that his smile could have been used in a toothpaste advertisement. Carlos Cook's wife, Thelma, declared, "Bob was so handsome he was pretty." Weber was also athletic, so that he was able to jump over pianos. Sometimes he would run on stage and then slide, like someone stealing second base—anything to get the audience going. Bobby Whitfield observed, "Bob was our clown. You wouldn't have thought it to look at him, but he was."

Calvin, on the other hand, was a nice-looking guy but had incredible social skills; he could chat up the girls better than anyone. In a matter of minutes, using an arsenal of come-ons that included flattery, teasing, touch-ing, questions, suggestions, and all the other flirtatious devices known to man, he could have a female either purring contentedly or flaring her nostrils passionately. Moreover, he possessed an indefinable magnetism that attracted women; his mere presence caused female palpitations.

Of Calvin's romantic proclivities and penchant for pushing the edge, author Walter Carter noted, "Calvin Newton would have fit better into a Jack Kerouac novel than a gospel quartet. He was not just driving fast; he was living fast. He took amphetamines to the point of addiction, and he took women where he found them—usually in the back of a Cadillac."

Calvin and Weber realized how they were perceived. "We were pretty much little gods to our fans and we took undue advantage sometimes," said Calvin. "Sometimes we'd get through a concert and a little girl would be lying back there on the floorboards, wanting us to take her home. We generally did. But while I may have taken advantage of a female or two, I never mistreated one and I never let anyone else do so either."

Thelma Cook stated, "I have seen Calvin and the quartet come off stage and he'd be walking along and not paying attention to anybody and there'd be about ten or fifteen women following him. They were like vultures." Calvin later referred to these women as "diesel sniffers," because they would usually be found hanging around a tour bus after a concert. With these gospel groupies, there was no need for candy and flowers or even wining and dining. Calvin said, "It was pretty much a direct route to sex," adding that strip poker sometimes served as both a get-acquainted activity and sexual foreplay.

9. The Battle of the Bands

The Blackwood Brothers and Statesmen quartets so dominated their field in the early-to-mid-fifties that it could be said that gospel music consisted of the Big Three: the Statesmen, the Blackwoods, and everybody else. This situation was due in large measure to the talent and professionalism of the two groups but also to the sharp and perhaps questionable business practices of James Blackwood and Hovie Lister. In 1952 the quartets struck a deal: they wouldn't appear at concerts unless they were both booked.

Gospel music promoters had no choice but to accede to their demands; after all, they were the two most popular gospel quartets. After the top market price was paid for them, there often wasn't any money left for other groups, and even if there had been, the Blackwoods and the Statesman additionally demanded the right to approve or veto any other groups that might be appearing with them. Had Ford and Chevrolet entered into a similar type of agreement, they almost certainly would have been hauled into court for restraint of trade and violation of the Sherman Antitrust Act. But in the world of gospel music, nobody challenged the Blackwoods or the Statesmen, at least not off stage.

The two groups' domination and the way they achieved it created a lot of bitter feelings. Decades later, Bob Weber still felt animosity towards the two quartets, especially Hovie Lister. "They [Statesmen and Blackwood Brothers] tried every way in the world to get us out of the business because they couldn't stand it that we were knocking on their door every night. Hovie's gonna be the biggest and the best ever—that was his attitude from the time he started in the business, and when anybody'd come and tromp on his feet a little bit, he'd do anything he could to hurt them—that was Hovie's action." However, the Blackwoods and the Statesmen did not intimidate the Oaks, particularly Weber and Calvin. Both athletes and highly competitive, the two would put all they had into outdoing the two groups whenever they appeared together, which was frequently. Calvin even went so far as to say, "Everybody was scared of us. We were that rebel-rouser group that nobody wanted to sing with."

The other quartets also worked hard to knock the two groups from their lofty perch. The Statesmen, especially, were the standard by which all other quartets were measured. The opportunity to show up the Statesmen and the Blackwoods was provided by Wally Fowler's all-night singings in Nashville, Birmingham, and Atlanta, especially the latter, which sometimes featured the Battle of Songs. According to the rules of the Battle of Songs, all the groups performed and were then judged by the amount of applause generated by the audience. Most of the quartet singers were overachievers and would go all out to win the contest. Today when the old-timers recall that period, they rarely do so with warm feelings. The Battle of Songs was cutthroat and often produced feelings of ill will. This harsh competitiveness had one positive benefit: it undoubtedly resulted in a higher level of singing, musicianship, and entertainment than would have otherwise existed.

Calvin recalls, "The Battle of Songs wasn't a singing convention. It was like, if you're the top man, I'm coming after you." Other Oaks recall the incredibly intense rivalry that characterized the period. "The Statesmen were the king of the hill; everybody was trying to match them," stated Bobby Whitfield, who added, "I think we held our own most of the time."

The Oak Ridge Quartet had a huge repertoire of tricks, jokes, gags, novelty tunes, and crowd-pleasing songs to capture and maintain an audience's attention. The group put on a floor show when they performed. The Oaks were also talented vocally and had two outstanding pianists—Livy Freeman, followed by Bobby Whitfield. Although Cook and Allred were both fine singers, the group got better when Les Roberson replaced Cook and Cat Freeman replaced Allred. In addition to being good vocalists, Roberson was good at arranging and Freeman excelled at comedy.

The Oaks would open their show with Bobby Whitfield breaking into a spirited up-tempo number. The athletic Weber would then vault over the piano to the delight and surprise of the audience. Calvin would be right behind, taking his coat off and flinging it across stage. Cat Freeman would then come skipping on stage like a four-year-old. The audience would roar with approval and the group hadn't sung a note! Freeman's humor made him especially valuable onstage. He had a routine based on two popular radio cornpone comedians—Lum and Abner—that would have audiences howling with laughter. If things started to lag, Weber would hiss at Freeman, who would then pick up his imaginary crank telephone and answer, "Jot 'Em Down Store—Lum Ed'erds speakin'." He could also do a takeoff on *Amos and Andy*. Affecting the accent of the popular Kingfish, Cat would begin, "Now, looka heah, Andy. I got duh deal of a lifetime fu' yew."

Freeman could also do mime; he would mimic a primping female putting on rouge and lipstick and then adjusting an unruly brassiere. Such shenanigans earned him the nickname "Sister Cat." But Freeman was also a top-rate first tenor who hit stratospheric notes that could have balanced the lowest of the bass singers—be it Arnold Hyles, J. D. Sumner, or London Parris. Indeed, some of his high notes sounded feline—hence the nickname "Cat." Freeman has the singular distinction of being the only vocalist ever to be a member of both the Blackwood Brothers and the Statesmen. The peripatetic vocalist also sang with the Melody Masters, the Oaks, the Revelaires, and at least a half dozen lesser-known groups. He was a cat with nine gospel quartet lives, maybe more. Perhaps the only criticism of the Sand Mountain singer was that he had a rather relaxed work ethic.

Most southern gospel quartets had at least one song that was a real crowd pleaser, referred to as a sugar stick or candy stick. A song that the group made popular ten years ago might still be the song the audience wanted to hear above all others. Incredibly, the Oaks came up with three candy sticks in three years. In 1954 they recorded "I Wanna Go There," an infectious upbeat black spiritual number that Carlos Cook said they got from Marion Synder and the Imperials Quartet. Bobby Whitfield, however, said the tune was one that was performed by the Golden Gate Quartet—the black a cappella group the Oaks toured with on several occasions. The tune undoubtedly has black origins—Calvin mimicked or perhaps carica-tured a black singer when he sang it, using a lot of falsetto. It is a hand-clapping, foot-stomping number that always got the audience on their feet.

The group's second sugar stick was the novelty tune "Go Out to the Program," recorded at a radio station in 1954 with only Bobby Whitfield's piano as musical accompaniment. "Go Out to the Program" was yet another black tune that Calvin took and arranged for the Oaks. The group got the idea for the song while listening to records at a Dothan, Alabama, record store. According to author Walter Carter, "It was barely a song, just a verse that encouraged the listener to go out to a gospel show. But in the middle, they mimicked their fellow gospel stars . . ." Mimicking the other groups is what gave the song its appeal. The Oaks took the top groups' candy sticks and sang a verse, using the other groups' phrasing and vocal licks.

It was on stage that "Go Out to the Program" proved to be so captiv-ating. The number featured imitations of five groups: Happy Edwards and the Harmoneers, the Blackwood Brothers, the Statesmen, the Chuck Wagon Gang, and the Oaks themselves. The two most popular segments on stage were those that spoofed the Chuck Wagon Gang and the Statesmen. When the group mimicked the Chuck Wagon Gang, Allred and, later, Cat Freeman would drape a fur around their shoulders and sashay on stage to sing the lead part of Anna Carter, an alto. Calvin stated that when the Oaks did the Statesmen's closer, "Get Away, Jordan," "I would roll up my britches' leg and I'd be wearing red socks like Hovie." Lister pretended to be flattered by Calvin and the Oaks' portrayal of him and the Statesmen, but Carlos Cook offers an anecdote suggesting that his true feelings might have been different.

"We were looking for another sugar tit to replace 'I Wanna Go There' and we came up with 'Go Out to the Program.' We had a Battle of the Songs with the Statesmen in Atlanta for two months in a row. Back in those days we were at one another's throats. Bob [Weber] was the manager and he said, 'Go out there and get it going.'" Cook was the Oaks' emcee at the time.

"So, I introduced it by telling the audience that these other groups had been singing songs and about half-doing it. I said, 'Let us show you how it's done.' It was mean-spirited. There was this ramp that went from the balcony backstage and I looked up there and that turkey Hovie was pacing like a wild Indian, and man, when we sang 'Get Away, Jordan' that place went wild."

"Get Away, Jordan" was the Statesmen's show closer. At the big venues Lister usually had the overhead lights turned off so that he could then have a spotlight turned on for dramatic effect. One night when Calvin and the Oaks were doing their version of "Get Away, Jordan," Calvin had the stage electrician turn off the lights. He then asked, "Hey, where's the spotlight?" Freddie Daniels of the Sunshine Boys ran out on stage and said, "I got it," turning on a flashlight and shining it on Calvin's face. The flashlight trick was another jab at Hovie, who had to grin and bear it.

It was the Oaks' third candy stick that became their most memorable. "Tearing Down the Kingdom" drew the longest sustained applause in the history of the Atlanta municipal auditorium, according to Calvin, who arranged the number. In order to perform the song, the Oaks would have a Bible hidden under a seat in the audience and then would begin singing the song, which was based on two premises: Jesus is the Rock, and we are looking for the Rock. When the number began, the four singers would go into the audience searching for the Rock, which wasn't easy, considering that this was decades before cordless microphones. Off the stage and down into the audience they would go, singing the song and looking for the Rock. Where was it? Father had the Rock; Mother had the Rock. The audience was then asked: Do you have the Rock? Excitement and anticipation would build as Calvin led the other three in search of it. As the spotlight followed them, they walked down aisles searching. The Rock was finally found. Calvin would proudly hold aloft the Bible and declare in song, "We have found the Rock that was hewn out of the mountain." The audience would erupt in pandemonium. Hallelujah!

Now, it was time for thanks. The Oaks would sing a chorus of "Thank God we found the Rock." The four would then gather together because it was time to pray to the Rock. The quartet needed to get back on stage, so they would sing "Let us rise with the Rock," then triumphantly,

"We're going home with the Rock." Back on stage they would end the song by telling the audience in song that they tore down the kingdom to find the Rock. Carlos Cook pointed out that the problem with a candy stick was that it was your closer or encore number, but the audience would begin yelling for you to sing it the minute the concert began. Before the Oaks got to their candy sticks they would sing their recent recordings, which usually featured Calvin.

10. Touring and Recording

The Oaks were road warriors during the period when Calvin sang with them in the early-to-mid-fifties. Bobby Whitfield recalled, "The road was hard. Just think, five guys in a stretch Cadillac with songbooks, records, PA system, luggage and no air-conditioning, although eventually we got that. In the beginning, we had two regular Cadillacs, but then the governor of Florida died and we bought his limo. That was the first stretch car we ever had." When the group obtained the late governor's limo, they bought a two-inch foam mattress and put it in the back. "With the foam mattress we could sleep three in the back while two rode in the front. We got on each other's nerves, living that close together," said Whitfield.

Carlos Cook said that the Oak Ridge Quartet performed as far west as Plainview, Texas, out in the panhandle, as far north as Detroit, and as far south as Miami. Recalling some of the other locales, Bobby Whitfield noted, "We did Texas, Oklahoma, Arkansas, Missouri, and Louisiana," adding, "We played New Orleans with Wally before Calvin came with us—a Grand Ole Opry-type show, and we went over like gangbusters. Hank Williams was there that night and next to Hank, we got the biggest applause of anybody. It set Wally on fire. He said, 'We'll come back here with an all-night singing and fill this auditorium.' So we came back and had about seventy-five people." Whitfield recalled, "We played the Shrine Temple in Detroit; we played Canton, Ohio, quite a bit. We always loved to go to Poplar Bluff and Cape Girardeau, Missouri. We played a lot of dates in West Virginia and sort of opened up that state to gospel music. Beckley, West Virginia, was especially good. We'd pack that auditorium ourselves. We covered Alabama from one end to the other. We played a lot of dates on Sand Mountain because of Cat, who was from there. We played dates in the Florida panhandle—Pensacola, Panama City, and De Funiak Springs."

The Oak Ridge Quartet also appeared monthly at the big Wally Fowler all-night singings in Nashville, Birmingham, Atlanta, and Winston-Salem, North Carolina. "Atlanta was best to us and one of our favorite spots to perform," said Whitfield. "Winston-Salem was good, too, with the Reynolds Coliseum usually being full when it was held there on a Thursday night."

The early-to-mid-fifties were the heyday of southern gospel music. The big auditoriums in Birmingham and Atlanta were almost always filled to overflowing, with seats often put onstage behind the performers, to squeeze in a few more. Nashville's Ryman Auditorium would be sold out, also. Fowler also began booking all-night singings into the cavernous Alabama State Coliseum in Montgomery, which featured a seating capacity of sixteen thousand and had horrible acoustics.

By 1954 gospel music had become so popular in the Deep South that Wally Fowler, ever the entrepreneur, conceived of the idea of "shuttle singing," which would allow as many as three groups to sing at three different locations, using the same talent in all three places. The process was so called because the talent shuttled from one place to another. The shuttle might involve two or three cities. If two cities were involved, it was known as a "bicycle" date; if three were involved, it was called a "tricycle" date.

By doing shuttle singing, Fowler could put on a lot more talent than he could ordinarily justify in a medium-to-small venue. As an example, a three-in-one shuttle sing, or tricycle date, was done in Huntsville, Decatur, and Sheffield, Alabama, in 1955 and featured the Chuck Wagon Gang, the Rangers, the Oak Ridge Quartet with Wally Fowler, the Statesmen, the Blackwood Brothers, and a new local group called the Charioteers. Logistically, it worked as follows. At least two groups would be at each of the three locations. The concerts would all begin at the same time. As soon as the three groups that opened at their respective locations finished their set, they would race to their automobiles and take off for the next destination while group number two began their set. In theory, the number-one groups would then arrive at the next location just as the second act was finishing, go onstage, do their set, then dash to their automobiles and make a beeline for the third destination. The crowds loved getting to see so many top-name acts, but the groups found it incredibly hectic.

Bobby Whitfield remembered, "They were pretty hard to do. Sometimes the PA system was hard to deal with. We wouldn't want to leave ours for the next group, so we'd tear ours down. A time or two we left them, and that was one of the problems. Sometimes the shuttle sings weren't all that successful, like when the audience would have to wait for the next group to get there." To prevent the waiting, Fowler encouraged the groups to drive as fast as possible to get to their next location on time, even offering to pay for speeding tickets. Calvin drove one of the Oaks' touring Cadillacs at that time, and when they were doing a shuttle singing, some of those who rode with him said the auto was moving so fast that it would have flown if it had been equipped with wings.

November 1954 was a busy but typical month for the Oaks when Calvin was with them. The quartet performed eighteen dates between November 4 and November 27, and played to packed houses at most of them. At that point Wally Fowler was still booking the group, and, as a rule, the distance from one show to the next wasn't great. They began with a shuttle date at Sheffield and Decatur, Alabama, followed by appearances at Nashville and Asheville, North Carolina. They then enjoyed a five-day rest before leaving on November 11 for dates in Huntington, West Virginia, Terre Haute and Indianapolis, Indiana, and one-night appearances in Columbus and Akron, Ohio. Fowler had them booked with the Sewanee River Boys, the Speers, and the Chuck Wagon Gang during this swing.

Tuesday, November 16, was drive day, and it was a killer—nine hundred miles—from Akron, Ohio, all the way to Nicholls, Georgia, just a few miles north of the Okefenokee Swamp in Georgia's southeastern corner. On the seventeenth they traveled to Cordele, Georgia, then rolled into Memphis on Friday night for a big gospel singing with the Blackwoods, the Statesmen, and the Chuck Wagon Gang. The next night they were in their favorite venue—the Atlanta city auditorium—for an all-night singing. On Tuesday, November 23, they did a date with the Chuck Wagon Gang. The Oaks and the Chucks were both booked by Wally Fowler, so they appeared together frequently and often socialized in their off-hours, including playing golf during the daytime. Calvin recalled, "Howard Gordon, the Chucks' guitar player, was a real quiet, mild-mannered person until he stepped on a golf course. On the links, you wouldn't believe how angry he would get—he would yell, throw clubs, you name it."

On Wednesday, November 24, the Oaks swung through North Carolina, doing a bicycle date with several other groups, including the Blackwood Brothers, plus an added attraction, songwriter/singer Stuart Hamblen. As a songwriter, Hamblen was hot at the time, having recently penned "This Ole House," a giant hit for the Statesmen and an even bigger one for pop singer Rosemary Clooney. In addition, Wally Fowler was riding high with Hamblen's novelty tune "Rusty Ole Halo." Both songs would have been sung at these locations, and James Blackwood probably would have gotten a standing ovation for singing one of Hamblen's most inspired numbers, "It Is No Secret," except that Hamblen sang it himself. At his best, the big cowboy was no great shakes as a vocalist, and, in the latter part of his career, when his voice had deteriorated even more, it was said that he didn't sing as much as bellow.

A converted alcoholic and tough guy—his best friend was macho actor John Wayne—Hamblen was saved in the late 1940s at a Billy Graham Crusade in Los Angeles. Although now a Christian, Hamblen, the singing cowboy actor, retained his irreverence. During the November tour, Calvin remembered, the Oaks met Hamblen early one morning to sing at a radio station. Perhaps a bit grumpy from having to rise at daylight, Hamblen greeted the quartet by making a grand gesture and proclaiming, "Piss on the world in little bitty drops." Hamblen got along famously with Calvin, whom he called "Boy." On their North Carolina swing, the Oaks had played Winston-Salem, Kenansville, and Charlotte, then finished out the month with a big all-night singing in Birmingham's city auditorium.

Carlos Cook vividly remembers the next-to-last week he was with the group. "We worked Beaumont on a Wednesday night, Houston on Thursday,

Memphis on Friday, and Rockingham, North Carolina, on Saturday night. At that time we were driving a limo and had a foam rubber mattress two-to-three inches thick, and three of us would be sacking it out in the backseat and the other two would be in the front seat. We got into Memphis about eight or nine o'clock Friday morning, and we got up about two or three o'clock Friday afternoon, and we didn't go to bed anymore until about 3 A.M. Sunday morning. We left Memphis about 1 A.M. Saturday morning and we drove steady until 9 P.M. Saturday night. We were there in Rockingham with the Chuck Wagon Gang; actually it was about a quarter to nine when we got there. We just run in backstage, sweaty and stinky, changed clothes and went out and sang, and got back in the car and drove to Statesville before we went to bed, and that wasn't unusual for us."

There were lazy days, too. Whitfield stated, "When we set it up like we liked it best, we would do three days a week for three weeks, then work a ten-day tour with the Chuck Wagon Gang, and we'd do our all-night sings during that ten days."

The Oak Ridge Quartet was extremely active in the recording studio during Calvin's three-year period with the group. Whitfield recalled, "All of our recordings were done in Nashville, except for 'Go Out to the Program,' which, the best that I remember, is that we stopped at a radio station and just laid that one down on tape. The quality was not near as good."

The group recorded on three labels: Oak Ridge, Gospeltone, and Dot Records, a small national label out of Gallatin, Tennessee, that made some big waves in pop music in the mid-fifties by recording local talent. Ragtime pianist Johnny Maddox, saxophonist/band leader Billy Vaughn, and singer Pat Boone were middle Tennesseans who had great success with Dot. "I think the ones we made on Dot were recorded at the old Castle; the others were at Owen Bradley's somewhere in Nashville before the barn," said Whitfield.

In those days, records cut in Nashville featured the A-team session players on all the cuts, which meant fine musicianship. The first Oak Ridge Quartet session that Calvin sang on was in 1953, when the quartet consisted of bass singer Bob Weber, baritone Carlos Cook, and first tenor Joe Allred. Calvin sang the lead, and "Lightning" Livy Freeman was the pianist.

Freeman had earned the sobriquet "Lightning" not from his considerable finger dexterity but because he was such a slowpoke. He was a great pianist, however, and drew accolades from gospel music critic Tim Gardner: "No doubt, Livy is one of the best all-around pianists to ever be a part of Gospel music . . . Livy possesses it all—style, technique, a smooth right hand and great rhythm. He plays a tremendous amount of notes, and he is equally adept playing other kinds of music like jazz, big band, and blues. In fact, he often incorporated other kinds of music into his Gospel playing."

Carlos Cook recalled that when Livy was with the Oaks he carried a small portable record player everywhere so he could listen to his collection of Art Tatum records. Freeman was totally enamored of the legendary jazz pianist's inimitable style, and much of what Gardner describes regarding Livy's playing style was the result of Tatum's influence and Livy's attempts to incorporate some of Tatum's piano licks into his own work.

According to Bobby Whitfield, Calvin's first session with the Oaks was in 1953 and featured four songs: "Crying in the Chapel," "I Believe," "This Heart of Mine," and "In the Sweet Forever." The songs were issued as 78 rpm records on the Gospeltone custom label, with the name Wally Fowler and the Oak Ridge Quartet. Wally's name, in large capital letters, appears above the smaller name, Oak Ridge Quartet. However, Fowler did not sing on any of the four numbers.

"Crying in the Chapel" and "I Believe" were covers of two songs that had been recent pop hits. Although three pop versions of "Crying in the Chapel" had been released, it was the Orioles, a black group from Baltimore, who put the song on the national charts. Issued by Jubilee, a small independent label, the Orioles' rendition was gospel tinged and featured the wavering tenor voice of lead singer Sonny Til. The song was one of the first crossover hits by a black group. In 1965 Elvis Presley ended a long dry spell on the charts by taking his version of the tune to number one.

The Oaks' vocal arrangement on "Crying in the Chapel" was basically street corner doo-wop. Calvin's interpretation is similar to Sonny Til's: soulful crooning sung with great feeling. In the background, Weber, Allred, and Cook also mimic the Orioles' falsetto swoops, although their ultra-tight harmonies come off sounding more like the Four Freshmen than the black group. Allred, a first tenor with incredible range, soared on this number. Bobby Whitfield noted that Allred could sing high C without falsetto, an impressive feat. Guitarist Grady Martin and bass fiddle player Ernie Newton—future legendary Nashville sidemen—enhanced the overall sound considerably.

The Oaks' arrangement of "I Believe" is true to the pop version recorded by Frankie Laine. Again, the quartet's harmonies sound more like pop than gospel. In addition, Grady Martin contributed some very tasty guitar licks. The group rounded out their three-hour session with two traditional gospel songs, "This Heart of Mine" and "In the Sweet Forever." Ernie Newton laid down a heavy boogie-woogie beat on "This Heart of Mine," which set the tone for that rousing number. Calvin sings the lead but Carlos Cook and Joe Allred both get step-outs. In keeping with Nashville recording values, all of the songs were under three minutes, with two of them—"I Believe" and "This Heart of Mine"—barely more than two minutes.

The second time Calvin recorded with the Oaks was in 1954 when the group was with Dot Records. Whitfield had replaced Freeman on piano, and the Nashville sidemen included Martin and Newton again, who were joined by keyboardist Marvin Hughes on the organ. This session included the group's first candy stick, "I Wanna Go There."

The Oak Ridge Quartet had two sessions in Nashville in 1955. The first one included "When They Ring Those Golden Bells," a solo by Calvin that was to become his signature song. Whitfield's piano work was superlative on this number as it was throughout his tenure as the Oaks' pianist. Music critic Tim Gardner commented that "Bobby is noted as one of the best pianists for adding original chords to improve the sound of simple songs, particularly fast tunes and spirituals."

Another song from this session was the oft-recorded toe-tapper "Rain, Rain, Rain." Chet Atkins played for the Oaks on the session, just as he did when he was a member of the Georgia Clodhoppers, the forerunner group of the Oak Ridge Quartet. Owen Bradley played organ. "We got 'Rain, Rain, Rain' from the Four Lads," recalled Whitfield, who stated that he purchased the sheet music for the song in a Louisville, Kentucky, music store. The Jordanaires also recorded it and got decent airplay. However, the song was an old black spiritual that had been around forever.

In late 1955 the Oaks returned to Nashville with a new lineup that featured Cat Freeman as first tenor and Les Roberson as baritone. Throat problems forced Allred to quit, whereas Carlos Cook's conscience got the best of him.

Recalling his decision to quit the Oaks, Cook said, "I hate to admit it, but I wasn't a Christian during that time. I was married with three small boys and I was gone all the time—six to eight weeks at a time." Bothered by his lifestyle of frequent absences from home and his family, Cook prayed, asking the Lord to come into his life. He came to feel that the Lord was telling him that he would come into his life only if he gave up his position with the Oaks and stopped being away from his family so much. After agonizing over the decision, Cook left the group while they were on the road. "I caught a bus out of Birmingham and went to Dothan and got straightened out. I felt no regrets about what I did, then or now." Since leaving the group, Cook has been active in the church for almost fifty years.

The new lineup cut two tunes, both solos by Calvin. The quartet chose "He," another religiously oriented song made popular by Duke Ellington's former lead singer, Al Hibbler, a powerful baritone with a full, rich voice. Hibbler's version of "He" made it all the way to number four on the *Billboard* pop charts in 1955. A comparison of the two versions shows that Calvin sang with more intensity, his voice soaring at times, whereas Hibbler relied on depth and power.

The other number to come out of the session was to become the quartet's third candy stick in as many years—"Tearing Down the Kingdom of This World," another old tune that Calvin cleverly arranged. It proved to be even more popular than the others. In fact, of the three, "I Wanna Go There" was good, "Go Out to the Program" was better, and "Tearing Down the Kingdom of This World" was the best. "I Wanna Go There" was simply a feel-good song, while "Go Out to the Program" was a spoof. However, the performance of "Tearing Down the Kingdom" was a faith-affirming experience—a religious skit that made the audience feel good, elevating their feelings and emotions so that the event resembled a revival meeting.

11. The Slide

It is said that the road to Hell is paved with good intentions. If so, it was the good intentions of a decent, respectable, middle-aged Christian woman that put Calvin on his own superhighway to the fiery lake. One often reflects on roads taken and not taken, but this one made all the difference in his life. The Oaks had just arrived back home from another one of their marathon tours that crossed rivers, states, and time zones, and they still had to perform that night in Statesville, North Carolina. They were all exhausted, especially Calvin, who always expended tremendous amounts of energy onstage. More than anything else, he just wanted to go to bed and sleep for about twenty-four uninterrupted hours.

Friends and family were there to meet them as they arrived. Calvin's fatigue was noticed by a concerned woman, who offered a pep pill to perk him up. Calvin recalled, "We came into Statesville for a concert. We'd been driving all night—a terrible trip, ten or twelve hours. I won't say who, but someone there had something called a Dexamyl. She said, 'Normally you take one, but you're awful tired; you might want to take two.' I took two and after I finished singing I could have driven to L.A. and back. I said to the group, 'Aw, come on, let's sing some more, fellas.' I thought I had found the elixir of life."

"I had no idea of the consequences, so I asked her if she had some more, and she gave me half a bottle. That got me started, and for a long, long time they were an elixir because they did what I wanted them to do. I had no idea they were harmful or psychologically addictive. I thought to myself, 'Anything that makes you feel this good can't be bad for you.' " That fateful night, Calvin discovered not an elixir but rather a substance that often destroys everything in its path—careers, marriages, and lives. The misery and unhappiness the drug exacted from him over the years was so devastating as to be incalculable. Certainly, the well-intentioned woman who gave him the pill is no more to blame for the substance abuse problem that followed than is a bartender who serves up a future alcoholic's first drink. Still, one wonders how Calvin's life might have differed if she had left them at home.

Dexamyl is an amphetamine, a stimulant that elevates mood and improves concentration, thinking, and coordination. It suppresses appetite, also, and was easily obtained from physicians, especially those associated with the weight reduction clinics that proliferated in the mid-twentieth century and catered primarily to overweight housewives. The woman who introduced Calvin to the drug was most likely taking them for that purpose. In addition to the enormous energy it engenders, the drug produces another pleasant sensation, too, which perhaps was why Calvin became so attracted to it. The elevated mood produces a feeling of well being that heightens self-esteem. Amphetamines caused Calvin to like himself, and for someone who never had, it was an amazing transformation.

Initially, it wasn't easy to tell when Calvin was taking the drug. A high-energy, good-natured sort to begin with, the pills didn't radically change his outward behavior. Bobby Whitfield observed, "If Calvin was doping when he was with the Oaks, I couldn't tell it." In the beginning it is doubtful that Calvin realized exactly how the drug affected him. He just knew that it made him feel better, and he wanted to feel that way all the time. Early on, he made a point of taking a pill before going on stage so that he could give a better performance. World War II soldiers and astronauts have taken amphetamines to sharpen their skills, also, and in the short term, amphetamines are not harmful. However, they have a high potential for abuse, particularly among people like Calvin, who have self-esteem problems and compulsive personalities.

Insomnia, tolerance, and habituation are among the negative side effects. Unless counteracted by other drugs, such as barbiturates or alcohol, sleep is almost impossible when amphetamines are in the body. Consequently, after a concert, try as he might, Calvin couldn't sleep. He found there wasn't much to do in the early morning hours—he was too fidgety to read and the television stations signed off at midnight in those days. Eventually, he began driving around aimlessly, his mind racing wildly with thoughts and ideas—some creative, some destructive.

Weber moved the group's headquarters to his hometown, Statesville, North Carolina, in 1955. Calvin lived in a hotel room there for a while but then bought a home in nearby Charlotte on the GI bill. The night of July 20, 1955, was a typical muggy southern night in Charlotte. Calvin had taken a Dexamyl earlier in the evening and couldn't sleep. Remembering that eventful evening, Calvin painfully recalled, "I was wild as a hare; I was doing pills, and I was single. There was this young girl, a teenager, that was interesting and I was looking for somebody that night. I knew where she lived; I had dropped her off there. So anyway, I went to the house; it was late at night, and a big air conditioner was going, making a lot of noise. I started to leave, but then I changed my mind when I saw a light at the side of the house. So I sneaked around the side and there she was, the girl, lying on the bed, dressed. I hollered, scratched on the screen, but nothing, she didn't hear me. So I proceeded to raise the screen and reached over and took her by the shoulder and shook her. She turned around and it wasn't her. It scared me and whoever it was, so I jumped back, bumping my head on the window. I took off running and some cops stopped me. I was frantic so I told them I was training for a fight; that was why I was running. Of course I had street clothes on, so they didn't believe me for a minute. It turned out that the girl's house was exactly like the one that I went to, but was a block over."

Authorities refused to believe Calvin's story, and he was charged with first-degree burglary. Burglary is the unlawful entry into a residence or business with the intent to commit a felony. Crime is classified according to its perceived seriousness; the nighttime entry of an occupied dwelling was the most serious of burglaries and also considered one of the most serious of all crimes. Calvin was panic stricken when he discovered how serious it was in North Carolina in 1955—it was a capital offense! He could be sentenced to a long term of imprisonment for the crime he had been charged with or even sent to the gas chamber.

Bobby Whitfield remembered the trial. "We all went to Charlotte to court with him and testified on his behalf. I sat through all of the trial. I don't recall what the prosecutor alleged that Calvin was doing or tried to do, but I remember the judge said, 'I am convinced that you were not there to cause any harm, but I do know that you have a total disregard for people and their private property.'"

Calvin and his attorney probably put on what is known as a mistake of fact defense, admitting that what he did was wrong but maintaining that there was no criminal intent. Calvin recalled, "I told the judge that I wasn't trying to break into some stranger's house but was trying to get the attention of someone that I thought I knew. What hurt me more than anything was that the girl's father wouldn't let her testify. If she had been there, she could have backed up my story and everyone could have heard that she lived a block over, and that I was just at the wrong place at the wrong time."

With great clarity, Whitfield recalls the conclusion of the trial and the judge's statements that preceded his pronouncement of sentence. "He said, 'What you have been charged with is a capital offense, because you burglarized a house in the state of North Carolina after dark.' He made a few other comments and then said Calvin was guilty of forcible trespass, a lesser offense. The judge then said, 'I sentence you to two years in the state prison,' and Calvin started crying. But the judge wasn't finished. The judge added, 'But the sentence is to be suspended for four years' good behavior.'" Calvin's close call with the gas chamber or incarceration had been averted. It was a wake-up call for him, and he slowed down on the Dexamyl. However, the problem with stimulants would later resurface again and again, and on those occasions he would pay dearly.

Just as Calvin's personal life took a hit, so did his career and that of the Oak Ridge Quartet. In 1955 the Oaks were composed of five guys who were talented, exciting, funny, energetic, and highly entertaining. Yet in 1956 the group disbanded. There was no dispute, no clashing of egos, and no disagreement about the song selections; they called it quits for one reason—money. They stopped making any. "The bookings dried up," said owner/manager Bob Weber.

By 1956 the Oaks had severed ties with Wally Fowler, except for appearances on his all-night singings. There were no hard feelings between Fowler and the Oaks; on the contrary, everyone got along fine. However, the group had begun to slowly distance itself from him when Weber made Fowler the ten-thousand-dollar loan in 1953. The group later moved from Atlanta to Weber's hometown, Statesville, North Carolina, about thirty miles from Charlotte. Then, recalled Carlos Cook, "Wally got into debt with us and he wouldn't let us book with any other agency. But we caught him at a weak moment; he owed us about six thousand dollars. We told him, we'll split it in half if you'll let us have the name and book with anybody we want to. So he took us up on it. We started booking with guys like W. B. Nowlin out in Texas and Lloyd Orrell in Detroit." It is not known whether the three thousand dollars written off was part of the original loan or yet another.

Several have commented over the years about Fowler's lack of business acumen, despite the fact that he is remembered more as a gospel music businessman than as a fine baritone who had many hit recordings. Weber said of Fowler, "He was gonna make millions and millions on promotions. I went with him in '49, when Wally was on WSM radio and he started off then booking other groups. He booked seven or eight groups every week there for a while and he went broke, and he just never could understand why he couldn't make any money. But the reason was, he wasn't a businessman; he didn't look at it like a business, therefore, he couldn't make it." When Weber was reminded of all the business enterprises Fowler created, he repeated emphatically, "Wally Fowler wasn't a businessman."

Fowler may not have been a good businessman, but no one can dispute his success with all-night singings, record companies, and television shows. His poor business practices perhaps resulted from being task saturated, to use a military term. Roy Carter of the Chuck Wagon Gang stated, "Wally wanted to do everything. What he did, he did well, but he tried to do too much himself." Apparently Fowler was a micromanager unable to delegate duties to others.

On the other hand, when it came to business, Bob Weber's managerial skills were marginal at best. When he took over the reins of a viable, successful quartet, he was a fun-loving twenty-one-year-old who was more interested in pairing up with a female after the concert than taking care of business. Oak Ridge Quartet members chuckle about Weber's filing system, which consisted of the pockets in his pants, coat, and shirt. He would have money, receipts, and invoices stuck away in every crevice of his clothing. Whitfield even remembered the time Weber dropped his cash roll in a urinal, which he hastily retrieved and then washed off. "When it came time to pay us, he would fish fifty dollars out of one pocket and then get some more out of another one. This was his bookkeeping system; it was horrible," said Calvin.

While the Oaks may have been battling toe-to-toe and holding their own with the Blackwood Brothers and the Statesmen onstage, when it came to managerial astuteness Weber was no match for James Blackwood or Hovie Lister, who not only watched every penny that came into their organizations, but were always looking for new business opportunities. Blackwood and Lister undoubtedly shared ideas, such as teaming up for appearances, but James Blackwood also benefited from the organizational expertise and vision of bass singer J. D. Sumner, who joined the Blackwood Brothers Quartet in 1954.

It was Sumner who introduced James Blackwood to the basic administrative concept of division of labor. Thereafter, the members of the Blackwood Brothers had specific offstage duties that made the organization much more efficient. Sumner also sold Blackwood on the idea of touring in a bus, an idea that was quickly copied by the Statesmen. Weber had no one in his organization who thought like Sumner.

James Blackwood persuaded RCA records to make him one of their distributors, which created immense profits for him and the Blackwood Brothers. Hovie Lister struck a television deal with Nabisco that was extremely lucrative and generated thousands of dollars for him and the Statesmen. The Oaks could have remained viable under such circumstances. Unfortunately, Weber not only lacked business savvy but also was surrounded by a group of young men with a very casual attitude about life and work in general. In looking back on his years with the Oaks, Calvin fondly recalls, "The Oaks were the most fun group I ever worked with. We had no earthly notion about what good business was and didn't care. We couldn't have cared less."

What hurt the Oaks more than Weber's loose management was that gospel music tightened up in the mid-fifties, and, to make things worse, the economy was in a mild slump. However, the real problem with gospel music was supply and demand. Because of the popularity of gospel music in the early-to-mid-1950s, many new groups formed and tried to make a go of it full-time. There were so many groups competing that bookings were harder to get and the promoters could pay less. In addition, the novelty of the all-night singing had worn off. The shows never seemed to change, so if you had seen one, you had seen them all.

Bob Weber quit the group before they finally broke up. The others could see it coming. Weber married an extremely attractive young woman who couldn't stand the thought of Bob being gone a week or two at a time. "She would just stand at the door and squall when we left to go on the road," said Calvin. Soon thereafter, Weber quit singing entirely and started booking the Chuck Wagon Gang out of Statesville.

Calvin quit both the group and gospel music, venting his feelings of frustration in a candid, emotional tirade at the all-night singing in Atlanta, Georgia, in December 1956. He told a shocked audience that he was leaving gospel music to sing rock and country in a nightclub. "I can't recall exactly what I said that night. It was something to the effect that I'm tired of the rat race. I told them, this is supposed to be a Christian thing but it isn't. I told them that a lot of people in the business are two-faced, and I'm sure that gave me a special place in Hovie's low-esteem department. My parents had heard me complain to them a lot about all the things that were happening because it was like most businesses; it was a terrible business. It was dog-eat-dog," said Calvin.

He was getting out, he told the audience. He had sung in nightclubs in the past and he'd do it again, this time at Hale's Supper Club in Atlanta, which had a house band and a stand-up comedian. Among other things, Calvin was completely put off by all the married gospel singers he saw who would give Christian testimony on stage either through speech or song and then commit adultery afterwards. At the time Calvin was, of course, a notorious skirt-chaser, too, but he was single. He also observed drinking and drugs among quartet members, which he found inconsistent with what the industry stood for. He was certainly no saint himself, but he wasn't a hypocrite, either. What you saw was what you got with Calvin; it wasn't that way with others.

Calvin wasn't the only person who was turned off by the hypocrisy and philandering. Gordon Stoker recalled that at one point during the 1950s the Jordanaires were considering a career change that would have put them full-time on the southern gospel music circuit. During that period, they traveled to Atlanta and appeared there at an all-night singing. Stoker remembered that while the group was backstage, a gospel music star—now an icon—came up them and said, "Boys, you sing those good gospel songs into their heart, and before you know it, you're in their pants." Stoker observed, "We're not nobody's bunch of angels, but when he said that, it was just like some-body throwing a cold bucket of water on us. Neal Mathews said to me, 'If you haven't signed any contracts—don't. I don't ever want to do another gospel all-night singing—ever!' We made up our minds to not ever do any again, and I just praise the Lord that he opened doors for us."

The last appearance for Calvin with the Oaks was December 1956. Weber had already quit the road. Bobby Whitfield had a wife and young child. He had had fun as well as a rich and rewarding experience with the Oaks, but he decided to give up the road and gospel music and take up barbering. Both Les Roberson and Cat Freeman joined the mighty Statesmen. Roberson, a natural baritone, moved into Jake Hess's second tenor role but was out of range and soon developed voice problems. Freeman replaced Denver Crumpler, who died in March 1957.

Wally Fowler stepped in immediately, and with Smitty Gatlin re-formed the Oaks. The new Oak Ridge Quartet began appearing a couple of weeks after the previous group had disbanded. Calvin moved to Atlanta and began singing at Hale's Supper Club, leaving gospel music behind him. As far as he was concerned, he would never perform at another all-night singing as long as he lived. What he didn't realize was that his biggest and best days as a gospel music singer were immediately ahead of him, offering a period of fame and adulation that would exceed his wildest imagination. It would have never happened if the Oaks hadn't broken up.

12. A New Era

Baseball historian Roger Kahn has referred to the years from 1947 to 1957 as "the Era." It was the period in which the three New York City teams—the Yankees, Giants, and Dodgers—ruled the baseball world. Kahn could have left out the Giants except for one brief shining season; the Era, for all intents, was about the total domination of major league baseball by the Yankees and the Dodgers, in that order.

Many times over the years parallels have been drawn between the Yankees and the Dodgers and the Blackwood Brothers and the Statesmen quartets. Just as the two New York City baseball teams dominated the major leagues from the late forties through the fifties, so did the Blackwoods and the Statesmen in southern gospel music. In 1957, however, the era came to an end for both the Yanks and the Dodgers as well as the Blackwoods and Statesmen. In 1957, the Milwaukee Braves beat the Yankees to become baseball's world champions. The Braves were, relatively speaking, an old organization; they had been in existence for decades. However, in the world of southern gospel music, a group of young Atlanta upstarts formed a trio that shot straight to the top in a matter of months, knocking the firmly entrenched Statesmen and Blackwoods from their lofty perch.

Nineteen fifty-seven was just beginning to unfold as Don Butler made his way into Atlanta one early January morning so he could have breakfast at his favorite eatery—Davis Brothers Restaurant, in downtown Atlanta, off Forsythe Street. Davis Brothers was popular; it was a good place to eat and a lot of swell people hung out there. When he got close, he parked his car and began walking to the restaurant. Although the sun was still low in the east, the traffic was already getting brisk and there were a lot of people on the sidewalks.

At the time, Butler was at a crossroads in his life. He had come out of college in the early 1950s and had gone to work in merchandising in Atlanta, his hometown, for the prestigious R. H. Macy chain of department stores. He had done well, but it wasn't what he wanted to do, so he quit and became a disc jockey. He liked playing and listening to gospel music but he enjoyed singing it even more, so he left his job and became the baritone singer for the Revelaires Quartet, a talented but short-lived group who disbanded in late 1956. Butler was a Renaissance man of sorts, but his true love was music. He was an introvert, and his mind was constantly filled with musical ideas; he toyed mentally with countless melodies and harmonies. Lately he had been preoccupied with an idea for a gospel music group that he knew was somewhat radical, but he was convinced it would work—if he could find the right singers.

As he waited for the light to change, he looked across the street and spotted the LeFevre Trio's piano player—Bob Robinson. Bob was striding briskly, head down, with a folded newspaper under his arm. He had a grim look on his face and appeared to have had a sleepless night. Don was surprised to see Bob because he knew that the LeFevres were in Philadelphia working as a house group for an evangelist named Thea Jones. Jones had been with the Church of God but had left and founded his own church in Philadelphia. Jones's church was in a large building that most knew as the Metropolitan Opera House, or Met. Jones had achieved great success as part of the charismatic religious movement that was sweeping the country in the mid-fifties.

As part of Jones's ministry, the LeFevres were regularly performing before ten thousand people in a building that covered almost an entire city block in downtown Philadelphia. The LeFevres had a strong Pentecostal background. Alphus and Urias LeFevre had studied music and academics at the Church of God's Bible Training School, in addition to having grown up in the church. Eva Mae LeFevre's father, H. L. Whittington, was said to have perhaps built more churches for the Church of God than any other person. In addition to being musically talented, the LeFevres were devout, fundamentalist Christians—zealots, in fact.

Thea Jones's services were in essence an open-ended affair, a nonstop revival running seven days a week. It was a rigorous and demanding schedule for anyone to follow, with practically no leisure time or off days. In addition, anyone playing for the LeFevres had Urias LeFevre to contend with—big Urias called the shots for the group, and he had a richly deserved reputation for running a tight ship. In fact, it was a well-known joke in gospel music circles that if you worked for the LeFevres, Urias believed that he should be able to dictate what you ate, what time you got up, what color socks you wore, and what time you went to bed. Bob Robinson simply didn't fit into such a structured, confining mold. Still a young man, Bob had acquired a reputation as a rising star in gospel music but also as someone who on occasion showed up late and sometimes not at all. Such behavior was unacceptable to the LeFevres and they let Bob go. He had just returned from Philadelphia that early Monday morning when Don Butler saw him.

Don didn't know Bob well, but he wanted to talk to him, so he got his attention and suggested they have breakfast together. Without any enthusiasm, Bob agreed. As they cut up their eggs and sipped their coffee, Bob confided that he was no longer with the LeFevres; when Don heard that, his mental machinery went into overdrive. He pitched Robinson on the idea that since neither of them was singing with anyone, they should perhaps try something together—maybe start a group. Don told Bob that he had always been impressed with Bob's voice, particularly on the LeFevres' hit "Stop and Pray," which featured a stunning solo by Robinson.

As dishes and utensils clattered in the background, Don explained that what he had in mind was a trio, and while he didn't mention who the third member would be, the person he was thinking of was the finest gospel music singer in the world, at least in Don's opinion. And in January 1957 the possible third member wasn't even singing gospel music. Don Butler was thinking of Calvin Newton. Bob listened respectfully to Don's suggestion and thanked him for complimenting his singing style, but he was too dispirited from just having been let go by the LeFevres to commit to anything. The breakfast conversation ended with Bob telling Don that he'd think about it.

Don was discouraged by Bob's lack of enthusiasm but thought the idea was a good one and he held on to it. He realized it was radical—southern gospel music had always meant four white men singing barbershop harmonies accompanied by a bouncy, smiling piano player. But Butler had come up with the idea of a trio, with each of the three men having a great vocal range, so that they could cover the four parts by sliding up and down the musical scale and could also trade parts, or invert harmonies, as it came to be known.

Six days later, on a mild Saturday evening, Don Butler was taking a leisurely walk along Peachtree Street in downtown Atlanta. Looking at the traffic, he spotted a 1955 Thunderbird convertible. The sleek, sporty automobile stood out from the other vehicles that were slowly moving down the well-known boulevard. The '55 T-bird had a detachable roof, allowing it to become a convertible. Butler noticed the T-bird was roofless and was being driven by someone he instantly recognized as Calvin Newton. Only Calvin Newton would drive a convertible with its top down in January, Don thought as he chuckled inwardly.

"Hey, Calvin," Don shouted. Calvin glanced quickly back over his shoulder and saw the tall young man whom he recognized as Don Butler. Butler motioned to him to stop. Calvin immediately cut his wheels hard to the left in a U-turn, creating havoc among other motorists on the busy Atlanta street. Maneuvering nimbly, he now was headed in the opposite direction. He drove past Butler and then swung sharply again to the left, tires screeching, coming back into the lane he had seconds earlier departed, making a complete circle. He pulled to the curb beside Don and killed the engine.

Calvin then raised himself up and sat on top of the seat. He fished a cigarette out of his shirt pocket, lit it quickly, exhaled, and then smiled. Don said hello, inquired of his well-being and asked him where he was staying. Calvin told him he was living with J. W. and Ruby Nelson out in Decatur. Don knew where that was—just down the street from Wally and Ginnie Varner's place. He had heard Calvin was singing secular music in an Atlanta nightclub, so he asked Calvin if he was serious about a pop career. Calvin responded rather absently that he had some people interested.

The two made a few more idle comments as they watched the Saturday night traffic promenade down the famous street, neon signs above them illuminating the skyline with a rainbow of colors. Don then told Calvin he had an idea that he wanted to discuss with him. What's that? Calvin asked, turning to face him. Butler mentioned his earlier conversation with Robinson. He suggested to Calvin that the three of them could get together and try something, just feel it out and hear how they sounded together. Who knows, they might sound pretty good. Calvin was skeptical. He had sung gospel music since the mid-1940s and he couldn't help wondering how the three of them could compensate for the missing vocal part. Besides that, he barely knew Butler; in fact, he had never even heard him sing.

But he was impressed by Butler's enthusiasm, and besides, he had already grown tired of singing to a bunch of noisy drunks in a dark, smoke-filled dive out on Memorial Drive, even though he had only been performing there for a few weeks. Moreover, he missed the all-night singings, especially the fans. At the various venues, he had thrilled thousands of men, women, and children with his inspired solos as well as his high-energy shenanigans. The more he listened to Butler, the more interested he became. "How will it work?" he asked Butler. Well, Butler explained, they would have to double some, switch parts around, but he, Butler, could sing either second tenor, baritone, or bass. And there was Robinson, who was a great piano player and an outstanding tenor. Bob could sing either first or second tenor, and baritone, too, for that matter. Calvin was familiar with Robinson and he agreed with Butler's assessment—Robinson certainly could play and sing. Calvin, of course, knew that he also had a three-octave range, as did Butler and Robinson. This thing about switching parts might work, and it might be fun.

Calvin thought about it for a few minutes, pursed his lips, then shrugged his shoulders and said, "What the heck, couldn't hurt to give it a try." That was all Don needed. The next day he contacted Bob, who by now was agreeable to the idea. They needed a place to rehearse, with a piano, of course. Don called a preacher friend who was holding services in an old Atlanta theater. The preacher agreed to let the three use the piano and the auditorium for their tryout. The following day they met and went to the old theater in downtown Atlanta. Don opened the door to the darkened building, made his way down an aisle and, after stumbling a couple of times, found the light switch to the stage. The building was musty and smelled like stale popcorn.

Bob found the piano. He pulled the bench back, wiped the dust off with his hands, sat down, and made a quick chord followed by a few runs and fills. The piano was woefully out of tune, but would do. The three looked at one another. So, anybody want to try one? Nobody suggested anything. Finally, Bob said, "What about 'Old Gospel Ship?' " The song had been a LeFevres' candy stick ever since Alphus LeFevre put new arrangements to it back in 1938. The LeFevres recorded the song and had a huge hit with it. It was almost always featured whenever the trio appeared. Having recently been with them, Bob could play and sing it in his sleep.

"Go ahead," said Don. "Old Gospel Ship" is a spirited, camp meeting tune. Bob immediately launched into it with some animated piano work. Bob began singing, "Oh, I'm a-gonna take a trip," and Calvin jumped right in, as it was a song he had sung many times in church. Don wasn't familiar with it but listened for a few seconds and joined in also. Three verses and a chorus later they concluded with the big ending they would use countless times over the years. They smiled and looked at one another, nodding— not bad, not bad at all. Ragged, of course, but that was to be expected. The LeFevres had just had their candy stick snatched from them, and the unnamed group had launched their career with an appropriate tune.

From there, rehearsals moved to J. W. and Ruby Nelson's new brick house in Decatur where Calvin was living. The house was convenient to all three, and the Nelsons had a piano. J. W. and Ruby Nelson loved gospel music and had been fans of Calvin since his days with the Oak Ridge Quartet. They had met Calvin and the other Oaks when the Nelsons were living in Rome, Georgia, and had invited the quartet over for dinner. For the rest of January and on into February, the Nelsons' house rocked with gospel music that was being sung differently from how it ever had been before. The trio would begin around eight in the morning and go hard until lunch. They would then break for an hour and come back and sing until around five or six, when they would stop and have dinner. Often, they would sing into the evening.

All three were perfectionists, and because of this, there was an unstated commitment to excellence that existed among them. Together they worked tirelessly on innovative arrangements and tight harmonies, in the process acquiring a distinctiveness that set them apart dramatically from all the other gospel groups. There was never a suggestion by any of them that they should try to be different from other southern gospel groups, in sound or arrangements, just a commitment to sound as good as possible.

From the outset there was an egalitarian quality about the trio. They became a true musical democracy with not one but three lead singers, which was highly unusual, especially considering their backgrounds. It seemed logical that Calvin would be the featured singer; after all, he had the marquee name. Calvin had been a member of the famous Blackwood Brothers Quartet at eighteen, and was the featured soloist and emcee of the talented Oak Ridge Quartet in the early-to-mid-fifties. It was widely known that he had one of the finest voices in gospel music; in fact, many, including Butler, thought he had the best. Yet, despite his success and reputation, Calvin accepted Butler and Robinson as equals and never sought separate billing, something most others in a similar situation would have probably insisted on.

Despite their not being as well known, both Butler and Robinson had strong credentials. Like Calvin, Bob Robinson had also been with a heavyweight group—the LeFevres—and in April 1955, the *Gospel Singing World* wrote, "According to the experts [Bob Robinson] is destined to become one of the greatest in gospel music." Two of the more prominent gospel music disc jockeys in the 1950s were Birmingham's Jack Jackson and Atlanta's Warren Roberts. Both wrote columns for the *Gospel Singing World.* Jack Jackson observed in his column in April 1955, "I never thought it could be done without Eva Mae, but the LeFevres have done it. With the help of Bob Robinson they have topped all the other groups with their recording of CLIMBING UP THE MOUNTAIN and it is terrific. In the middle, Bob slows it down and heads for the top of that terrific range of his. Boys, take a bow . . . The other side, I have a feeling will soon be out by other groups when they hear it. It's just that kind, STOP AND PRAY . . . " "Stop and Pray" was the song featuring Robinson's voice that so impressed Don Butler. In addition, Robinson's superb piano style was remarkably similar to Eva Mae's.

Don Butler's credentials were more modest. The Revelaires had been as talented as some of the more popular groups, but lacked name recognition. However, the truth was—and the world would soon find out—that Butler was perhaps the finest baritone singer in southern gospel music. Calvin came to be enormously impressed with Butler's singing, but also with his assertive, take-charge attitude on stage. Butler did things with a flair, as did Calvin.

Early on, Calvin, Don, and Bob adopted a simple formula for determining who sang the lead on a number: it was settled by challenge. A singing contest was held and after everyone had sung, a vote was taken and a winner declared. There were never any hard feelings and the person singing the best rendition always won. However, with most of their songs each member soloed on a particular verse, with the other two joining on the chorus. It worked out well, as most gospel songs were three verses long, giving all three a solo on each number. As rehearsals continued, the group's harmonies became tighter, and they came to have an uncanny ability to sense one another's spontaneous improvisations. The three developed or perhaps discovered that they had a remarkable chemistry and cohesiveness that was present every time they sang together, even later when years lapsed between performances. Don Butler summarized what happened during this formative period, stating, "We became a unit."

13. A Matter of Style

Some groups dared to be different, and those groups that dared to be different brought about the changes.

—*Bob Terrell*, The Music Men: The Story of Professional Gospel Quartet Singing

The Sons of Song had an unusual and unique sound. When attempting to describe it, most people—even music experts—simply say that it was different. While that may be true, at least one of the reasons they sounded so different was that everyone else sounded the same. By 1957 a rigid framework for singing southern gospel music had evolved; it was nothing less than an orthodoxy or dogma. Within this framework, there was to be an exaggerated emphasis on enunciation and diction because of the lyric content. Gospel songs were inspirational and were considered to have an important message; therefore, it was essential that the words be clear and easily understood. A deaf person would have had no problem reading the lips of James Blackwood or other practitioners as they performed onstage. Furthermore, the song was supposed to be sung just as it appeared on the page, with absolutely no deviations. Consequently, there was to be no interpretation of a song other than that dictated by the musical notes and words on the song sheet. Any student slurring up to a note could expect a stern lecture about the proper way to sing a gospel song.

All of these musical ideas and philosophies came from the gospel singing schools where most of the singers had been trained, particularly the large Stamps-Baxter and Vaughn music schools. Students there developed skills that improved their singing but limited them. The Stamps-Baxter and

Vaughn singing schools made no allowances for individuality; in fact, they stoutly forbade it. On the one hand, the contributions of the Stamps-Baxter and Vaughn singing schools were essential to the development of southern gospel music; without them there probably wouldn't have been such a musical form. Yet, on the other hand, their teaching and musical philosophies resulted in a cookie-cutter, assembly-line method of turning out singers who sang in the same manner—with the same techniques, phrasing, intonations, and inflections. This style of singing evolved into nothing less than a paradigm: it became the way gospel songs were supposed to be sung.

Beginning in 1957, the Sons of Song broke the paradigm and defied the rules that had evolved from Stamps-Baxter, Vaughn, and others. The three didn't consciously or deliberately set out to violate these sacrosanct rules, yet they clearly ignored the conventions despite the fact that Butler and Robinson were both Stamps-Baxter graduates. Butler's singing style was an eclectic mix of opera, jazz, and southern gospel. He had over fourteen years of vocal training, which included world-class high school glee clubs, large church choirs, and private lessons, plus the three weeks he spent at the Stamps-Baxter School of Music. As a result he had superb vocal techniques, especially the ability to project his voice, utilizing his diaphragm and lungs. Butler's voice, notably his diction and inflection, probably benefited from his years as an announcer and disc jockey. His vocal deliveries sounded urbane, sophisticated, and silky smooth. Butler sang with a certain flair, or panache, more reminiscent of a jazz vocalist than a gospel singer, undoubtedly a result of his emulating jazz great Billy Eckstine. "Billy Eckstine was my man. He was the one that taught Sarah Vaughn how to sing. He was my idol, and he could sing blues, pop, or jazz," said Butler.

Particularly impressive was Butler's phrasing and intonation. He would sometimes stretch words out, adding syllables like fifties pop star Johnny Ray. Yet, he would also attack words in staccato fashion, leaving them compacted and clipped. His vocal performance on the Sons of Song's recording of "In the Garden" showcases his unique phrasing. In the 1970s when he was managing the business affairs of the Stamps Quartet, Elvis Presley invited him to come to Lake Tahoe and emcee one of Elvis's shows. After the performance, Don boarded one of Elvis's private jets—the Lisa Marie—and went to the refrigerator for some orange juice. While he was there, someone sneaked up behind him and sang, "Guhhhhoooooooooooooood Bless America," then said, "Man, you thrill my ass when you sing that." It was Elvis, commenting on Butler's phrasing on the well-known patriotic tune.

Butler's musical tastes were diverse. As a boy, he became enamored with opera and seriously considered pursuing a career as an opera singer, having received strong encouragement to do so from his voice teacher. He would listen spellbound for hours to the recordings of operatic star Richard Green. He was similarly amazed at the vocal prowess of Paul Robeson. In addition, Butler loved jazz, especially Eckstine, Sarah Vaughn, Roberta Hunter, and Art Tatum, the fabulous blind piano player. However, when, as a teenager, he chanced upon hearing and seeing the Rangers Quartet at an Atlanta radio station, he realized he had found the type of music he wanted to sing and perform thereafter.

Calvin, on the other hand, was a pop stylist with incredible range; in fact, using falsetto, he could sing A flat above high C. He could also drop down and sing baritone; he began as a baritone with the Oak Ridge Quartet. Calvin always considered his control to be his biggest musical asset. Don Butler stated that Calvin was the only singer he ever heard who could bridge a full-throated sound with falsetto without a break. "When I was with the Sons, I could slide from a full-throated sound to falsetto on the same *note*," said Calvin.

Gospel music songwriter Sammy Easom characterized Calvin's voice as both "pretty" and "smooth." Writer Walter Carter said he sang with a lot of "dynamic swoops." Easom and others are convinced that Calvin could have been a successful pop singer. Explaining his so-called pop style, Calvin commented, "It wasn't a purposeful thing. I didn't say, 'I'm gonna sing pop style.' I just sang." Don Butler added, "He sang like he felt. It was inside him." Calvin, of course, sang pop and country tunes in Phenix City, Alabama, in the late forties, in Japan in the early fifties, and in Atlanta in the mid-fifties and recorded a rock ballad to great critical acclaim in 1959.

Calvin's vocal style of smooth crooning mixed with lots of falsetto is similar, if not identical, to that of the Ink Spots' lead singer, Bill Kenny, who influenced countless others, including the Platters' Tony Williams and many of the various doo-wop groups that proliferated in the 1950s. Calvin was not being imitative of Kenny; he merely adapted his style to his capabilities, and, as Butler noted, he "sang it as he felt it." Yet since Calvin had grown up as a Holy Roller, he could also throw his head back and rattle the rafters; that was second nature. He could croon sweetly and smoothly, but he could sing with spirit and feeling as well. He was so versatile that he could sing any type of music any way he wanted to—rock, country, or gospel; he was comfortable in all genres. Calvin has stated that no music particularly influenced him, and, unlike Butler, he had no music heros whom he wanted to emulate. However, like Butler, as a young man he saw a southern gospel group that amazed him with their sound—the legendary Rangers Quartet. "When I heard them, all I could say was, 'Gaaaaaaaalee—they were fabulous,'" he said, echoing Butler's sentiments about the group. Calvin's wife has stated that, in fact, Calvin probably did have influences from the world of music; he just wasn't aware of them.

Bob Robinson provided the perfect counterpoint for Calvin and Butler, who, with their crooning and jazz stylings, sometimes sounded more like they belonged in a nightclub lounge than at an all-night singing. Robinson's musical interests were narrower than those of the other two members. He had grown up playing and singing in the Church of God, and that was his main music influence. In addition, he was a Stamps-Baxter graduate, having made the sojourn to Dallas, Texas, as a young man, following the same route many others did who eventually hooked up with major gospel groups.

As a child, and as a college student at Western Carolina, he studied and played classical music. When he joined Calvin and Butler in 1957, Robinson was an accomplished pianist who deliberately and wisely used restraint in playing with the Sons of Song. Robinson realized that the strength of the Sons' sound was their voices; therefore, most of the time he chose to play simple rhythms and chords to give the group structure and keep them on pitch. Much of Robinson's piano work with the Sons was simply chording along with the vocals, although some of his musicianship was both sophisticated and complex. It would have been a grave mistake for him to have played piano in the flamboyant overkill fashion of Jackie Marshall or Wally Varner, and it is to his credit that he realized it and was willing to hold his musical talent in check.

In addition, Robinson was an excellent arranger. Although Calvin, Butler, and Robinson all contributed to the arranging of Sons of Song material, Robinson did the lion's share. When discussing the distinctiveness of the group, most focus on their unusual sound, but their remarkable, complex, and truly innovative arrangements also set them apart from other gospel groups. That Robinson became a stylist despite his Stamps-Baxter training is probably indicative of his creativity. As an artist, he wanted to put his own individual stamp on his work.

Like Calvin's and Butler's, Robinson's vocal range was three octaves, allowing him and the other two to switch parts, or invert harmonies, as it is more commonly known. The Sons became noted for this and, according to Butler, were the first group in gospel music to invert harmonies in a syncopated rhythm. Calvin and Robinson became so adept at inverting harmonies that they would sometimes switch parts in midsentence, creating a musical shell game of who's on first tenor. Sons of Song fans have played parts of records over and over trying to determine if it is Calvin or Bob Robinson who is singing a particular part. Shortly before his death, Robinson joked that he and Calvin inverted harmonies because neither was capable of singing first tenor all the way through a song, and while he may have been kidding, he nonetheless gave the chief reason that most groups do so: because of the singers' limitations, they occasionally have to switch parts.

Robinson frequently sang with an anguished urgency—a glass-breaking crescendo accompanied by room-shaking vibrato. In the early 1950s, while practicing at his parents' home, Robinson actually shattered a thick glass globe on a lamp when he sustained a high note for several seconds. Robinson sang with such intensity that occasionally, like a train jumping the tracks, he would go off pitch and flat a note. "When he did, me and Calvin would flat the note, too," said Butler, adding facetiously that maybe that might account for their unusual sound.

The Sons of Song were not only gospel music's first all-male trio but were also the first group in which all of the members were soloists. A song sung by them was as likely to begin with Butler's booming baritone out front as it was to feature one of the others, which was unusual. Southern gospel baritones are usually hummers and harmonizers. As Calvin pointed out, "Any one of us could have given a concert by ourselves. We were all soloists." There were never any arguments over who would be the featured vocalist. As Don Butler emphasized, the Sons were a unit, not unlike a basketball team composed of unselfish team players. With the Sons, no one cared who took the shot, as long as the ball went in the hole.

While the group was a trio composed of soloists, it was another trait that set them apart from the Stamps-Baxter trained gospel singers and made them so distinctive: all three were stylists. Stylists are singers who interpret both lyrics and music, infusing songs with their own distinctive musical personality. Bing Crosby's crooning, Frank Sinatra's backphrasing, Buddy Holly's hiccupping sound, and Sam Cooke's unique type of yodel are all examples of individual styles. Elvis Presley's version of "Blue Moon of Kentucky"—in which he put a driving rockabilly beat on what had been a slow, wailing, bluegrass tune—is an excellent example of a stylist interpreting a song. However, the term "stylist" is not always complimentary. Some people differentiate stylists from singers, saying that stylists are those who cannot sing. For that reason, among others, the Sons of Song were not everyone's cup of tea.

Gospel Music Hall of Fame producer, conductor, and arranger Ralph Carmichael identified what made the Sons of Song stand apart from other individual singers and groups. Carmichael observed, "Generally speaking, when you are singing in a group, the group has its own style, and you have to submit to that if you are a group singer. Many times a group singer would not be able to carry the aplomb that is necessary to step out and do a solo. The guys [Sons of Song] could step out and do a solo, but at the same time they knew how to discipline themselves for group singing, and they made a beautiful blend, plus they had the rhythmics and everything. They were good group singers, so I would pay the guys a double compliment: I wouldn't want to say they were only stylists, because many soloists are only stylists; they could never keep in step with a group. On the other hand, many group singers, when you take them away from the printed page and the disciplines of sight-reading, they aren't able to express themselves or project with that solo quality that is necessary. But I would say the Sons of Song were adept in both departments."

This, then, was what truly set the Sons apart. They were not just three soloists who sang together and tried to make do on harmonies, but three divergent stylists, who could also meld their voices together in a highly unusual but seamless harmony. A listener is treated to four interpretations—those of each singer and of the group.

Although their sound was inimitable, the Sons of Song had a dramatic impact on the way gospel music was perceived and performed. Through their innovative stylings, inverted harmonies, and unusual arrangements, the Sons demonstrated that gospel music didn't have to be done by the book. Fans and experts alike referred to what the Sons of Song were doing then as "cutting edge," and some, such as *Singing News* editor Jerry Kirksey, say they were the first contemporary gospel music group.

The Sons of Song profoundly affected a group that ultimately became better known than they did—the Singing Rambos. In his 1992 book, coauthored by Bob Terrell, Buck Rambo wrote, "The Sons of Song were completely different from the others. All the rest were all-male quartets with piano players. The Sons of Song were a trio using a piano. *When they sang, it completely wiped that audience out* [emphasis added]. They sang with such beautiful harmony that you never seemed to realize the piano was there . . . We marveled at the way they sang. We bought one of their albums . . . then drove back to Evansville, about 130 miles, and spent the rest of the night listening to that album. *That record probably affected our lives more than anything we'd done or known . . .*" [emphasis added].

The Sons of Song were not the first stylists in southern gospel music; that distinction probably belongs to Jake Hess, who began interpreting lyrics when he became a member of the Statesmen. Hess, of course, has perhaps the most identifiable voice in southern gospel music and many consider him the best. As a west Texas youngster in the 1950s, Gary McSpadden was a great fan of Jake Hess. McSpadden related the following story on his syndicated radio show in 1999.

"One Sunday morning, I was about thirteen years old, and I'd been listening to Jake for four or five years and just loved his music. A song came on that morning called 'Something Within Me.' I screamed for my mom and dad about halfway through the song. I said, 'Come here and listen . . . you gotta come here and listen to this—all of these guys sound like Jake Hess.' And what I meant by that was they had all of these inflections, moves, and slides and a stylistic way of singing. Unbelievable!" The excited west Texas youth had just heard the Sons of Song for the first time. He went on to have a distinguished career in gospel music, singing with such popular groups as the Oak Ridge Boys, the Imperials, and the Bill Gaither Trio, as well as having a fine solo career.

McSpadden added, "That song still excites me. I called my mom this morning and told her we were taping the Sons of Song, and I asked her, do you remember that morning, and she said, 'Yes, that's the most excited I've ever seen you.'" McSpadden continued, "What made them different was the way they approached the songs. They emphasized different things. Of course, they all three had great voices, particularly when Don Butler was with them. Overall, I think the things that impressed me most were their use of staccato, the way they blended, the way they seemed to do things all together in a different form, the way they phrased their lines, and the way they said their words. As a youngster, I had all of their records—a couple of copies, in fact, on the vinyl. I loved their music, and they shaped a lot of what we aspiring singers did at the time." Bill Gaither noted that when McSpadden joined the Gaither Trio, he was a "different kind of vocalist." That difference would seem to be at least partly attributable to McSpadden's having grown up listening to the vocal stylings of Jake Hess, Calvin Newton, Don Butler, and Bob Robinson.

"Something Within Me" was one of the Sons' most popular songs, and serves to showcase their interpretive stylings. The tune opens with Butler's booming baritone. He sings the first verse with a warm, easy assurance. He then passes the vocal baton to Calvin, who croons his part; he is smooth and relaxed and also does his patented vocal lick of going from the full-throated sound to falsetto. Robinson sings the last verse with more intensity than either Butler or Calvin. Robinson packs his voice with urgency, and, whereas Butler and Calvin caress the words, he bites them off sharply. Then, on the chorus, all three come together, their voices crescendoing and then fading.

The Sons of Song had a unique style as a group, and the individual members had unique styles as well. As for the sound of the group, Butler said, "It had a pop feel to it. Calvin had an affinity for the pop style of music, even when he was with the Oak Ridge [Quartet] because he put that pop flavor into it. I have an affinity for jazz and pop and I love the music, and it [the pop sound] came easy for us, more so than it did for Bob, because Bob's background and music appreciation was more into the church style of music, although he had the interpretation in his voice—stylistically that added to that special effect."

Indeed, more than anything, it was Robinson's crying, wailing intonations that imbued their sound with melancholy. Many of the Sons' songs have a sad, mournful quality about them. Above all, Robinson sang with great passion and feeling. In that regard, comparisons could be drawn between Robinson and Johnny Ray, the 1950s pop sensation who was dubbed "the cry guy," for his emotional rendering of such songs as "The Little White Cloud That Cried," "Cry," and others. Ray's sound had more of an edge to it than Robinson's, and Ray's voice—burnished by years of cigarettes and bourbon—was harsher. All three of the Sons of Song could bring a high level of intensity to their voices. Bill Gaither observed that the Sons of Song were perhaps the first southern gospel group to truly sing with emotion.

While these three unique voices were pleasing and interesting to listen to individually, it was when they joined together that the Sons of Song's unusual sound emerged. Sammy Easom sagely observed, "They were explosive vocally, but at the same time, perfectly as one, they sang each word simultaneously, crescendoing and then dropping together to a whisper." Similarly, Calvin recalled, "One prominent deejay said, 'They could sound like a symphonic orchestra on one phrase, then whisper the next phrase like a baby's sigh.'" Their ability to stay together through complex vocal arrangements is attributable to chemistry, intuition, and long and intense rehearsals.

The three had an almost clairvoyant ability to sense when one was about to depart in a particular musical direction. It was as if each had a musical sixth sense enabling him to intuit or divine what the other two were contemplating. "We never sang a song on stage the same way twice," remarked Butler, adding, "Calvin and I were so in tune that no matter what one of us did, the other one knew it before they did it, and could change and follow without anybody ever realizing. It was just so unreal that I've tried many times to analyze it and figure it out, but I've never been able to." Bob Robinson noted, "We all thought the same way. We read each other so perfectly. Somebody else would jump ahead and take something that someone else was bound to miss." In Robinson's obituary in the *Singing News* Bob Terrell observed, "The Sons of Song were totally compatible, totally dedicated, and produced one of the greatest and most unusual blends of voices ever heard on gospel stages."

By late February 1957 the three had a dozen or so songs polished and ready to perform. They felt it was time to get an expert opinion on how they sounded, so they asked neighbor and gospel music pianist Wally Varner to listen and tell them what he thought. Varner was completely knocked out. He'd never heard anything like it—the vocal energy, the soaring harmonies, the emotional intensity. Still in awe decades later, Varner stated, "They all looked at me when they finished, and all I could say was 'Wow' . . . They were amazing!"

"Wow" became an oft-repeated term associated with the dynamic trio. This group was set apart from others not only by their unusual sound but also by their physical appearance. The Sons of Song were young—Bob was twenty-six, Don twenty-seven, and Calvin twenty-eight—and were all good-looking men with athletic physiques. In fact, Bob Robinson was drop-dead handsome. When Robinson walked into a room, heads turned and people began trying to figure out what movie they had seen him in. Robinson's son, Dan, stated that Bob had an offer to be Elvis Presley's double in a movie. Four decades later a waitress looked over someone's shoulder in a restaurant and caught a glimpse of the group's first publicity shot, now yellowed with age. She responded, "Wow, who are those handsome guys?"

After practicing for several weeks, they began to cast about for a name. The Men of Music and several other names were considered and rejected.

Friends and family offered suggestions; nothing seemed right. Finally, Alphus LeFevre volunteered, "Why don't you call yourselves the Sons of Song?" Alphus thus provided them with both their name and their biggest early hit—"Old Gospel Ship."

After a few weeks of concentrating on singing, they began to work on stage presence. There wouldn't be any jumping off piano benches as the Statesmen did nor would they do "Go Out to the Program" or anything similar. In fact, there wouldn't be any humor at all, other than little snippets thrown out by their emcee, and it was a foregone conclusion that Calvin would handle those chores. They had no plans to do anything other than sing their hearts out. Years later, Roy Pauley, attempting to put the group's awesome presence into the proper perspective, concluded, "They just stood there and sang."

By the end of February they knew it was time to try out their wings before an audience. They came up with the idea of going to the all-night singing in Birmingham the following Saturday night and seeing if Wally Fowler would let them sing. They wouldn't expect to be paid; they simply wanted the exposure. But how would they get there? Other than Calvin's T-bird, which was too small for three people, they didn't have a car. Aware of their dilemma, J. W. and Ruby Nelson offered to loan them their car, a brand new Chevrolet. J. W. and Ruby were proud of the car and held their breath as they handed Calvin the keys, hoping that it wouldn't get wrecked. But they thought the world of those three boys and would do anything to help them. However, since the three had not been working—all they had done for six weeks was rehearse—they didn't even have gas money. But J. W. took care of that, too, loaning them money for gas and food. Despite their financial plight they were unanimous about one item: they had to have tuxedos. They felt that looking good was part of a stage presence, so money was scrounged up for rentals.

On Saturday afternoon, March 9, 1957, dressed in their rented tuxes, they left Decatur, Georgia, and drove down U.S. Highway 78 to Birmingham in J. W. Nelson's new Chevrolet. The old two-lane blacktop, full of curves and hills, had the usual Saturday traffic: large trucks hauling freight, pickup trucks with farmers' families going into town for groceries and to socialize, a Greyhound bus taking passengers to Atlanta. At a couple of rest breaks en route they drew some stares. When they stopped for gas and a Coke in Bremen or Heflin, Calvin, the flirtatious one, probably melted a female teenager's heart with a wink and a smile. If so, it would be the first of many for the new group.

14. The Magic of Their Singing

They sang with a magic that held crowds in rapt attention.

—*Bob Terrell*, Singing News

By 1957 Wally Fowler's all-night singings were firmly entrenched in Nashville, Atlanta, and Birmingham. Birmingham City Auditorium was the largest venue of the three stops and was a hotbed of gospel music. Once a month, a huge, enthusiastic throng of seven thousand people queued up in long, serpentine lines to see their favorite acts. Overflow crowds could be accommodated with folding chairs placed on the stage, behind the entertainers. The price of admission was a bargain, considering the bevy of talent Fowler always had on hand. The low admission price and glut of talent resulted in the gospel groups not making very much money, and grousing was inevitable. Bob Weber, the bass singer and owner of the Oak Ridge Quartet in the mid-fifties recalled, "There was too much talent. Us and another group, we could have probably filled Atlanta ourself. And he'd [Fowler] have ten to twelve groups there. And you know, there's not that much to be squeezed out of a dollar bill—that's about what we charged back then."

The wealth of talent posed another problem for the Sons of Song. How were they going to persuade Wally to let them be on the show? Bob and Don had only a passing acquaintance with Fowler and were depending on

Calvin to get them onstage. Calvin had known Fowler since he joined the Oak Ridge Quartet in 1953, and the two had a good relationship. Calvin was confident Wally would put them on.

The trio arrived in Birmingham, parked the car, and managed to get in free through the back entrance. Backstage they chatted with members of the groups who were appearing that night and told them of their hopes of getting a spot on the show. The performers wished them good luck and told them they looked great in their tuxedos. On that particular evening— Saturday, March 9, 1957—the show consisted of Wally and the newly formed Oak Ridge Quartet; soloist Jake Hess, who had temporarily left the Statesmen and was also singing that night with the Homeland Harmony; the Happy Two (Shorty Bradford and Lee Roy Abernathy); Happy Edwards and the Harmoneers Quartet; the Cavaleers Quartet; the Johnson Sisters; and the Stamps Plainsmen Quartet from Dallas, Texas.

The Sons recall that Wally was incredibly busy that night; there was a full house, and the usual large show. There were a million details to attend to, and Wally insisted on trying to do them all himself. The concert quickly fell behind schedule. Nonetheless, the Sons managed to corner Wally and made their request. They only wanted to sing a few songs—for free, of course. Fowler dismissed the request out of hand. There were no spots on the show and the program was running behind already. Backstage was a beehive of activity. Others were waiting to talk to Wally. Before they could plead their case further, someone said, "Wally, we got a problem," and he was gone, leaving the group in midsentence. Things didn't look good for them.

However, the three young men were determined, even desperate, to go on. They were broke and had to have some bookings if they were going to become a viable group. To get bookings they had to have exposure; to get exposure they had to get onstage. Fowler continued to flit about, announcing groups and concert dates, hawking records and souvenirs, and then hurrying backstage to tend to the next minor crisis. He was aware that they had driven over from Atlanta and desperately wanted to sing. He'd known Calvin for years and wanted to accommodate them, but he just couldn't! Calvin stayed after him, however, and finally Fowler threw his hands up in despair.

"I told y'all I don't have a slot for you," he began. "But," he continued, frowning, looking at his watch, and then shrugging resignedly, "we're running forty-five minutes late for a concession break now, but forty-five minutes or an hour is not gonna make that much difference. I'll let you sing two or three songs right before we break for intermission." The Sons were elated. A few minutes later, Fowler came out and said to the audience, "Folks, we got a brand-new group and a brand-new idea we want you to see and hear tonight—a gospel music trio. You people remember Calvin Newton, who sang for several years for the Oak Ridge Quartet. He's appeared on all-night singings many, many times. He's here tonight with two other fine singers—Don Butler and Bob Roberson [sic]. They call themselves the Sons of Song. They weren't scheduled to sing tonight, but as a treat we're gonna let you hear from them right before intermission. Here, they are, making their first appearance, let's give a big hand and make 'em welcome—the Sons of Song."

Although he mispronounced Robinson's name, he had given them an enthusiastic buildup. However, people headed for the lobby. Don Butler recalled what happened next. "People started to get up wholesale and leave for intermission. We hit the stage and opened up with 'Old Gospel Ship,' and they froze in their tracks." Hunger, thirst, and other needs were quickly forgotten as people scurried back to their seats to hear the group. They sang with such emotion and energy; their harmonies were unbelievable, and they were so good-looking. Caught totally unawares, the audience was mesmerized.

A young woman from Birmingham, Mary Ann Price, was one of the herd that was stampeding to the lobby when she heard the group. She became infatuated with them from the first note and quickly made her way back to her seat. Within a few months, she became the president of their new fan club.

Concluding the catchy, uptempo number, the Sons then immediately launched into "Sometimes I Cry," destined to become one of their most popular songs. The tune began with Calvin crooning the first verse in soft but husky strains. Then, Bob Robinson, "the tenor with a tear in his voice," closed his eyes and took the lead, singing notes that soared across the stage and out into the spellbound audience. The Sons' pop-like sound appealed to the teenagers, who by that time were seeking out their own type of music. Then the group performed a tune that Bob had sung with the LeFevres entitled "On and Underneath You." The applause grew with each number. They wound up singing every song they had rehearsed, but the audience wouldn't let them stop.

In the meantime, the concessionaires, who weren't being patronized, became livid. Ice melted in cokes, popcorn and hamburgers had gotten cold and greasy, and the usual lengthy lines were nonexistent. The lobby was deserted. The concessionaires were angry at Fowler; they had a contract and it specified breaks. Calvin stated that the concessionaires filed a lawsuit against Fowler the following Monday for violating the contract regarding intermissions.

In *The Music Men*, Bob Terrell noted that the Sons were on stage for forty-five minutes, and by that time the quartets were lined up in tandem in the wings, watching and listening with wonder and envy. After many encores, the Sons exited to thunderous applause. Their first appearance at an all-night singing had been met with the same raucous enthusiasm that Hank Williams had received at his Grand Ole Opry debut. All three were ecstatic and happy beyond belief.

History was made that late-winter night as the audience witnessed the birth of contemporary gospel music. In the coming years, it became fashionable to claim to have been there on that historic occasion. Lee Kitchens, who would one day become a member of the Sons of Song himself, witnessed the event that night. "I had never heard anything like it—they were incredible," he said.

Afterwards, as the Sons were backstage accepting congratulations from a beaming Fowler, they were approached by a promoter—"Pop" Myers—who wanted them to sing the next day, Sunday, at the cavernous Garrett Coliseum in Montgomery. Flattered by the offer, they were nonetheless hesitant; after all, they needed to return J. W.'s and Ruby's new car. "I'll pay you $150," Pop boomed. That was big money for a gospel group in 1957; it was what the top acts—the Blackwoods and the Statesmen—made. That cinched it; they had to go.

They would have to call J. W. and explain. They could stay overnight with friends in Birmingham and drive down U.S. 31 the next day. Pop could front them some gas and hamburger money. They asked themselves—was this really happening? While other gospel groups toiled for years in the obscurity of small churches and tiny school auditoriums, the Sons of Song were that rare phenomenon—an instant success. Their gospel ship had indeed blasted off.

The Sons got a great reception at Montgomery the following day. They returned to Atlanta from the wonderful weekend in Alabama with enthusiasm, determination, and vigor. They knew they had something special and were going to capitalize on it. Calvin began calling churches, schools, and other familiar haunts, booking them for appearances. Promoters were hearing about them, too. They began a full schedule almost immediately after returning from Alabama. Their ascent to stardom was incredibly rapid.

Shortly after the Sons began making public appearances, an Atlanta talent scout who worked part-time for music executive Bill Lowery advised Lowery that he had just heard a new gospel trio that was going to be the most sensational group ever assembled. The talent scout just happened to be the Statesmen Quartet's former lead singer, Jake Hess. Hess wanted to learn more about the business end of music, particularly copyrights, and had begun working with Lowery when he wasn't touring with the Statesmen. Hess had left the Statesmen towards the end of 1956 and had opened a piano store in addition to his work with Lowery Music.

Lowery had already been active in recording and publishing in Atlanta during the fifties, and in the sixties he would develop such acts as Jerry Reed, Billy Joe Royal, Tommy Roe, Ray Stevens, and Dennis Yost and the Classics IV. Lowery's publishing company provided Sonny James with "Young Love," the 1957 career-making monster hit for the young country music singer from Hackleburg, Alabama.

Based on Hess's sunny representations about the Sons of Song, Lowery offered to have the group cut a single on his Fox label. The Sons subsequently recorded two songs at Superior Recording Studio in Decatur, Georgia. Despite the regal-sounding name, Don Butler recalls that it was in fact "a little rinky-dink studio in a room over an office in Decatur." "Old Gospel Ship" was the first song recorded by the Sons, backed with "He Knows Just How Much You Can Bear." "Old Gospel Ship" was the first song the trio sang together and the first they performed on stage together; now it was their first recording. It would become one of several candy sticks for them over the years.

Surprisingly, their first recording of "Old Gospel Ship" is rather pedestrian, at least by their standards. That may be because they sang it at a slower tempo than they would in the future. Subsequent recordings would have the spark and energy that this version lacks. Robinson's piano work, however, is absolutely superlative and features some sophisticated jazz fills and runs. The "B" side, "He Knows Just How Much You Can Bear," is also a bit tentative but gives a glimmer of things to come; for instance, the Sons alter the tempo when Calvin does his solo, slowing it down, as they would do in the future, and allowing the three stylists to interpret the song to their liking.

Jake Hess wasn't the only person with a gospel music background who wanted to learn more about the music business from the knowledgeable Bill Lowery. Young Polly Grimes, a Californian, moved to Atlanta during the 1950s to work for Lowery. She explained, "The reason I worked with Lowery Music was to learn everything I could about the secular music world and how it was promoted, so that I could use these techniques and strategies to begin promoting gospel music. I never wanted to do anything but serve the Lord." Polly Grimes achieved her goal and subsequently became the biggest gospel music promoter on the West Coast, booking groups not only there but worldwide as well. She was working with Lowery Music when she first heard the Sons of Song. "To me, they had the greatest sound that had come along in gospel music. They really knocked me out. They had such incredible harmony and professionalism, and their style was so unique. I think so often we imitate the styles of the world and the sounds of the world, and the only difference is you hear the lyric. They didn't do that. They were innovators and they had so much heart," she said.

Although Wally Fowler was acquainted with all three, it was undoubtedly because of his close ties with Calvin that he had allowed the Sons to perform at the all-night singing without having heard the group. Several months later it was Don Butler's turn to help the trio by calling an important contact he had made when he had been with the Revelaires. In 1956 the Revelaires embarked on an ambitious five-month tour encompassing twenty-five hundred miles and most of the western United States. Along the way, they sweltered as they sang in 120-degree desert heat in Nevada and Utah. Later, they sang in one of the world's largest tents in Odessa, Texas. However, the centerpiece of the tour was their first stop: an engagement at the renowned World Church in Los Angeles, which was pastored by the internationally known minister O. L. Jaegers. Dan Huskey had met Jaegers when he was singing with the Blackwood Brothers and had used his acquaintanceship to get the Revelaires an appearance at one of Jaeger's non-stop revivals. Now Butler intended to do the same.

Butler recalled, "I called O. L. and told him about the group and he invited us to come out and sing at his church. Bob, incidentally, had also been exposed to him through a trio that he had with his wife, Mary, and a girl named Finette Dake. They sang at some meetings where Dr. Jaegers was speaking, so he was familiar with Jaegers, too. The only one who Jaegers didn't know was Calvin."

The trio still lacked transportation, so Calvin bought an old car that had enough miles left in it to get them to the West Coast and back. The group began appearing at the nightly services, singing songs and occasionally giving brief testimonies. The church itself was elaborately decorated and extremely ornate, containing, for instance, an altar covered with a sheet of beaten gold. The white grand piano had an etched gold trim overlay. As a rule, outsiders weren't allowed to play the instrument, but an exception was always made for Bob Robinson. It was to be the first of many appearances by the trio at the World Church, and later Jaegers always sent them first-class airline tickets, which they promptly redeemed for coach so they could pocket the difference.

Religious music was popular in California in 1957; in fact, Phil Kerr had a television program in Pasadena airing on Monday nights that featured traditional church music sung by groups and individuals whom he had invited to appear. One of Jaegers's young staff members called Kerr's attention to the Sons of Song and they were extended an invitation to be on his show. The Sons were told that this was a real break because Kerr was rather selective about his guests. "When we sang, a guy in the audience lassoed us afterwards and said, 'I want to do something with you guys. Let me see if I can get you a record deal. Let's just see what happens,' " recalled Don Butler.

"I can no longer remember the guy's name, but he knew Earle and Ailene Williams, who owned Sacred Records and who had recorded some great stuff," said Butler. The man contacted Earle Williams and set up an audition for the Sons. The Williamses were tremendously impressed with the three young men and wanted to have them record an album immediately.

Good things were falling into place rather quickly for the trio. Earle and Aileen Williams advised the Sons that a man named Ralph would coproduce the recording session along with Earle. Ralph, the Sons were told, would write the lead sheets, help with the arrangements, and handle the orchestration. Ralph would get together with the Sons the day before recording to rehearse the numbers.

The pairing of the Sons of Song and Ralph was another of the timely events that occurred during the group's early days. Like the Sons, Ralph was strikingly different, and by 1957 he had developed the reputation of being a musical maverick. His thoughts and ideas on religious music and how it should be played were so revolutionary that he was forbidden to perform his music in many churches. Like the Sons of Song, he was ahead of his time. Ralph wanted to take secular music, ideas, and instruments such as brass, woodwinds, and drums and wed them with religious lyrics. Ralph and the Sons of Song together in a recording studio was a match made in Heaven—the man who came to be known as the dean of contemporary Christian music working with the group considered by many to be the first practitioners of the art form.

15. Ralph Carmichael—A Contract with God

As soon as he could grasp objects, Ralph Carmichael had a violin and bow thrust into his hands by his two adoring parents. He soon became fond of playing the instrument and had weekly lessons from the time he was three and a half until just past his seventeenth birthday. He had grown up in the Pentecostal church, hearing, playing, and singing its music. From the outset, his pastor father, also a musician, had encouraged him to embellish his violin playing when he performed in church. Accordingly, young Ralph would take an old religious chestnut and play it more softly, more slowly, or perhaps an octave higher than it was usually played, and he would frequently include double and triple stops and lots of arpeggios. Early on he began to question whether God really required Christian music to be as staid as the way it was being performed in church.

As a teenager, Carmichael became enamored with big band music, particularly the orchestras of Gene Krupa, Tommy Dorsey, and Stan Kenton. In his head, he began merging the melodies of traditional hymns with large orchestral accompaniment. "I would sit in class and daydream about endless combinations of instruments and voices," he wrote in his best-selling autobiography *He's Everything to Me*.

In 1947 Carmichael heard an armed forces music show on KFWB radio called *Sound Off* that was conducted by Mark Worneau. The sound emanating from the big orchestra set him on fire. In his autobiography Carmichael wrote, "I had never heard anything like this. The strings were as smooth as butter and seemed to ooze through all the cracks and empty spaces left by the horns. I was transfixed . . . On the way home I talked to God . . . The gist of the conversation was that there had to be a way to use the sounds I had just heard to proclaim the gospel. Why not? All melody, harmony, pitch, and rhythm belonged to Him. Instead of using lyrics about 'people love' and 'people things,' I could use lyrics about 'God love' and 'God things.' I made a deal with God: If He would help me out on this project, He could have complete ownership of it. Furthermore, I'd agree to a lifetime contract . . . Just as sure as I shook hands on a deal, I shook hands with God that day."

Carmichael then formed an orchestra and chorus at Southern California Bible College, where he was a student, and began arranging and conducting religious music in his unorthodox manner. Despite much resistance from certain individuals and churches, he quickly experienced enormous success, winning an Emmy in 1950. During the fifties he began writing and arranging secular music, primarily to learn the medium so that he could transpose it to the type of music he wanted to make. His learning experience also earned him huge sums of money. He soon was arranging and producing all of Nat "King" Cole's sessions as well as those of pianist Roger Williams (both of whom, coincidentally, were preachers' sons). In addition, he wrote or conducted for Peggy Lee, Jack Jones, Count Basie, Duke Ellington, Stuart Hamblen, Pat Boone, Eddie Fisher, Lena Horne, Frankie Laine, Bing Crosby, and many other well-known singers and performers.

A like-minded friend of his, Earle Williams, formed Sacred Records, a small Los Angeles company that specialized in recording and publishing religious music. Carmichael wrote, "Earle gave me the chance to experiment with new kinds of gospel music even though he would be criticized for it and almost go broke financing it. Earle kind of shared my dream and turned me loose. Somewhere along the line I talked him into a full orchestra, and that's when we recorded 'Rhapsody in Sacred Music.'"

"Rhapsody in Sacred Music" was an instrumental album that featured a full symphony: four trumpets, four trombones, three or four French horns, five or six woodwinds, a huge string section of at least twelve violins and four violas, two Arco bass harps, and percussion. Carmichael observed, "It was the first all-instrumental sacred music recording with that size orchestra. We recorded it at Capitol Records Studio A, and used one of the best mixers in Hollywood—Val Valentino. It was a scary experiment and I nearly broke the record company." It was also a highly acclaimed artistic success and a landmark album that helped pave the way for others who wanted to depart from the norms and expectations associated with religious music.

As a composer, he was much in demand, to the extent that he usually took on more than one person should attempt. Consequently, he would often work feverishly at composing and orchestration for as long as sixty hours nonstop. He would then frantically shave, shower, and dress and make a mad dash to a television or recording studio to meet some deadline, composing the final bars with one hand as he drove with the other.

Carmichael was an eccentric in the most delightful sense, periodically becoming so preoccupied with his work that he would neglect to replace burned-out lightbulbs in his bachelor quarters until he was down to his last one and in almost complete darkness. He was also a perfectionist and a workaholic, having been admonished as a child by his father to always do his best. His total commitment to music cost him a marriage and nearly wrecked his health. For a brief period he relied on amphetamines to provide energy through his grueling three-day work periods, but quit them after suffering an incident with his heart.

He had much in common with Bob, Don, and Calvin, particularly Calvin. Both had been born in Illinois—Ralph in Quincy, Cal in West Frankfort. Their fathers were Pentecostal preachers, and they both had grandfathers and uncles who were preachers. Both had attended Pentecostal church schools where their musical skills were nurtured and where in various ways they tested the patience of their respective faculties. Yet if Carmichael had a wild streak, he nonetheless was always a committed Christian with a lifelong agenda of honoring God through music, even though his method was considered heretical to many.

His unorthodox approach to music was based on his musical philosophy, and that was what he had in common with Don Butler. After Butler became head of the Gospel Music Association in the 1970s, he wrote an introduction to Bob Anderson and Gail North's *Gospel Music Encyclopedia*. In it Butler says, "To me, music is music and what makes it gospel is the lyric content which contains the message of Good News, Hope, Promise, Faith, and Assurance . . . Is it imperative that religion be sad, somber, reserved? Or may it be alive, vibrant, vital and electrifying?" His answer to the latter question is yes. He disagrees with those who would assert that gospel music is getting too worldly. "The gospel message will always remain the same because it is truth."

Don Butler's and Ralph Carmichael's views on religious music made them musical soul mates. Don and Ralph felt that as long as people were singing praises to the Lord, they could be accompanied by a kazoo, a set of bongos, or wind chimes. Such thinking now is commonplace; in the 1950s it was revolutionary. Eighteenth-century evangelist Rowland Hill once asked, "Why should the devil have all the good tunes?" As far as Butler and Carmichael were concerned, he shouldn't.

What Ralph Carmichael and Bob Robinson had in common was that they were both formally trained musicians. Carmichael began his lessons when he was barely more than a toddler; Robinson's training began when he was seven and continued through college. Both performed in Pentecostal churches throughout their childhood and both were married to musically talented wives. In addition, Carmichael and Robinson were both superb arrangers who created musical pieces that were highly innovative and unconventional.

Carmichael met with the Sons in their hotel room the day before the first recording session. "I remember meeting around a piano there at the hotel and discussing routines of the titles, and getting keys, and how many verses they sang, and if there were any particular chord changes that were altered from the original of the tune," said Carmichael. There was a meeting of minds. Carmichael discovered immediately that the Sons were not a paint-by-the-numbers group but rather musical innovators who were different from other gospel groups; the Sons realized they were in the presence of genius. "Our relationship with Ralph was one of mutual respect," said Calvin, who marveled at the speed with which Carmichael took the dictation.

Don Butler declares emphatically that the Sons' arrangements were theirs and that Ralph simply copied down the notes and chord changes as the trio dictated them to him. That may be true, but to his credit, Carmichael didn't object to any of the Sons' unique stylings. On the contrary, he found them imaginative and refreshing. Carmichael's creativity on the project centered on the orchestration—that is, the choice of instruments and the notes that were played. Ralph wrote the charts for the rhythm section that backed the Sons, and he coproduced the album with Earle Williams.

For the recording, Carmichael chose the finest session men on the West Coast, including the talented keyboardist Bobby Hammack. "Bobby ended up as music director at ABC [the television/radio network], and those were in the days when the major studios had a staff orchestra. He had a fine staff orchestra, and in those days I did some ghosting for him. In later days, Bobby would do some ghosting for me. If I got stuck on a session or a show, I'd call Bobby and he'd do some ghosting for me." Carmichael recalled that the talented Lloyd Lennom played bass, with Bobby Gibbons handling guitar. The renowned Les Barnett played organ.

The Sons insisted on recording at night, which, according to Don Butler, was somewhat unusual on the West Coast. "Ralph and his studio musicians played on every song but one, but we ran overtime and still had one song to go, so Bob played the piano on that," said Butler. Then as now, musicians belonged to a union that specified a standard three-hour session for a set amount of pay. With one song to go, the trio relied on Bob Robinson's musicianship for instrumentation. Although a fine piano player, Bob Robinson normally didn't play piano in the recording studio, which allowed him to concentrate on vocals.

The album featured six cuts on side one, including three songs that the Sons would perform countless times to appreciative throngs of fans: "Sometimes I Cry," "Open Up Those Pearly Gates," and "Heavenly Love." Another song, "He'll Make a Way," serves as a showcase for the trio, with each interpreting the lyrics in his own inimitable style. Midway through the number, Calvin departs from crooning to engage in some intense, Robinson-like singing, setting the stage for Bob's vocal entrance. Like a relay runner passing the baton, Bob picks up on Calvin's intensity and kicks it up another notch. He sings a lyric line, intensifies it a second time and then passes the baton back to Calvin, who begins ratcheting down. This interplay between Calvin and Bob is similar to that of two rock guitarists trading riffs.

"Open Up Those Pearly Gates," destined to become one of the Sons' most popular recordings, was an old novelty song from the black genre. The rhythm section, especially Lennom's thumping doghouse bass, provides a funky upbeat sound. The tune explodes with the opening line, "Open up those pearly gates." Calvin has the solo, and he employs his silky-smooth crooning style, again reminiscent of the Ink Spots, to implore, "Now all you gamblin' sinners, better quit saying 'seven-'leven' and git yo'-self prepared for judgment day." The lyrics are facetiously aimed at the lapsed Christian who spends more time on his knees shooting craps than praying. It's a fun tune with humorous lyrics and a catchy rhythm. The Sons conclude with one of their patented strong endings, hitting a crescendo and then fading, leaving the guitarist repeating a jazz riff that diminishes and fades.

Vep Ellis's short, spirited "Heavenly Love" is given a doo-wop flavor by the trio, with Butler and Robinson coming in as a chorus a beat behind Calvin. Although there was piano accompaniment to the song on this album, the Sons occasionally performed it a cappella, giving the number a street-corner sound.

Side two features the immensely popular "Something Within," a John T. Benson composition. Bob Robinson's intense, soulful singing is sandwiched in between two smooth solo performances by Calvin and Don Butler. The sequencing demonstrates that the latter two are basically finesse singers while Robinson does it with heart. (This was the tune that would set young Gary McSpadden on fire when he heard it played over a west Texas radio station.) "We had a lot of fun with 'Something Within,' inverting harmonies and toying with the arrangements," said Calvin.

Another side-two cut, the old standard "Since Jesus Came into My Heart," features the rapid-fire staccato singing described as "herky jerky" by gospel music columnist and critic Roy Pauley. Pauley meant that the group would take words and stretch them by repeating certain syllables. On this song they did it by singing "Since Jesus came into my ha-ha-ha-ha-ha-heart" in a manner similar to the hiccuping style used by rock singer Buddy Holly. Actually, this cut is a medley of three songs: "Since Jesus Came into My Heart," "This Little Light of Mine," and "Come and See Me When You Get There."

The most unusual tune on the album is "Roamin' River," an inspirational number written by ace pianist/composer/neighbor Wally Varner. The number is Gershwinesque—the chord progressions, languid tempo, and overall effect are reminiscent of the Gershwin classic "Summertime." The lyrics contain imagery of a big river flowing and winding—"River wide, keep on flowing (flowing, flowing, flowing)." The construction of this song follows a pattern used by the Sons on other numbers, building to a climax that ends with a Robinson vocal slide—a musical dénouement, as it were.

This first album, Sacred LP 9053, was entitled simply *Sons of Song*. To draw attention to the group's uniqueness, the album jacket heralded the group as "The South's Most Colorful Gospel Singers." Another marketing strategy used by Sacred involved the album jacket. It was pale pink, and behind individual pictures of the three men was a facade of an old plantation mansion with a southern belle standing in the doorway, armed with a parasol. This motif was ostensibly designed to emphasize the regional flavor of gospel music. The Sons always referred to their first Sacred recording as the "pink" album.

Apparently the Williamses—both Californians—saw the Sons' music as a type of "darky" music sung on the plantation. While in the first album this is only hinted at, in the subsequent one—*Riverboat Jubilee*—the suggestion becomes an outright theme. Although Sacred was a religious label, the Williamses had never been exposed to southern gospel music until they signed the Sons. Consequently, they had a different perspective, focusing on the origins of the music.

The final act of flamboyance by Sacred was to cast the record itself in a transparent plastic vinyl of hot red, similar to records issued on the RCA Camden label. The album is impressive. The Sons' unusual arrangements, Ralph Carmichael's masterful instrumentation, the excellent accompaniment, the superb vocals, the good mix of tunes, and the design and packaging of the album all suggest that the Sacred Records people were knowledgeable professionals who knew how to create and market a product.

With their "pink" album, the Sons made musical history by being the first southern gospel group to record in Hollywood, doing so in the same recording studio where Elvis Presley cut his *Blue Hawaii* album a few years later. They had a great time on the West Coast but were eager to get back on the southern gospel circuit where big things lay in store for them.

16. The Fat Lady Sings

The Sons returned from California and quickly became the hottest southern gospel group, displacing even the formidable Blackwood Brothers and the mighty Statesmen. In a *Birmingham News* advertisement for the September 1957 all-night singing in Birmingham, there were four headliners—Wally Fowler, of course, then the Sons of Song, the Blackwoods, and the Statesmen—with pictures of all. It seemed nothing short of incredible that a group that had debuted only six months ago was now starring with established heavyweights. Both the Blackwoods and Statesmen, though extremely talented, had had to pay dues before achieving stardom. The Sons of Song were stars from the time they sang the opening strains of their first song onstage.

Several of the songs they recorded in Hollywood, notably "Something Within," "Open Up Those Pearly Gates," and "Sometimes I Cry," garnered heavy radio airplay when they were first released as 45 rpm records. Gospel music promoters were after them, also. Don Butler recalled, "When we got back, we were in demand. Wally Fowler, Lloyd Orrell, W. B. Nowlin, 'Pop' Myers and Tilford Salyer all wanted to book us." They received standing ovations and encores no matter where they performed. As Buck Rambo wrote, they tore the audience up.

But the location where they were the hottest and the crowds were always the most responsive was Birmingham's municipal auditorium, later named Boutwell Auditorium in honor of Birmingham mayor Albert Boutwell.

"We owned Boutwell Auditorium lock, stock, and barrel," recalled Butler, who said that crowds would wait in long lines to purchase tickets to see them. Obviously, the other quartets had their admirers also, but the Sons of Song were the prime draw in the big Alabama city. Jimi Hall, who later sang temporarily with the group, said he was amazed at how popular the Sons were in Birmingham and that the dates there were the high point of his brief tenure with the group.

It wasn't just the audience who listened to and watched every sound and gesture the group made while performing. Backstage, almost all of the other quartet members stood in the wings when the Sons were on stage. Butler recalled, "The highest compliment I ever had was when James, Jake, and Hovie came to me and said, 'Can you get me a copy of your album? Can you get me one? You guys are twenty years ahead of your time.' That was a high compliment coming from them because they didn't like competition. We were—and I'm not boasting when I say this, 'cause I have no reason to boast—but we were cleaning their plate every night. No matter where we sang, when we came off stage, you knew the fat lady had sung."

The Sons of Song worked hard on their stage presence. Terms such as "colorful," "flamboyant," and "different" were applied to them not only because of the way they sounded but also because of their appearance. When the group began making money, they reinvested it in their act, setting new fashion standards. Don Butler noted, "We set the pace in clothing. Before us the wildest thing ever worn on stage was a red formal jacket [by the Statesmen] that caused a lot of people to talk. We took it to the next three levels because we came out with custom tailor-made clothes, including a gold lamé coat which would change colors when the light hit it, from a gold to a blue to a purple. We had a powder-blue tux that we wore with a satin lapel. We also had a purple formal jacket that we wore with a striped bow tie and striped cummerbund. We had an all-wool suit that was imported from England. We had ties custom made, lace overlaid over a floral design." So fastidious were they regarding their appearance that they once directed a florist to dye their carnations black to match their coats. And while their clothing was tasteful and costly, their shoes were the pièce de résistance—expensive unborn calf.

When the Sons took stage they did so with a confident air. While performing, they were relaxed, but their music, as well as their presence, was charged with energy and charisma. Their relative youthfulness and dashing good looks made them extremely popular with teenage girls. Jack Clark stated that a lot of their popularity was "a teenybopper thing." Gospel music journalist Bob Terrell stated, "They brought something new to the business, a new style of singing, a new freshness, a new sound that eventually helped forge a total change of face for Gospel Music as other groups broke away from the traditional male quartet format and, like the Sons of Song, explored new areas of sound."

As the emcee, Calvin kept the show moving, tossing in little jokes, making witty remarks about the city they were appearing in, flirting with the females in the audience, teasing others in gentle badinage. He was mentally quick, friendly, and engaging, always knowing the right buttons to push and the proper mood to evoke. His emceeing was effortless and polished after years of handling such chores for the Oak Ridge Quartet. Like any master of ceremonies, he had his share of canned comments, but he frequently shot from the hip, too, with spontaneous utterances that drew raucous laughter on some occasions and reactions of shock on others. "You never knew what Calvin was going to say," remarked Butler.

He sometimes made references to the Lord and religion, although he usually turned the mike over to Butler for such comments, since he was the group's ordained minister. Butler stood out on stage. He was several inches over six feet and had a wavy mane of straw-colored hair. He also had a regal, patrician-like bearing that was accentuated by his deep voice. When he sang, his appearance and voice imbued him with an aristocratic bearing that was impressive. Calvin would sometimes step aside and let Butler share his religious testimony with the audience. The big baritone was eager to tell what the Lord had meant to him and how the Sons deeply appreciated the abundant blessings that had been bestowed upon them. In addition to his singing with the Sons of Song, Butler also preached at church revivals during this period.

Robinson, of course, sat at the piano and was content to let the other two make most of the conversation; his brooding good looks masked the intensity that usually manifested itself when he sang. Robinson was, if anything, a shade taller than the towering Butler, which often made Calvin appear shorter than he really was.

Mary Ann Price, president of the Sons of Song fan club, made sure that all the members knew about the trio's latest activities. The club issued a newsletter that highlighted the group's recent concerts and new recordings as well as their tour schedule. A network was thus formed, and it became customary for fan club members wherever the Sons were performing on a given night to have them over for dinner and fellowship. Other gospel groups had their fan clubs also. Eating at the home of a fan was a well-established tradition on the gospel circuit and several singers developed paunches as a result of the frequent feasts.

The chemistry both on- and offstage among the three was remarkable, especially considering that Robinson could be temperamental and quirky, Butler was given to moodiness and introspection, and Calvin was rebellious and lived life right on the edge. Gospel music historian Jack Clark wrote, "The only thing that kept them from becoming standard bearers for the industry was the simple fact that they were three collision course personalities, each bent on doing his own thing."

Yet in 1957, the Sons were in perfect synch, and were not only the darlings of gospel music fans but were also Wally Fowler's favorite sons.

In 1957 the career of country music singer Sonny James exploded with his recording of "Young Love." The song was what is known in the industry as a "ten-pounder," and was so strong that Randy Woods, owner of the small but formidable Dot Records, enticed actor Tab Hunter, who was not a singer, into recording a pop cover of the tune. Hunter's bland version went all the way to number one on the pop charts, and, amazingly, Sonny James's version was number two. The owner of the valuable copyright was Lowery Music, the company that owned the Fox label on which the Sons' first record was released. Bill Lowery had, of course, issued the first Sons of Song product earlier in the year when he released "Old Gospel Ship" on his Fox label.

Sonny James was from the north Alabama community of Hackleburg, and when "Young Love" was released, his version got especially heavy air play from Alabama disc jockeys, particularly the large fifty-thousand-watt Birmingham station WVOK. The station promoted frequent concerts in Birmingham during the fifties, usually showcasing a package of country and rock stars. James headlined some of their shows, known as the "Shower of Stars," and appeared on others. In 1957 Sonny James was hotter than the proverbial two-dollar pistol.

Wally Fowler, ever the visionary and imaginative entrepreneur, decided to seize on James's enormous popularity at the time by signing him on for one of Fowler's all-night singings. Birmingham was the logical choice, since James was an Alabamian and had recently appeared in a WVOK-promoted concert. Since the all-night singings were already attracting overflow crowds at the municipal auditorium, Fowler rented cavernous Legion Field, the Birmingham football stadium where the University of Alabama and Auburn University played several times each fall. At the time Legion Field had a seating capacity of forty-four thousand.

Fowler scheduled the singing at Legion Field for August 1957. James headlined the show. Fowler brought in the southern gospel heavyweights to round out the program. The Sons of Song, the Blackwood Brothers, the Statesmen, the Speer Family, the Chuck Wagon Gang and Big Jim Waits were all booked to appear, plus some local talent, including the Johnson Sisters. The event was somewhat marred by an ugly incident that occurred before the concert began.

Calvin recalled, "Before it started, I was standing backstage, which was just a grassy area behind the stage. Without any warning, James [Blackwood] and Hovie [Lister] walked up on the platform and announced that they would not sing on the program with anyone who was a secular singer. The crowd seemed surprised by this; there was no applause, and everything was extremely quiet after their statement. Wally was already on the platform when they walked up and he was absolutely dumbfounded. That was the first time I had ever seen Wally speechless, but he was. I kept waiting for Wally to make some sort of reply. It was extremely puzzling to me because Sonny James was a very fine Christian man. What ran through my mind was, 'How can they be such hypocrites?' The Blackwoods and the Statesmen both had performed secular songs in the past—never in church—but in municipal and high school auditoriums, lots of times. After a while—it was probably seconds, but it seemed like minutes—when I realized that Wally didn't know how to respond I walked on stage and took the mike out of Wally's hand and said very humbly, 'Let he who is without sin cast the first stone.' The audience broke into applause. Then I said, 'You know, this seems like much ado about nothing to me,' and with that I gave the mike back to Wally and walked off stage. To this day, I don't remember whether the Blackwoods and Statesmen sang that night or not, but they probably didn't."

Blackwood's and Lister's statement seems little more than pompous grandstanding. Sonny James, as Calvin pointed out, was a devout Christian, to the extent that in the course of his career he passed up millions of dollars in revenues because he refused to sing in nightclubs and other establishments that served alcoholic beverages. Moreover, he would not record songs with negative themes, such as cheating and drinking, which were commonplace in country music. His nickname, "the Southern Gentleman" was appropriate and well deserved. Calvin's rebuttal to Blackwood and Lister was simply another instance of his crossing swords with Hovie Lister, and he was one of the few who were willing to do so openly.

Over ten thousand people flocked to Legion Field to hear Sonny James sing "Young Love" and other tunes. James, whose real name was Sonny Loden, had sung gospel tunes earlier in his career with other members of his family; they were called the Loden Trio. He undoubtedly sang some gospel numbers at Legion Field, also. The Sons performed their hits— "Old Gospel Ship," "Something Within," "Open Up Those Pearly Gates," and others. Fowler, of course, emceed the show and probably did his usual good job after the shaky beginning. Fowler was an excellent baritone and had a repertoire of hits himself, including his two-sided hit, "Rusty Ole Halo" and "The Valley of Prayer," plus the tune that became his signature song, "May the Lord Bless You Real Good," which he cowrote with Atlanta disc jockey Warren Roberts.

The Legion Field throng was the largest crowd that the Sons ever performed before. It turned out to be the first of several dates the Sons did with Sonny James, because Fowler booked them on a tour together throughout the South and Midwest following the Legion Field concert. Butler remembered the Sons doing concert dates with Sonny James as far away as Indiana. The symbiotic relationship of Fowler with the Sons of Song would continue, culminating in 1958 in the most whirlwind tour ever for the dynamic trio—the frenzied Alabama governor's race of 1958.

17. "We Sang at Every . . . Pig Trail in the State"

In 1958, the large field of fourteen candidates for the Alabama governor's office ranged from "the sublime to the ridiculous," according to George Wallace's biographer, Stephen Lesher. The governor, James E. "Big Jim" Folsom, was forbidden by law from seeking reelection. In those days, the state's weak Republican party didn't even bother to provide opposition, so the winner of the Democratic primary would become the state's next governor. Because of the large and colorful field and the unique campaign style that most of the candidates used—live rural-flavored entertainment—the contest attracted widespread attention. Several national publications covered the race, gently lampooning the merrymaking and provincialism that characterized the campaigning.

Life magazine, then the predominant periodical in the United States, made it one of five feature stories in the May 5, 1958, edition. The article reported that "[a]nything goes for governor in Alabama, as 14 candidates put on an election revelry with pitchforks, hillbilly bands, kinfolk and mules . . . Almost every candidate has a guitar, a group of hillbilly singers or a gag. Before a candidate and his entertainers come to town, a loudspeaker car usually precedes them, giving equal billing to the politician and his performers. Before the show starts, the candidates often get lost in all the singing and shouting." The tongue-in-cheek article made no pretense of being serious, but focused on the entertainment used by the frontrunners and the clowning or the eccentricities of the candidates who had no chance of winning.

With its big-for-pictures format, *Life* assigned veteran photographer Frank Scherschel of their Chicago bureau to cover the campaign. The renowned Scherschel had previously taken assignments all over the globe for the magazine, including combat action. The six-page article on the campaign featured thirteen photographs, including one of Grand Ole Opry entertainer Minnie Pearl and one of a portly baritone gospel entertainer—Wally Fowler—who is standing on the back of a brightly painted flatbed truck singing, accompanied by three younger men—Calvin, Don, and Bob. It was in this milieu that the Sons of Song spent ten grueling yet exciting weeks in the spring of 1958.

As the *Life* article mentioned, the accepted method of campaigning was for a candidate to barnstorm the entire state making stump speeches from the back of a flatbed truck on the town square. Early on, someone might make as few as five appearances a day. However, as the May 6 deadline approached, the campaigning became a whirlwind of hectic events, sometimes with twenty speeches in one day—or twenty concerts for the vocal group hired to warm up the crowd. The key to the speechmaking was to have a big turnout, and there was probably no one in the southeastern United States better at drawing a crowd than Wally Fowler. He had been doing it since the first time he filled Nashville's Ryman Auditorium on a rainy, icy November night in 1948—the night of the first gospel music all-night singing in the South. A portion of the Nashville all-night singing was broadcast by WSM, the fifty-thousand-watt clear-channel station that broadcast the Grand Ole Opry. Fowler soon established Birmingham, Atlanta, and other large southern cities as sites of monthly all-night singings. As a result, almost everyone in the South knew or had heard of Wally, and would rush to the town square to hear him sing, especially for free.

Fowler's onstage mannerisms were deliberately folksy, because he knew what appealed to the audiences with their mostly rural roots. Fowler claimed to be from "Possum Trot, Georgia," and when directing traffic onstage as emcee of his all-night singings he would encourage audiences

to be sure and buy "some of them good-tasting goobers" from the concessionaires. However, the hayseed personality people saw onstage masked a
shrewd promoter's mind, and by 1958 Fowler was widely known in powerful circles as a mover and shaker—a big-time promoter who could get
things done.

It was Fowler's ability to draw a crowd that attracted the attention of
the most viable of the 1958 Alabama gubernatorial candidates, Jimmy
Faulkner, a wealthy media executive who had run second to James "Big
Jim" Folsom in the 1954 race. Faulkner was the odds-on favorite. He knew
Fowler; in the mid-fifties the *Birmingham News* had featured a picture of
the two shaking hands as a photo opportunity for Faulkner, who had never
stopped running since his near-win in 1954. However, as it turned out,
Fowler worked for one of Faulkner's main opponents in the 1958 race.

The eventual winner—John Patterson—was the state attorney general.
Patterson had risen to political prominence after his father, Albert Patterson,
had been slain because of his efforts to clean up the brothels and gambling
dens in Phenix City, Alabama, a few years after Calvin Newton had sung
there in two of the more popular clubs. Patterson won because he used the
entertainment formula to draw crowds and because he astutely determined in the early going that segregation was not just the main issue; it
was the only one that voters paid attention to or seemed to care about.

The degree of their opposition to integration was the candidates' litmus
test. Refusing to make stump speeches from the back of a truck, retired
Rear Admiral John Crommelin ran his campaign from a rocking chair on
his front porch. With a sweep of the hand, the crusty Crommelin dismissed
the whole lot of his opposition as "pink-tea segregationists," pretty strong
stuff considering some of the outrageous promises made by the other
candidates. Another arch-segregationist—Public Service Commissioner
C. C. "Jack" Owen—vowed that, if necessary, he would deputize the entire
white male population to preserve segregation. Perhaps to emphasize his
commitment, he had his music group, Shorty Sullivan and the Confederate
Colonels, decked out in Confederate uniforms.

Most of the candidates were unknown and had no chance of winning,
but it was they, in part, who made the race so colorful and attracted the

media attention. They included a farmer who was running "on a bet," a Baptist preacher who refrained from calling himself "Reverend" lest people think he was running a revival instead of a political campaign, and a pint-sized state legislator nicknamed "Shorty," who once complained that a dog had more rights than he, following his arrest for urinating on a fireplug during one of his frequent intoxicated episodes. Another long shot, Montgomery jeweler Shearen Elebash, provided his own entertainment by singing what *Life* referred to as songs "both corny and sophisticated," while pounding a piano that had been anchored to the bed of a pickup truck. With diplomas from such elite institutions as Choate and Yale, he was a favorite of the state's aristocracy.

The *Life* article stated, "Three men appear to have pulled ahead of the big field: John Patterson, Jimmy Faulkner and George Wallace, all staunch segregationists. Among the other candidates, A. W. Todd stands out because he bears down heavily with gospel music but does not have much of a chance."

Todd was the state commissioner of agriculture. He had lost a hand and was nicknamed "Nub." Todd's campaign motto, "From Farm Boy to Governor," resonated well with the largely rural voting population. He was a viable, well-financed candidate who at the outset had a legitimate shot at winning. Like the other serious office seekers, he intended to stump the state's sixty-seven counties with live entertainment to attract voters. Todd and his supporters realized that gospel and hillbilly music were the two most popular entertainment forms, and in the days that predated shopping malls and cable television, people in small towns would turn out en masse to hear some free live entertainment. A savvy political insider, Todd hired Wally Fowler for the express purpose of providing musical entertainment to attract a crowd that would ultimately hear Todd's stump speech. Fowler realized the best way to draw a crowd was to hire the most popular group in gospel music, which, in the spring of 1958, was the Sons of Song. While they were popular throughout the South, the Sons were absolutely idolized in Alabama.

Beginning in mid-March and continuing up until May 5, election day eve, the Sons performed from the back of a brightly painted red, white, and blue flatbed truck that had Todd's motto boldly emblazoned for all to see. Bob Robinson played an electric piano because it was light and could be transported easily. Calvin recalled a typical campaign day: "We'd start in the morning around 9 A.M. We would warm up the crowd, doing fifteen minutes to a half-hour, or we sang until A. W. got there. There were some occasions where we sang for an hour 'cause he might be late. We'd go all day like this, performing a short set, then pulling stakes and heading for the next little town. Every night there would usually be a large rally held in a large town. We'd do a full concert there."

In the northeast Alabama town of Scottsboro, the first Monday of each month was known as "Trade Day," when farmers came to town to swap knives, coon dogs, guns, guitars, and other items of value or to peddle homegrown vegetables and fruit out of the backs of pickup trucks. Consequently, there were more people in downtown Scottsboro on Trade Day than on any other day of the month. Early in the campaign a big political rally was held in Scottsboro on a Trade Day to allow the candidates to take advantage of the crowd, which swelled to over five thousand. More than a half-dozen gubernatorial candidates spoke that day, including Todd. Candidate Laurie Battle stated that at the Trade Day rally he shook hands with "2,000 farmers and one dog." Calvin remembered, "There was a real big turnout, with people standing in the square as we put on our show. The streets had been cordoned off to keep cars out of the area. That day I sang a solo and afterwards this ole rough-looking hillbilly came up to me with tears running down his cheeks. He grabbed me in a bear hug and then said, 'That was the prettiest goddamn singing I ever heard.' I've always remembered that because the man wasn't trying to be irreverent; it was simply the only way he knew how to express himself."

Calvin continued, "We had some great crowds. Back then there was no cable TV nor a lot of other diversions that we have today. We had a caravan of supporters that followed us, mostly young men and women, and they'd have cowbells they'd ring. When the caravan of cars rolled into the small towns whistling and cheering with horns blowing and cowbells clanging, it created a pep rally–like atmosphere. We'd come on and do our songs and then Wally would sing some of his and by then the audience would really be fired up for A. W. With all the young, spirited, energetic people traveling with us, it was like a traveling house party. At night all of the Todd people would have an entire floor of motel rooms, and there would be lots of fun and frivolity. The three of us [Cal, Don, and Bob] always rode in different cars from one town to the next with some of Todd's supporters and lots of them became our fans, too. By splitting up, we had a chance to visit with everyone. The race was so wild that everybody had a gospel group or hillbilly group. I remember Minnie Pearl being at several of the rallies."

All the major candidates utilized some type of down-home entertainment. George Wallace used Grand Ole Opry comedienne Minnie Pearl plus a band that played hillbilly and rock and roll. On other occasions he used the Willis Brothers. Jimmy Faulkner, the early favorite, used the Blackwood Brothers and the Statesmen. John Patterson used country singer Rebe Gosdin and his Sunny Valley Boys. And, of course, Todd used Wally Fowler and the Sons of Song. Other candidates used lesser-known local talent.

Gubernatorial candidate Karl Harrison didn't use live entertainment and spoke out against the "overcommercializing" of the governor's race. Assessing the voters' feelings, Harrison stated, perhaps incorrectly, "They resent much of the bandwagon and sideshow campaigning at the expense of hitting the real issues." Throughout his campaign he lambasted his opponents for using "hillbilly bands and gospel singers," adding, "Those bands and singers don't perform for nothing. I like music but I don't like the obligations that go with it." Harrison's remarks may have been sincere, but he ran a shoestring campaign and probably couldn't afford live entertainment.

The typical format was for the Sons to open up the show and perform a few of their big numbers. "Old Gospel Ship," "Open Up Those Pearly Gates," and "Something Within Me" were all popular at the time. As the Sons' emcee, Calvin would talk to the audience between numbers, complimenting an elderly woman on her pretty bonnet or teasing a farmer about his new brogans, always giving a personal touch to the Sons' performances. After ten or fifteen minutes they'd bring Wally out and provide background accompaniment for him. "We never rehearsed with Wally; we'd just sort of hum in the background," said Calvin. Like Calvin, Fowler was a master emcee. He could communicate with the mostly rural audience in a manner that was both sincere and light-hearted, sensing when to joke and when to be serious. Fowler's immensely popular signature song, "May the Lord Bless You Real Good," was rewritten into a campaign song for Todd. It and other gospel tunes were featured in a songbook that included pictures of Todd and that was handed out by the Todd campaign. Fowler always heaped praise on his candidate, but, ever the promoter, he would also find a way to mention an upcoming all-night singing.

A portion of Fowler's all-night singings at Nashville's Ryman Auditorium were broadcast live on WSM radio. During this segment, station officials expressly forbade his mentioning all-night singings at other locations, as this would amount to free advertising. Fowler cleverly skirted their injunction by mentioning the other singings when he offered up prayers: "Lord, watch over us as we go to Atlanta next week for our singing there, and Birmingham the week after that." For listeners who might be curious as to which groups would be there, Wally would add, "And Lord, provide safe passage for all the folks that turn out to see us, and Heavenly Father, please be with the Blackwood Brothers, the Statesmen, and the Sons of Song, as they make their way to those two cities." There is no record of how station management reacted to Fowler's ingenuity, but Wally never stopped praying for his all-night singings during the period when they were broadcast by the large Nashville station.

During a typical campaign day the Sons would stay a step ahead of Todd. As Calvin mentioned, they usually would pull into a small-town square before 9 A.M. and sing until Todd got there. They would depart as soon as he took stage to head out for the next town to start the process anew. "We wouldn't break for lunch or anything," Butler recalled. "We would stop and get some Vienna sausage or some cheese and crackers and bologna and eat it on the run. We wouldn't get a decent meal until we'd finished." Before the Sons began singing in a particular town, Don Butler would ride in an automobile equipped with loudspeakers, and, in his deep, disc jockey's voice, announce the upcoming event (this was called ballyhooing).

The Sons performed nonstop six days a week for approximately eleven weeks—from mid-March to May 5. It is not possible to determine how many people saw them, but if it was an average of 5,000 each day, they would have performed for 330,000 people during that period. They undoubtedly gained many new fans through this tremendous exposure and strengthened their hold as the top group in gospel music. Don Butler noted, "We sang at every city, town, four-way stop and pig trail in the state." The major Alabama newspapers provided detailed accounts of the candidates' activities, publishing each one's daily campaign schedule. A review of these published accounts supports Butler's claims—it is possible that the Sons and Todd appeared in every community in the state during that period.

On April 7, 1958, the Todd juggernaut was rolling. A huge rally was planned at the Sheffield Community Center, twenty miles from Russellville, Todd's hometown. Todd pulled out all the stops at this rally, and Fowler brought in the Chuck Wagon Gang to beef up the entertainment. Approximately three thousand turned out to hear the music of Wally Fowler, the Sons of Song, and the Chuck Wagon Gang, and then Todd's speech, wherein he promised to build a north Alabama governor's office if elected. Preston Porter, Sheffield's recreation director, was quoted in the *Birmingham News* as stating that the combination entertainment/political event attracted more people than Elvis Presley had two months earlier, a noteworthy achievement, since in 1958 Elvis was at the height of his popularity.

By April 19, the pace had accelerated even more. The Sons sang "Old Gospel Ship" and other popular tunes in a marathon swing through mostly small northwest Alabama towns where they had appeared a couple of weeks earlier. Todd concentrated on north Alabama because he was from that area and would run better there than elsewhere. The day began in tiny Phil Campbell, and then the caravan went on to Haleyville, Hamilton, Guin, Winfield, and Fayette; from there it was back on the road to Vernon, Millport, Reform, Carrollton, Aliceville, and Northport. Next they crossed the Black Warrior River and entered Tuscaloosa, home of the University of Alabama. The good-sized turnout there included businessmen, farmers, factory workers, housewives, retirees, school kids, and a sprinkling of college students.

Although they had already been in fourteen municipalities that day, there was much campaigning still to be done. The Sons, along with Todd's supporters and campaign team, proceeded to Walker County—coal mining country—where they spent the remainder of the day warming up crowds in Oakman, Parrish, Cordova, Dora, and Sumiton. By then, the Sons had probably sung themselves hoarse and Todd's hand undoubtedly ached from all the flesh pressing, but a big rally was still ahead at Jasper, the Walker County seat. On that day, the Sons of Song performed in nineteen different municipalities before crowds that probably ranged from one hundred to three thousand or more at the Jasper rally. Towards the end of the campaign, fifteen to twenty cities a day became the norm.

Ironically, for Todd, the second week in April was probably when his popularity peaked, also. His picture appeared on the front page of the *Birmingham News* twice in three days, following the big Sheffield rally and then two days later in Birmingham where he and a beaming Wally Fowler were standing under an umbrella in the rain. Pollsters had him among the front-runners, and one large state newspaper—the *Decatur Daily*—endorsed him. From then on, he began slipping badly, either because he failed to perceive the importance of segregation as an issue or because he deliberately chose to ignore it, which in this race was tantamount to political suicide. While his opponents were railing against integration and its enforcer—the federal government—Todd was urging passage of federal laws that would allow for inoculations of swine and other livestock, and chastising the U.S. secretary of agriculture. As some might say, Todd just didn't get it, which is surprising, since he was considered an astute, savvy politician.

John Patterson, although a political newcomer, picked up quickly on what was important to the Alabama voters. Patterson recalled, "Within a matter of weeks after the campaign started, it turns out that the main thing people are interested in is the segregation question . . . If you happened to be a politician or somebody running for public office and you were perceived by the white majority to be weak on the black question, then you wouldn't be elected ... The fellow who wants to be elected governor ... has got to articulate the issues the public is interested in."

That was Todd's failing. Either through ignorance or as a matter of principle, he wouldn't speak out against integration, at least not forcefully. There is no indication from newspaper coverage that he mentioned it at all in his speeches, although it was a topic that would have been difficult to avoid completely. Consequently, on election day, he ran a distant fourth, which was actually a decent showing in a field of such strong candidates (George Wallace, who would later become a nationally prominent politician, ran second).

For the Sons, it had been a great experience. They had put a lot of effort into the campaign, perhaps singing more in those two and a half months than in any other similar period, but they had been paid well. Each earned $250 per week plus expenses, and in 1958, that was good wages for gospel singers. In addition, they had enjoyed tremendous exposure in a state where they already had a large number of fans. Clearly on a roll, the group took a week off and traveled to Miami for a vacation in the sun—Don Butler knew someone who ran a hotel that would put them up for free. In contrast to the frantic pace of the past ten weeks, in Miami they'd lie on the beach, catch some rays, and charge their batteries for their next big venture three thousand miles away—another trip to the West Coast to record their second album.

18. Gentlemen Songsters off on a Spree

The Sons came back from Florida tanned, rested, and eager to pick up where they had left off. On Saturday night, June 15, 1958, the trio delighted gospel music fans at the all-night singing in Atlanta, then caught a 3:40 A.M. red-eye special to Los Angeles to record their second Sacred album. They had worked up a lot of new material and were eager to meet with Ralph Carmichael again and give him their arrangements for the project. As he did on the first album, Carmichael would take the arrangements and write out the instrumentation for all the songs that were planned for the session. Carmichael intended to use the same session men who had played on the previous Sons album: pianist Bobby Hammack, Les Barnett on organ, and veteran sidemen Lloyd Lennom and Bobby Gibbons on bass and guitar. Earle Williams and Carmichael would coproduce, as they had on the Sons' first album.

Carmichael was pleased to be working another recording session with the Sons. He remarked, "The last half of the 1950s impresses me as the time that recordings of gospel music really took a giant step forward." According to Carmichael, the two albums made in Hollywood by the Sons of Song were part of that giant step forward.

Now established stars, the Sons were beginning to enjoy the perks of their fame. The three were lodging at the luxurious Knickerbocker Hotel, situated on the corner of two of the most well-known streets in America: Hollywood and Vine. Located within the hotel was the world-famous Brown Derby nightclub, a favorite playground and watering hole for movie stars and other famous people. Sacred Records was picking up the tab for room and board. In addition to recording the album, the Sons would appear at O. L. Jaegers's World Church while they were in the Los Angeles area.

The lobby of the Knickerbocker, with its expensive Persian rugs, rare art, and dark, rich mahogany paneling and woodwork, was stately and elegant. At almost any time one could see famous entertainers, athletes, politicians, and stars and starlets; June 1958 was no different. Count Basie, Johnny Cash, Sam Cooke, and the middleweight boxing champion of the world, Sugar Ray Robinson, were guests at the Knickerbocker when the Sons were there. Sam Cooke had recently scored high on the *Billboard* charts with his pop hit "You Send Me." Before becoming a pop singer, Cooke had forged an outstanding reputation by singing lead with the fabulous black gospel group the Soul Stirrers.

Cooke and the Sons met and then had a leisurely lunch in the Knickerbocker restaurant where they swapped stories about their lives and careers. Don Butler was a big Soul Stirrers fan, having played their music daily on his black gospel radio show on WEAS when he was an Atlanta disk jockey in the mid-fifties. Calvin and Cooke learned that they had much in common. Both their fathers had been Holy Roller preachers in Chicago, and, as a consequence, they had grown up singing spirited and soulful church music. In addition, Cooke and Calvin were both vocal stylists. The distinctive yodel heard on Cooke's pop records actually originated when he was with the Soul Stirrers and can be heard on those recordings as well. Once encouraged by a pop music producer to insert the sound at a particular point on a recording, Cooke rebelled, saying, "Nobody tells me when to do my whoa-whoas."

The June 1958 recording session would culminate in the second Sacred album, which would be entitled *Riverboat Jubilee*. It was a concept album that focused on the origins of gospel music, particularly black spirituals and the so-called camp meeting songs of a bygone era. To emphasize the album's old-timey aspect, the jacket features a drawing of a nineteenth-century paddlewheel steamer captioned "Mark Twain." The back shows the steamer pulling up to the dock while southern gentlemen in top hats and derbies and females in bonnets await its arrival. The theme of the album has to do with the antebellum South and its plantation blacks, fatigued by the shackles of slavery and a life spent in the fields, leaning on the Lord to make it through the day.

The liner notes proclaim that the songs are "interpreted with such uninhibited twang and 'plantation fervor,' that one can almost visualize groups of weary Negroes gathering at sundown on a Saturday night, after their week's work, for a traditional 'all night sing' to their 'Lawd' for freedom from man's imposed bondage." Earle and Aileen Williams, owners of Sacred Records and coauthors of the liner notes, had obviously never heard Caucasians sing with the spirit, animation, and emotion of the Sons of Song, and that is basically what they are trying to convey to the listener: that the trio sang with a "plantation fervor" associated with blacks. In the 1950s, singing with emotion was something that blacks did and whites didn't. Johnny Ray and Elvis Presley were the first two white singers to sing with what Aileen Williams described as "plantation fervor." Before Ray and Presley, if a white man sang with emotion, he was expected to blacken his face, like Al Jolson and others.

The Sons could imbue their voices with a weariness and melancholy that was central to their distinctive sound in general and to this album in particular, and two songs on *Riverboat Jubilee* stand out because of the evocation of these two feelings—"Lonesome Road" and "Lord, I Want to Go to Heaven." Don Butler insisted that both songs be included on the album, and he was featured on each. "Lonesome Road" was written by depression-era artist/writer Gene Austin, who also penned the popular "My Blue Heaven." A review of the lyrics to "Lonesome Road" suggests that Austin may very well have been inspired by thoughts of "weary Negroes" when he wrote the tune.

Butler stated, "We all liked 'Lonesome Road,' but I was the one who suggested it; it was one of my favorites. I said, 'Let's sing this song; I can feel it.' And so we did, and it happened to be President Eisenhower's favorite song, so I sent him a copy of it and he acknowledged it graciously. It was played on a lot of pop stations, and if we had had a record label that was promoting it to radio at the time it would have probably been a chart buster, because Ralph Carmichael already had a feel for the song. You could hear it when I gave that ad lib blues start to it and then he came in with that shuffle, and then Calvin took off."

"Lonesome Road" is another musical vehicle that showcases the Sons' vocal interpretations. The song begins with Butler singing slowly and soulfully. When he reaches the lyric line "Weary totin' such a heavy load," he packs the phrase with an inflected fatigue that seems both physical and spiritual, making it appear that such lyrics could not be sung with any other inflection or phrasing. However, when Butler completes his solo, Calvin immediately kicks the song into double tempo. Instantly, the song is transformed into an upbeat, finger-snapping number. Moreover, Calvin's upbeat performance doesn't violate the substance of the lyrics. It's as if he is suggesting with his bright mood that things may be bad but you can still be happy. "Calvin sang it like he felt it" was how Butler explained the radical departure in mood and meter. After Butler's and Calvin's solos, the song climaxes with an incredible vocal slide by Robinson. "Lonesome Road" became Butler's signature song and also one of the most popular songs performed by the trio. The Sons' arrangement showcases the diverse interpretations of three singers and is also an intricate, superbly crafted piece of musical architecture.

Another strong number to come from the session was "Lord, I Want to Go to Heaven," composed by James "Big Chief" Wetherington and Mosie Lister. According to Lister, Wetherington brought the song to the great tunesmith for scrutiny and possible revision. Wetherington had originally entitled it "Hell's an Awful Place," and Lister knew in an instant that a shift in focus was necessary. After Lister's revisions, the song was recorded first by the Statesmen and then by the Sons.

"I insisted on us recording that song," said Butler. The Sons' version of "Lord, I Want to Go to Heaven" has a strong rhythm-and-blues–like arrangement and is loaded with vocals exhibiting fatigue. Butler asked organist Les Barnett if he could create a windswept effect to begin the song, and the Sons came in right behind the unusual sound at full blast. Butler's deep voice goes all the way down on the line "I've been bending way down low," allowing the listener to realize the extent of his range. Pianist Bobby Hammack played choppy riffs on the piano, creating a bluesy sound. Without the singing, the melody is actually a good slow-dance number.

The songs on *Riverboat Jubilee* were an excellent mix of upbeat camp meeting songs and slower, heartfelt numbers. Among the former were "Heaven's Jubilee," only fifty-five seconds long, and "Old Camp Meetin' Time," which, as Aileen Williams noted, was more familiarly known as "I Cried and I Cried to the Lord." A new song introduced on the album became a southern gospel classic, recorded countless times over the years by many different groups. Don Butler remembered, "We were singing in Dalton, Georgia, and a man came up to us with a song written on a napkin. He said, 'I hate to bother you fellows, but I wrote this song and I'd like to talk to you about singing it.' His name was Henkle Little, and I will never forget the man. He was so humble and not wanting to intrude in any way. We took the song back to Atlanta and starting moving around with it and singing parts here and there until we came up with an arrangement we liked. It became one of our most requested songs." The tune brought to the Sons by the humble north Georgia preacher was "Sorry, I Never Knew You," which is the straightforward story of a man who dies without having been saved and is told by his maker on judgment day the words to the title of the song. The song features a recitation by Calvin, who in a humble, sincere voice assumes the role of God and delivers the bad news to the supplicant. Recitations became a staple for the Sons, and Bob Robinson does a touching personal testimony on "Amazing Grace," another tune on the album.

Riverboat Jubilee is regarded as the Sons' best album and is a collector's item today. The Sons of Song fan newsletter, which summarized their second Sacred recording session, stated that the trio recorded a total of eighteen tunes and that "[a]fter working all day Thursday, they left for Birmingham at 1:30 A.M. and arrived at 10:05 A.M., just in time to prepare for a sing in Gordo, Alabama." The newsletter added that the group had a flat tire on the way, which made them late to a steak and chicken dinner at the home of Sam House, one of their biggest fans. After the dinner, they performed before a packed auditorium and "the audience responded wonderfully."

It was June 1958. In fourteen months the Sons had gone from being totally unknown to being the most popular group in southern gospel music. Their songs filled the airwaves of radio stations. When they performed, they packed tiny schools and large auditoriums with enthusiastic, responsive audiences. With their unusual sound, good looks, and flamboyant clothing, they had become trendsetters who impressed fans and influenced other groups. They had the world by the tail and they knew it. In fact, following a clothes-buying spree in downtown Atlanta, the trio joined hands and skipped merrily down the street, like three happy children, blissfully unaware of the life-altering misfortune that awaited them.

On June 27, 1958, the Sons piled their suitcases and other articles into Calvin's new car to begin their trip to a disc jockeys' convention in Miami, Florida. Bob Robinson was wearing the gold Bulova watch that had been given to him by the Sons of Song fan club only a few days earlier at a surprise birthday party in Birmingham—he had just turned twenty-seven.

From Atlanta to Miami was a grueling seven-hundred-mile trip, and one the Sons had made just a few weeks earlier when they went down for a vacation. This time it was work, and the disc jockeys' convention was an important date because it would give them a lot of exposure to a group of people who could exert tremendous influence over their careers. The Sons would be performing at the convention and then would probably go to some of the many parties that were always a part of such a gathering. The event offered the Sons a chance to show the deejays how talented and dynamic they were, and would also give the trio a chance to become personally acquainted with record spinners from all over the United States.

To sing gospel music professionally meant spending many days traveling, and for most gospel groups in the 1950s that meant riding in an automobile. The two exceptions were the Blackwood Brothers and the Statesmen, who traveled in customized buses. In the early 1950s the Blackwoods flew to dates in their own private twin-engine plane, piloted by their baritone singer, R. W. Blackwood. Blackwood and bass singer Bill Lyles were killed in Clanton, Alabama, in June 1954 as they were practicing takeoffs and landings at a small airstrip before their concert that night. James Blackwood sold the Blackwoods' remaining plane after the crash, and the quartet returned to automobiles for a period before being persuaded by bassist J. D. Sumner to customize a bus.

Calvin's new car—a shiny Chrysler Imperial with large rear fins—was roomy and comfortable. It was a big automobile, with lots of interior space; a lone passenger in the back seat could easily stretch out and sleep. The huge eight-cylinder engine provided power and riding comfort, which was important on a long trip and had been a big consideration for Calvin when he shopped for a new car. Like all cars during the fifties, it lacked most of the safety features found on twenty-first-century automobiles. The dash was metal, the steering wheel was a steel circle encased in hard plastic, and there were no safety belts or air bags.

According to Sacred Records publicity, the Sons traveled over a hundred thousand miles per year, all of it by car except trips to the West Coast. The weeks, months, and years of seemingly unending travel had become for them a stuporous, monotonous drudgery that had to be tolerated and endured. The trip to Miami began as just a soon-to-be-forgotten journey down another narrow, winding asphalt road that was four lanes in only a few places. In 1958, the nation's interstate system was just in the planning stages. One section of the highway on which they were traveling—U.S. 27—was known as "suicide lane," because of the frequency of fatal wrecks on the curving, winding road.

Don Butler recalled, "I felt really ill at ease the entire trip. When we left I was in a heavy, blue, depressed state, so I didn't drive during the day." When the Sons traveled, one of them would ride in back and two in the front. The person in back often stretched out and slept; the person in the front passenger seat would either talk to the driver or snooze. Every four to five hours, the three would rotate positions, although there was no formal arrangement governing how long each would drive. Butler got in the backseat when they began and slept much of the day.

As they headed south they encountered the small Georgia towns that dotted the landscape: Perry, Cordele, Ashburn, and others. The highway ran straight through cities in those days, so there was no avoiding traffic lights and slow-moving vehicles. The Sons poked along behind muddy pickup trucks hauling pigs and cattle to livestock sales, and then, especially since Calvin was driving, sped by noisy diesels hauling lumber and steel. The trip became a series of jerky motions, speeding up and slowing down. They would stop every few hours to eat, stretch, relieve themselves, and buy gas. The trio crossed the state line into Florida in the early afternoon. Calvin had been at the wheel for the entire trip and was still pretty alert, so he kept driving.

"Finally, when night fell, Calvin turned it over to Bob," Butler recalled. "Bob drove for a while and got tired and sleepy and said, 'You're gonna have to drive,' so I said, 'Let's stop and get some coffee.' It was raining and just a miserable night. We got just past Ft. Lauderdale to a little place called Andytown. I was driving down the highway and all of a sudden in the rain I saw a flash of lights. By the time I realized what it was, I couldn't swerve enough to miss it, 'cause there were cars coming on the left and canals on both sides. So, I did the only thing I knew to do—I hit the brakes." The "it" was a semitrailer truck plodding along in front of them transporting a load of watermelons. When Butler braked, the car lurched abruptly to the left, causing the right front side to absorb the initial impact of Calvin's car striking the truck. The result was a grinding crash of colliding metal and unrestrained bodies propelled violently forward. Situated several feet from the point of impact, the truck driver was uninjured.

According to a Fort Lauderdale newspaper, the wreck occurred on U.S. 27, south of state road 84, just a few miles from Miami—their destination. The article also mentioned that Butler was given a traffic ticket for not having the car under control. Butler steadfastly denies having fallen asleep, blaming the weather conditions for the wreck. Whatever the reason, the wreck occurred because he drove right into the rear end of a slower-moving vehicle; there was no question that Butler was at fault. He fully accepted the blame and has harbored a tremendous amount of guilt over the years for the accident, which dramatically altered the lives of three people. "They were both asleep when it happened," said Butler. "Calvin was lying down in the backseat. Bob was in the front seat doing something I had asked him a thousand times not to do: he had his head lying on the window and his knee propped up on the dashboard. I told him many times, 'Bob, if we ever have a wreck, you don't stand a chance.'" Butler had no idea how prophetic his warning was.

Photos of the wrecked automobile show that the collision totally demolished the entire right front side of the car. The metal holding the roof in place was sheared, bringing the top down to dashboard level. The front and side windshields were reduced to glassy fragments.

When the collision occurred, the sleeping Robinson was catapulted like a limp rag doll against the metal dash. His right leg, which had been propped there, was snapped at the hip; his face and chest also struck the dash and windshield, and then he was thrown back violently against the seat. There, he became sandwiched between it and the twisted metal that had been knocked backwards by the impact. A particularly grisly newspaper photo taken at the site of the wreck shows a comatose Robinson upright in his seat, his face and chest drenched in blood. He was forced to remain there, penned and helpless, until officials could pry him from the wreckage. Considering the amount of trauma inflicted upon his body, it was a miracle that he survived. Butler fared better only because he had a brief moment to brace himself and because the passenger side bore the brunt of the impact. However, photos revealed that Butler's chest slammed against the unpadded steering column so hard that the steering wheel was bent outward on the top and bottom. "The impact threw me out of the car, but not before I had hit the steering wheel and my elbow had been pushed through the window," Butler stated.

Calvin had been asleep in the back and was thrown over the front seat, with his head hitting the ashtray. Because he was lying down, he first hit the back of the front seat, which slowed down his forward motion and made impact with his ultimate stopping point—the front dash—less violent. In an instant, Calvin was suddenly awakened and then came close to being rendered unconscious by the crash. Looking back on that fateful night, he recalled, "The truck loaded with watermelons had just pulled out of a truck stop. I was sound asleep in the back, and I wasn't even aware that we had wrecked. I looked up and saw the truck stop sign and said, 'I don't want anything to eat; I'm going back to sleep.' However, nobody answered and I heard these strange sounds—groans, the sounds of people outside the car—so I roused myself and got out of the car."

Calvin was too dazed by the injury and the suddenness of the event to be able to use any of his army emergency medical training, but he did offer assurances to the distraught Butler and then helped the ambulance attendants load Bob and Don into the back of the ambulance. He rode in the front with the driver as the vehicle sped to the hospital.

Butler recalled, "Calvin came to me on the side of the road and helped me up. I felt like I was passing out. I told Calvin, 'I think I'm dying,' and he said, 'No, you'll be all right.' Then I asked, 'What about Bob?' So we both made it to where we could see Bob, and he appeared to be dead. The scene just looked like death. It tore me all to pieces, to think that I was driving and here was this guy in that kind of shape." Forty years after the accident, it pained Butler tremendously to relive those horrible moments in south Florida.

Compared to today's standards, emergency care in the late fifties was somewhat primitive. Ambulances dispatched to wrecks were often owned by a funeral home and manned by personnel with little or no first aid training. Victims were scooped up and taken to the nearest hospital. Medical care in emergency rooms sometimes wasn't much better. In fact, when Bob Robinson arrived at the hospital he was apparently given a cursory examination, pronounced dead or hopeless, and then wheeled into a darkened room. Lying motionless on a gurney, he was considered funeral home fodder.

Lee Kitchens lived in Tampa and was in Miami for the deejay convention. He somehow heard that the Sons had been in a wreck and immediately made his way to Broward County General Hospital. He located Don and Calvin and asked where Bob was. "In there," he was told by a grim-looking hospital official, motioning to a closed door. Kitchens opened the door and heard Robinson moaning in the darkness. He turned immediately and yelled, "This man needs help!" Nurses came running and began administering aid. In all likelihood, Kitchens's discovery saved Robinson's life.

Robinson's injuries were the worst. He was unconscious when he was admitted to the hospital. He had a broken hip, a broken nose and jaw, and severe facial lacerations requiring 167 stitches, as well as numerous cuts and bruises elsewhere. A pin was inserted into his hip, and his teeth and jaw were wired together. Butler was pretty banged up, too. One of his legs had been severely injured, he had a deep cut on an elbow, and the cartilage in his chest had been crushed. All three of the men had suffered broken noses from being thrown forward. In addition to his broken nose, Calvin suffered severe facial lacerations that took 48 stitches to close.

Calvin needed to be hospitalized, although for a shorter period than the others. However, he insisted on being discharged; he wanted to sing at the convention. A heated discussion ensued, with the hospital administration, concerned about Calvin's health and their liability, adamantly refusing to discharge him. But Calvin persisted, and after several minutes of his animated protests, a compromise was reached. He was given a pass that would allow him to sing at the convention, but he would have to return to the hospital by 10:30 P.M. that night. Reflecting on Calvin's recalcitrance, Butler remarked, "That's just the kind of person Calvin was. He was always on the edge, pushing it, and he wanted to make that appearance, thinking that if he did, they'd pay it."

During Calvin's solo performance at the disc jockey convention while he was bathed in the stage spotlights, blood began trickling down his face from the gash on his forehead. He made it through the show, however, and then, his spirits buoyed by the convention camaraderie and because he was away from the gloominess of the hospital, he decided to socialize a bit with some of the other entertainers. He was sitting on the bed in Marty Robbins's hotel room when there was a loud knock on the door. Robbins opened the door and was advised by uniformed police officers that they had a warrant to pick up Calvin Newton for not returning to the hospital as promised. Calvin rode in a police cruiser back to the hospital, where he was greeted by somber-faced nurses and physicians who ordered him to bed. However, he was discharged the following day.

Butler was hospitalized for eighteen days but suffered complications with his leg that lasted over a year. He had to wear a brace for a lengthy period and at one point almost lost his leg because of a staph infection. Robinson was hospitalized in Fort Lauderdale for a month but required additional convalescence at home. The wreck devastated all three, and though Calvin sustained the fewest bodily injuries, he was emotionally traumatized as much if not more than the others.

The accident was a turning point in the career of the Sons of Song and in the life of Calvin Newton. Their first appearance in Birmingham on March 7, 1957, and their automobile accident on June 27, 1958, served as dramatic bookends for their brief, meteoric rise and flameout. In typical Sons of Song fashion, both events were spectacular. Because of the wreck and its aftermath, the Sons lost the enormous momentum that they had built during their brief period together. Soon thereafter, Calvin seemed rapidly to lose his tenuous grip on life.

19. Picking up the Pieces

Bob Robinson's injuries would require an extended home rest and Don Butler would be laid up for at least a few weeks. In the meantime, there were concert dates to fill and commitments to be kept. The Sons were immensely popular and were booked solid for the next several months. Life had to go on and bills had to be paid, so Calvin had no choice but to seek replacements for his two injured comrades. During the next four years, various combinations would be used, with Calvin being the one constant member and others shuttling in and out. Initially, Jimi Hall, a high school classmate and fellow member of the Kingsmen Four, joined Calvin. Hall had been playing piano recently with the Harmoneers Quartet. Hall recalled, "Newton had booked some dates out in Texas, so the two of us went out there to cover those." Hall, a talented pianist and fine tenor, filled in for Robinson. On that particular trip, there was no baritone.

Butler came back to the group after the Texas trip—sooner than expected—although he had to perform supported by leg braces for a period of time. Calvin and Butler decided to contact a talented teenage pianist from Lenoir City, Tennessee—L. David Young—about serving as Bob Robinson's replacement. Young stated, "I graduated from Mars Hill Junior College in '58, moved to Nashville and had a music scholarship to Belmont College. Don Butler called me and said they'd had a wreck and they needed me to come down and help them. I quit my job at Aladdin Industries in Nashville and left my scholarship to join Calvin and Don.

At that time, they were a sensation; they had rose up faster than anybody had ever heard of, so this was just too good an opportunity to pass up. I got a copy of their second album—*Riverboat Jubilee*—and learned everything on it until I knew it note for note. That's the songs we did when I went with them. We had one rehearsal at J. W. Nelson's house, and we went over some stuff and Calvin said, 'That's all we need to rehearse; that's enough to do a program.' So, our concerts consisted of only six songs, which we encored about two or three times."

Actually, the Sons performed a few songs from their first album, too. Young recalled that a Sons of Song concert basically consisted of "Open Up Those Pearly Gates," "Old Gospel Ship," "Sorry, I Never Knew You," "Heaven's Jubilee," and Calvin's solo signature song "When They Ring Those Golden Bells," with perhaps one or two others. However, he added that they were doing lots of package shows with the Blackwood Brothers, Statesmen, and others, and in such a situation would do a forty-five-minute set, a considerably shorter performance than when they were doing a concert by themselves.

Young's period with the trio was especially memorable and exciting. The Sons were not only popular but now had the sympathy of gospel music fans, who were aware of the horrible accident. One of the high spots for the Sons of Song occurred during their first appearance in Birmingham at an all-night singing following their accident. A packed auditorium of enthusiastic, supportive fans yelled themselves hoarse during the Sons' set; then someone suggested a donation be taken up to help them with their medical expenses. Over a thousand dollars was collected for the group, a huge sum for an impromptu offering in 1958.

With Calvin Newton there was never a dull moment, and Young discovered just how exciting life could be with him shortly after he joined the group. "We were due to sing at Mt. Zion Baptist Church in Powder Springs, Georgia—Hovie's church. We had flown to Gordo, Alabama, to speak to Sam House about an idea that Calvin had about having gospel singings on a riverboat. We left out of Gunn Field in Atlanta in a Tri-Pacer that was piloted by a guy named Chuck Singer. Coming over, Chuck let Calvin fly the plane. We heard this racket all around us—it sounded like explosions. We later found out that we were flying over an air force base that was firing all this artillery up in the air. We made it through that, but when it came time to land, there was no airstrip in Gordo, so we just landed in Sam's cow pasture. We came in right over some treetops; it was scary. Then, when we left, we ran into a storm on both sides of us, and we couldn't get down anywhere—not Atlanta, Chattanooga, or Birmingham. So we went back and landed at Sam House's pasture and had to cancel our concert at the church." Fearing a plane crash, people at the church were frantic with worry until they heard that the aircraft was safely on the ground.

Young continued, "We were very busy, and were singing regularly at all the large concerts—Nashville, Atlanta, Birmingham, and some big dates out in Texas. We traveled in that big purple Cadillac that Calvin bought from Hovie Lister after their wreck in Florida. Calvin used to let me use that car to date a girl that I'm married to now. We always stayed in the most glamorous hotels and ate at the most expensive restaurants. Everything the Sons of Song did was first class, and I guess I had stars in my eyes, joining them right out of college. I was with the Sons of Song for four or five months."

Things obviously weren't the same following the wreck. Although a fine pianist, L. David Young couldn't sing Robinson's part convincingly and that, plus his youthful looks, made him seem like what he was—a fill-in. Robinson, Butler, and Calvin had all contributed to the Sons' sound and look in equal measure. The loss of one-third of that combination was obvious and telling. However, Robinson's absence was only temporary, so the problem of the missing original member would be corrected. Yet no sooner had Robinson rejoined the group than Don Butler dropped a bombshell: he told Calvin and Robinson he was quitting. According to Butler, his injured leg was continuing to bother him; in fact, he said he developed a staph infection at one point and nearly lost it. Furthermore, he stated that he had wearied of living out of a suitcase, being always on the run and gone from home all the time. Frequent absences from home can cause problems in marriages, and problems in marriages can create emotional problems. Although he didn't say so, others indicated that Don was caught up in such a cycle; he had additional reasons for dropping out, as well. His resignation was a death knell. The Sons of Song broke up when Don Butler decided to drop out of the group at the end of 1958.

All of the original Sons—Calvin, Butler, and Robinson—were dealing with emotional fallout from the wreck, and they responded to their psychological problems in different ways.

Since Calvin had been injured the least, the responsibility of keeping the Sons' flame lit had fallen completely on him. He had to find another car and then locate substitute performers and get them rehearsed. He also had to deal with the promoters and assure them that the original group would be back soon. There were numerous details to attend to, and Calvin—flighty by nature, with a short attention span—was not a detail-oriented person. In addition, he missed the emotional comfort that Butler and Robinson provided when they were both healthy. He knew that when it was the three of them onstage, there were none better, and he was sometimes embarrassed at how he and the various substitutes sounded. Certainly, they could all sing on key and the pianists could play the right notes, but they sounded nothing at all like the Sons of Song. He did his best but found the situation extremely stressful. Always an insecure person, he now felt vulnerable, inadequate, and overwhelmed. Calvin desperately needed someone to lean on but had no one to turn to. There was no wife, no steady girlfriend, not even a best pal that he could confide in or share his mounting problems with. He was alone and looking for support, and he soon found it—a chemical crutch. He began abusing amphetamines. In the past, he had taken them occasionally when he had missed a night's sleep or to give him energy onstage. After the wreck, he took them for stress and depression.

During this period, Calvin was not coping well at all, and it affected his behavior. He became difficult to be around. An emotional person, he at times lost his temper in a quick eruption that subsided immediately. Butler—whose nerves were on edge following the wreck—stated that Calvin's difficult, erratic behavior was a big factor in his quitting the Sons. "It got to the point where I just didn't want to be around Calvin," he explained. Butler, introspective by nature, needed some distance and a lifestyle change. "I was totally bummed out following the wreck. I just didn't want to travel anymore." Part of Butler's depression was undoubtedly guilt—he had been driving when the wreck occurred and the accident was clearly his fault. Fortunately, there were other avenues for him to pursue. An experienced, talented announcer, he knew he could always work in radio, and, as an ordained minister, he could begin preaching on the weekends. Butler had physical, emotional, and personal problems, and quitting a job that required constant travel would go a long way towards alleviating them. There were simply too many reasons to quit and not enough to make him want to remain.

Calvin accepted Butler's resignation stoically, forced a smile, and wished "Big Daddy" good luck. But inwardly he was devastated at losing his "basso profundo." Butler was the best baritone in southern gospel music at the time, certainly the most popular. He was the only baritone in gospel music who was a featured soloist. He had won the prestigious America Youth Singers Outstanding Gospel Singer award for 1958. Butler had not only a booming voice but also a charismatic stage presence—he sang with panache and attitude, and, like the other two, with lots of emotion. He was irreplaceable and Calvin knew it, which only added to the emotional luggage Calvin was toting at the time.

Calvin felt that there was another reason for Butler's quitting—perhaps the real reason. He thought, and was told by others, that Hovie Lister probably had something to do with it. Calvin said rumors were rampant that Lister had offered Butler ten thousand dollars to quit, solely for the purpose of breaking up the Sons of Song. Butler heatedly denies being given money by Lister to quit. "When I quit the Sons, I didn't have a job or even the prospect of a job. It wasn't until after I quit that I spoke with Hovie," said Butler. However, an anonymous source close to the Statesmen and the Sons of Song during this period—someone with no axe to grind with Hovie Lister—thinks that Hovie was behind the Sons' breakup, that he enticed Butler into quitting with some sort of promise. Whether he did or didn't, it was true that Butler developed a close relationship with Lister and the Statesmen right after leaving the Sons. Butler recorded an album with three members of the Statesmen in 1958, which would have been a few weeks at most after he quit the Sons of Song. To avoid any legal wrangling with record labels, the three Statesmen called themselves the Sentinels. The album was entitled *No Greater Love*, and was listed as being by Don Butler and the Sentinels. In addition, Butler also became associate pastor at the Powder Springs Baptist Church, where Hovie pastored.

After Young left the Sons of Song, he moved to Winston-Salem, North Carolina, took a day job at a service station, and joined a local gospel group—the Victors. Young had been in Winston-Salem for only a brief period when he was contacted by Don Butler, who informed Young that he was helping put together a quartet for Hovie Lister, which would open for the Statesmen on tour. He invited Young to become the group's pianist. The group would be known as the Ambassadors, and if he joined, Young would be in a lineup that included Don Butler, Cat Freeman, Jim Hill, and the recently recovered Bob Robinson. Hovie Lister gave Butler the authority to put the group together. "I hired Bob Robinson and Little David Young," said Butler. "I also hired Bill Huey and Cat Freeman. We toured out west and all over with the Statesmen." Although the Ambassadors had two former members of the Sons of Song, the group had a traditional quartet sound, borrowing more from the Statesmen than the Sons. They selected the word "ambassadors" for their name because it is a synonym for "statesmen"; it was Hovie's idea.

Lister ostensibly put the group together to complement what the Blackwood Brothers were doing with their Junior Blackwood Quartet, a group of second-generation Blackwoods who were learning the ropes. The Junior Blackwoods opened up for the Blackwoods. Since the Blackwoods and Statesmen appeared together frequently, Hovie Lister wanted what amounted to a junior Statesmen group.

Calvin strongly suspected an additional reason, at least for having Butler and Robinson in the group. If those two sang with Hovie's "pet" quartet, there would not be a Sons of Song to compete with, and as Butler himself mentioned, if there was one thing that James Blackwood and Hovie Lister disliked, it was competition. Butler adamantly insists that such wasn't the case, but Hovie Lister—preacher or not—was capable of such a ruse. Commenting on the possibility of Hovie's destroying the Sons of

Song by co-opting two of the members, more than one gospel music old-timer from that period stated, "That sounds just like something Hovie would do." Indeed, such chicanery sounds similar to what he did with the Melody Masters Quartet in the late 1940s, encouraging them to relocate in Greenville, South Carolina, instead of in Atlanta, Georgia.

During this period, Les Roberson contacted Calvin about a job singing with the Sons of Song. Roberson had a distinguished career in gospel music, having sung great harmony for the Weatherfords, and was the Oak Ridge Quartet's baritone in the mid-fifties when Calvin was the lead singer and emcee. Roberson subsequently became the Statesmen's lead singer when Jake Hess left the group in 1956. However, as lead singer, Roberson had been forced to sing in a higher-than-normal range for him and he damaged his voice. Roberson subsequently left the Statesmen and was without a job when he contacted Calvin. Calvin not only gave him a job, but also allowed Roberson and his wife, Rae, to move in with him, providing the two with free room and board. Decades later, Rae Roberson Whitley recalled with gratitude Calvin's generosity. Her memories of that period also included eating Calvin's delicious chicken, fried in sizzling hot butter.

While Butler and Robinson performed with the Ambassadors, Calvin got Jimi Hall to return, and Calvin, Hall, and Roberson went on the road as the Sons of Song. However, bookings began to drop as promoters realized that, though Hall and Roberson were talented, this group was a far cry from the original Sons of Song, with their unusual sound and onstage charisma. Roberson's voice lacked the depth of Butler's, and, said Butler, "Roberson didn't fit in—music-wise or personality-wise." During his period with the Sons, Hall sang in a quivery vibrato in an effort to put the tear in his voice as Robinson did. He could do a passable imitation, but it was just that—an imitation. Nonetheless, Hall was extremely talented. His piano work and arranging skills were the equal of anyone's in gospel music. Calvin's solos carried the group during this period, but that simply wasn't enough. As the bookings declined and the crowds grew smaller, Calvin became increasingly worried, anxious, and despondent. He responded to the emotional turmoil by taking more amphetamines. Whereas in the past he had used amphetamines on occasion, now he began using them daily. Calvin,

Roberson, and Hall had individual publicity pictures taken during this period, and in them Calvin looks absolutely wasted. He had lost weight and his face had prematurely aged and was wrinkled. When asked what the Sons were like when the group consisted of him, Roberson, and Hall, all Calvin would say was, "It was sick."

Research has shown that abuse of amphetamines goes through predictable stages. In most instances a person starts out using them only occasionally but soon begins taking them regularly. From that point, a vicious cycle ensues. An increasing dependence develops which interferes with work and relationships. By this time, the person is either unable to stop or suffers withdrawal symptoms when he or she attempts to discontinue use. From there, the amphetamines begin to dominate the person's life, and the user starts to lose interest in daily activities. The abuser's body begins to become tolerant of the drug, requiring a larger amount to produce the good feelings. The deterioration continues in a paradoxical web of illusion. The abuser gets high each day as his life spirals downward. He becomes obsessed with the drug, and suffers from impaired thinking, poor judgment, and loss of will power. Soon thereafter, he begins to neglect his physical health, personal hygiene, and appearance, and stays intoxicated for long periods of time. During this final phase, or "bottoming out," the person undergoes marked personal, social, and physical deterioration. Except for the brief comebacks he would make, Calvin followed this vicious and destructive cycle of addiction from 1959 to 1963.

Calvin may have had worries about the group, but his lifestyle was nothing less than glamorous—at least on the surface. To replace his wrecked Imperial, he purchased Hovie Lister's purple Cadillac, a highly distinctive vehicle in keeping with the Sons of Song's flamboyant image. Despite the antagonism Calvin and Hovie felt for each other, they maintained a civil relationship on the surface. In addition, he purchased a luxurious house in Sandy Springs, Georgia, from a real estate agent who was a big Sons of Song fan, and who made him a great deal. "The guy must have thought I had a lot of money since I was a member of the Sons. He told me he had this beautiful five-bedroom home I might be interested in. It had a swimming pool that was both indoor and outdoor, with a huge sheet of glass as a partition. You could swim under the glass from outdoor to indoor." Whereas he had boarded with J. W. and Ruby Nelson in the past, this time it was they who moved in with him. In addition, Kathy and Miriam, two good friends and fans, also rented a room from Calvin. Les and Rae Roberson lived with him for a period, too. "The price of the house was fifty thousand dollars with no down payment. The guy told me to pay whatever I could each month. Sometimes I paid a lot, sometimes not much at all." Calvin kept it for about a year and then let it go back.

Meanwhile, the lineup of Calvin, Hall, and Roberson didn't have much success. The new Sons of Song simply weren't accepted by either audiences or promoters. "Our dates started drying up. Most promoters wanted me, Bob, and Don—not substitutes," said Calvin. Under the influence of the stimulants, Calvin's thoughts and behavior became radically altered. When he was high, he had grandiose visions of the original Sons getting back together and mesmerizing audiences as they had done in the past. Yet during those moments when he wasn't on pills the reality became clear: he was now part of an ersatz group that simply could not captivate audiences as the original trio had done in the past. Things finally got so bad that Calvin had to pull the plug. "I had to let Hall and Roberson go because I just didn't have the money to pay them."

He was now at loose ends, without employment or a game plan, and with escalating amphetamine abuse. Calvin's world began to lack structure and purpose. He began living with friends and fans for short periods of time. L. David Young recalled that Calvin stayed with him in Smyrna, Georgia, for a couple of weeks during the period when Young was performing with the Ambassadors. "I remember he started calling all of his friends, telling them he was broke and needed money. He'd get a hundred from this person, a couple of hundred from another. In just a few days, he had over two thousand dollars. Calvin was just absolutely charismatic, and he had a lot of friends."

Soon thereafter, Calvin quit singing altogether, moved to Birmingham, and began a lifestyle of simply hanging out with friends. Among his closest Birmingham friends were Bib and Dot Chandler, whose two little boys were extremely fond of Calvin. The Chandlers were good people but were heavy drinkers. One time, both in their cups, the Chandlers got into a heated argument that ended when Dot hit Bib in the head with her spike-heeled shoe. Bib began bleeding profusely and Dot, fearful that she had mortally wounded her spouse, got Calvin to drive her to the hospital as she held Bib's bleeding head in her lap. Hysterical with fear and remorse, Dot insisted that Calvin sing "When They Ring Those Golden Bells," since Bib's demise seemed certain. As Calvin roared down First Avenue, changing lanes, with tires squealing and smoking, he sang a very uneven rendition of his favorite song. They somehow made it to the emergency room without being arrested, and Bib was stitched up and taken home.

A few weeks later the three went to Panama City, Florida, where Bib and Dot argued once more on the beach. This time, Bib decided to resolve the dispute by walking straight into the lapping waves, seeking solace in a watery grave rather than continuing the nonstop disagreements with Dot. "Come back, Bib, I'm sorry," wailed Dot. "No, by God, this is it. You can say goodbye to Bib Chandler forever—I'm outta here," he replied, as he slogged through the thigh-high water. Calvin and Dot both called out to him as the water rose higher and higher on his diminishing figure. Then, after a few minutes, Bib came back, everyone made up, and the party continued.

While Calvin was killing time down in Birmingham, Bob Robinson dropped out of the Ambassadors and formed a group called the Velva Tears. The Velva Tears were nothing less than a Sons of Song copycat group, deliberately imitative of the originals. Although some say that no other group ever sounded remotely like the Sons of Song, the Velva Tears did a more-than-passable imitation, mostly because of Robinson's singing, piano playing, and particularly his arrangements. In addition, Bill Morris, the baritone, had a voice that was uncannily similar to Don Butler's. Morris's phrasing was also virtually identical to Butler's.

The Velva Tears consisted of Robinson, Morris, and Al Harkins, a fine tenor who sang with intensity. Although they were together for only a short period, the Velva Tears recorded an album and appeared in concerts with the Blackwood Brothers and the Statesmen. The high point of their brief existence was an engagement at Dr. Ralph Sanders's huge Seattle Revival Center. Their album—*His Velvet Touch*—included "Highway to Heaven" and "Old Gospel Ship," two of the Sons' candy sticks. Another fine song, later recorded by the Sons of Song, was Al Harkins's "Had It Not Been for You." The group used all of the Sons' tricks and techniques, including liberal doses of syncopation, staccato, crescendos, and slurs. Although they were not as good as the original Sons of Song, they were probably better than some of the combinations that Calvin sang with after Butler left.

After a few months of idleness, Calvin decided to return to music. He moved back to Atlanta and made a phone call.

20. From Rock 'n' Roll to Rock Bottom

With his gospel music career at a standstill, Calvin decided to switch gears and take a shot at rock and roll. He had sung pop and country music in nightclubs in the late forties and mid-fifties, so the transition to rock wasn't as radical as it would have been for anyone else in southern gospel music. To initiate the transition, Calvin contacted Atlanta music executive Bill Lowery to see if Lowery might be interested in recording him. Lowery had been on the Atlanta music scene for a decade and was beginning to experience enormous success, particularly in publishing. Lowery had begun working full-time in music publishing and record production in the mid-fifties, and scored big right off the bat, publishing Gene Vincent's all-time rock classic "Be-Bop-A-Lula." In 1958 Lowery Publishing blasted off with the huge hit "Young Love," which Tab Hunter and Sonny James jointly rode to number one on the country and rock charts. Lowery's reputation blossomed, and soon both songwriters and artists were seeking him out. Calvin was one of them.

"I had known Bill Lowery for some time, so I just went and asked him if I could record something." It was Lowery's Fox label that had put out the first record by the Sons of Song in 1957, so Lowery indeed knew about Calvin. "Bill gave me a couple of songs that Cotton Carrier had written, and we went into the studio and cut them." Carrier was Lowery's right-hand man during the period of Lowery's enormous success, which included the development and career management of such artists and songwriters as Billy Joe Royal, the Classics Four, Joe South, Tommy Roe, and Bertie Higgins. (Both Lowery and Carrier were inducted into the Georgia Music Hall of Fame years ago.) The two songs—"Just As You Are" and "Every Feeling I Have"—were both rock ballads, tunes particularly suited to Calvin's talents and vocal style. His vocal style was remarkably similar to that of the Platters' lead singer, Tony Williams, during their period of great success; Williams in turn had modeled his style on that of Ink Spots tenor Bill Kenny. "Just As You Are" was proclaimed the "A" side, but Calvin's performance on "Every Feeling I Have" may be his most remarkable feat in a recording studio. Calvin imbues the lyrics with a passionate intensity that builds until he peaks in falsetto, just as Kenny or Williams would have done.

Released on Lowery's Scotti label, both tunes were bubblegum love songs that captured the essence of rock records during the late fifties. The production on both numbers was professional, but "Every Feeling I Have" suffers from a heavy-handed arrangement that detracts from the love song mood Calvin was trying to convey. Calvin recalled that Ray Stevens and his wife sang backup on both songs.

As soon as the record was pressed, Calvin went on the road promoting it to radio and television stations. One of his stops was at WDBM radio in Statesville, North Carolina. Advertising executive Joe Price recalled, "I was a disc jockey at WDBM at the time and Calvin brought me a copy of 'Just As You Are.' I played it on the air a few times and it got some response, so I called Bill Lowery and ordered a couple of hundred records, and we put them out at various music stores there in the area. Lowery told me, 'When you sell the first one of these records, I want you to call me collect.'" Joe Price's younger sister was starstruck over Calvin, so she and several of her teenage friends starting calling area radio stations and requesting "Just As You Are." If the station didn't have it, they were told they should get it, because it was a great song and was destined to be a hit. The telephone campaign apparently was successful, as all the Charlotte stations worked the song into their playing rotation.

"Some other people started requesting it at radio stations in Charlotte, so we sent some around to different broadcast facilities. Then it picked up some regional popularity and ultimately it ended up being previewed on the Dick Clark show. Dick would take those regional recordings and spotlight them," Price said. During his promotion of "Just As You Are," Calvin appeared at a southern Illinois television station afternoon sock hop show where he lip-synched the lyrics as teenagers swayed in the background. Calvin's younger cousin, Artie Dillon, was home watching the show that day and was ecstatic that his relative was singing on television. Artie said, "I just couldn't get over it; Calvin was on TV singing his rock and roll song, and he was my cousin."

" 'Just As You Are' made it all the way to number one in Birmingham, then Della Reese had a big hit that knocked it from the perch," recalled Calvin. Popular Birmingham disc jockey Joe Rumore of WVOK had used Calvin's "When They Ring Those Golden Bells" as the theme song for his gospel music show for years, so the powerful Birmingham station already knew about Calvin and subsequently gave the tune heavy airplay. Della Reese's hit—"Don't You Know"—peaked at number three on the *Billboard* pop charts the week of November 16, 1959; therefore, it can be surmised that Calvin's rock and roll activity occurred during the fall of the same year.

Often during the late 1950s, a recording on a small label such as Scotti Records would become a regional hit; then a big radio station out of New York or Chicago would begin playing it, and it would break nationally. "Just As You Are," was getting heavy radio airplay in the South and might have become a national hit until, in characteristic fashion, Calvin experienced another instance of rotten luck: the pressing plant that manufactured Scotti Records—Bill Lowery's National Recording Company—went bankrupt. With no product to ship to wholesalers, "Just As You Are" died on the vine, along with Calvin's rock and roll career.

Calvin had the talent, energy, and sex appeal to be a major rock star, yet for the second year in a row, his career ground to a halt. If "Just As You Are" had broken nationally, Calvin would have been on his way. Joe Price indicated that Lowery was monitoring the sales and airplay of "Just As You Are," and at that point had the resources and acumen to help make the song a national hit. However, for the brief period during which he had financial problems with his pressing plant, Lowery was forced to cut back, and Calvin was one of the casualties. It was unfortunate, because Lowery had nothing but the highest respect for Calvin's singing abilities. "In the 1960s I met Bill Lowery on a sidewalk in downtown Nashville. He turned to the person who was with him and said, 'I want you to meet the finest singer I ever recorded,'" said Calvin.

Even if factors over which he had no control had not sabotaged his career, Calvin might have self-destructed because of his abuse of amphetamines. What he sorely lacked at this point was a manager/mentor not only to provide career guidance and support but also to counsel him about his lifestyle. The Sons of Song had likewise suffered from not having a manager, or for that matter, a leader. Their relationship had always been that of equals, which worked well onstage and in the recording studio, but offstage someone needed to take charge. Occasionally, Butler would assert himself. During his period with the Sons he was called "Big Daddy," because of his large stature, booming voice, and commanding presence. Yet Calvin assumed most of the management duties, such as handling the bookings and other details, but the Sons lacked a leader/manager.

A strong, no-nonsense, autocratic manager, such as Elvis Presley's Colonel Tom Parker, might have been able to give the group the focus and direction they needed, both personally and professionally, particularly during the period following the accident when all three were emotionally devastated. (Although, as strong as Parker was, he couldn't save Elvis from self-destruction.) During this period, Calvin needed not a manager, but an angel.

If the Sons of Song had been savvy businessmen, they would probably have been able to strike an alliance early on with the powerful Statesmen and Blackwood quartets. Both James Blackwood and Hovie Lister were well aware of the popularity of the group, and working with the Sons instead of having them for competition would probably have appealed to the two astute businessmen. If such an alliance had been in place at the time of the wreck, the Sons probably would have been able to recover without damage to their careers. However, instead of an alliance with the two groups, there was fierce rivalry, exacerbated by the Sons' gleefully "cleaning their plates" every time the three groups appeared together.

By 1960, after Calvin had cast aside whatever dreams he had of being a roll and roll star, his heavy amphetamine consumption had become the one constant in an increasingly unstructured and chaotic life. He was no longer singing music of any type, nor was he engaged in any other productive activity. He had no income and basically depended on the kindness of his many friends and fans who provided him room and board. The pills he consumed in ever-increasing quantities dulled his appetite and robbed him of sleep. He lost weight and had dark circles under his eyes. His pupils were as dilated as a dead man's. With no job and no meaningful activities, he began to ignore his appearance, even his personal hygiene, often going days at a time without shaving.

He began showing up at all-night singings, where he would stand around looking pitiful, wanting attention and affection yet feeling unworthy of it. He chain-smoked, and when he ran out of cigarettes, which was often, he would bum them from fans or entertainers. When someone asked if he was doing anything or had any plans, he would usually utter some vague statements about getting a group together.

"At this point I was taking thirty pills a day," said Calvin. "I'd generally take five or six at a time. I would often go three or four days without sleep, then crash, even though my body was full of amphetamines. I felt like my life was getting away from me and this made the drug abuse even worse, because I felt I had to be 'on the alert' to try and stay on top of what was happening to me." On the continuum of amphetamine abuse, Calvin had just about bottomed out—the only step beyond was death.

Lee Kitchens heard about Calvin's plight. Kitchens had first met Calvin back in the mid-1940s when the quartet from Bible Training School—Kingsmen Four—came to Florida seeking fame and fortune. Kitchens was a charter member and the first lead singer of the Melody Masters. He recalled, "In 1946, Mosie Lister, James Wetherington, and I separated from the Sunny South Quartet and formed the Melody Masters. Calvin and Wally Varner soon joined us. I knew then that Calvin had a promising future in gospel music." The two developed a strong friendship from their days together with the Melody Masters. Kitchens had already saved the life of one member of the Sons of Song—Bob Robinson. Now, he was prepared to do it again.

Kitchens recalled, "By 1960 I was no longer traveling with a singing group. Word came to me that Cal was seen at a gospel singing in North Carolina. I was told he was in pretty bad shape, with many needs—healthwise, emotional, the whole ball of wax. Through friends of mine, I located him in Statesville, North Carolina. I told them to put him on a nonstop flight to Tampa, Florida." The friends Kitchens referred to were the members of the Rebels Quartet, whom Kitchens had recently sung with and who were appearing at an all-night singing in Winston-Salem, North Carolina. There they saw Calvin and reported to Lee that he "looked awful." Calvin was getting his pills from a truck driver who was a big gospel music fan and followed all the singings. When Kitchens learned this, he contacted the truck driver and told him not to let him have any more amphetamines. The truck driver agreed and further agreed to put Calvin on a nonstop flight to Tampa as soon as Kitchens wired the money. Kitchens was emphatic about it being a nonstop flight to prevent Calvin from deplaning at Atlanta to go in search of pills. Kitchens's motive for coming to Calvin's aid was purely altruistic. Forming a singing group with Calvin was the last thing on his mind; he was simply trying to help an old friend in desperate need.

Kitchens stated, "I brought him to my home and me and my wife, Ginger, fattened him up with chocolate ice milk—his favorite. After a couple of weeks of sleep and eating right, Calvin perked up. Both of us still had singing in our veins. We attempted to form a quartet, but it didn't work. Cal suggested we call Bob Robinson. We did and he came to my home. We rehearsed and the Sons of Song 'sound' was still there. We decided to give it a try." Initially, Calvin and Kitchens attempted to get Jerry Redd and Gerald Adams to join them in forming a quartet. Neither Calvin nor Kitchens remembers why, but the quartet didn't jell, so they called Bob Robinson, asking him initially just to come down and practice. The three began rehearsing Sons of Song material. The practice sessions revealed that there was virtually no difference in the trio's harmonies with

Kitchens singing baritone instead of Don Butler. Calvin and Robinson decided to activate the Sons of Song once more with Lee Kitchens as their baritone.

Lee Kitchens had grown up in Gravelly, Arkansas, hearing and singing southern gospel music. His father was a songwriter, music teacher, and circuit-riding preacher, who on a Sunday might travel fifty miles, sometimes on horseback. His dad taught him how to sing in the orthodox singing-school style, and Lee was an apt student. As a young adult, Kitchens sang second tenor with the Sunny South and Melody Masters in the 1940s, and was also second tenor for the Rebels Quartet in the 1950s, a group that included one of the greatest gospel bass singers of all time: London Parris. By 1960 Kitchens's voice had matured considerably, to the extent that he had become a baritone, and a deep one at that. He differed considerably not only from Butler—the original Sons' baritone—but from Calvin and Robinson as well. First, as a vocalist, he was not a stylist. Kitchens sang straight ahead, without flourish, in the manner of a singing-school-trained vocalist. However, his fine voice blended so well with Robinson's and Calvin's that one has to listen closely to the trio's harmonies to tell that it was he singing baritone instead of Butler. Like Butler, Kitchens could step to the mike and either do a solo or sing as a soloist for an entire concert. The difference was that Butler interpreted the lyrics; Kitchens sang them as they appeared in the songbook.

Kitchens was not a stylish person, either. Unlike Butler, whose confident bearing and demeanor were just short of swagger, Kitchens saw himself as a pretty regular guy, someone who is invaluable in a support role. "Don came out with a more aggressive stance and gung-ho attitude. Lee was content to stay in the background," recalled Calvin. With Butler there was style and substance; with Kitchens there was only substance, but a lot of it. Unlike the original three, there was nothing flashy or charismatic about Lee Kitchens. However, he was a good dependable person, with solid character and good vocal skills. His steady presence helped anchor and stabilize the Sons of Song during a thirty-year on-again, off-again existence.

Kitchens had no illusions about the huge shoes he was trying to fill. Years later, he stated, "I knew I couldn't sing as good as Don Butler, but nobody else could, either." However, Lee Kitchens was both skilled and talented, had good vocal range, could sing on pitch effortlessly, and most important, could sing great harmony with Calvin and Robinson. A fan of the Sons stated that the group lost some of their "oomph" when Butler left, but, all things considered, the group couldn't have found a better replacement. Kitchens became the group's straight man, and the fact that he wasn't a stylist actually gave them a dimension they had previously lacked.

In 1960, Wally Fowler was still the most powerful person in southern gospel music. His all-night singings remained popular; he had a publishing company, a record label, and television programs on stations in Atlanta and Birmingham which featured live southern gospel music. He also had regained control and ownership of the Oak Ridge Quartet. Fowler was a classic entrepreneur, always looking for good business opportunities. He was aware that the Sons of Song had hit hard times but knew they were still a highly marketable commodity. Calvin and Fowler met to discuss how to strike a mutually beneficial arrangement between Fowler and the newly reconstituted Sons. "Wally pitched us a song called 'Wasted Years,' and said if we would sing it, he would arrange for us to get our next album recorded and released," said Calvin, who realized that it was a good tune and that it made sense to remain in Fowler's good graces, as he had begun booking the group. Fowler's company, Gospeltone Publishing, published the song, and Fowler was listed as the writer/composer.

However, Fowler didn't write the song and the Sons knew it. In the future, they would be coy, smiling and shrugging their shoulders when asked who did. They either didn't know or wouldn't say, but one thing was certain—it wasn't Fowler. Finally, in August 2000 it was revealed at the Grand Old Gospel Reunion that Albert Williams, an employee of Fowler's, actually wrote the song. Williams had formerly played piano with the John Daniel Quartet when Fowler sang with the group. "Albert was Wally's utility man," explained Calvin. "He was quiet and timid, and sort of did whatever Wally needed done in their office." There was nothing unethical per se about Fowler claiming authorship; people frequently sell rights to songs, and Williams may have sold or assigned the rights to Fowler through some sort of financial agreement. Williams wrote another song, "Little Boy Blue" (recorded by the Sons on the same album as "Wasted Years"), for which he was listed as the composer; it was destined to become one of the Sons' more requested tunes.

The Sons signed with Bill Beasley's Songs of Faith record label and began reviewing material for their third album, which would be entitled *Wasted Years*. Since the release of their second album, *Riverboat Jubilee*, Sacred Records had gone out of business. The twelve songs selected for the first Songs of Faith album constituted an eclectic mix of old and new, upbeat and blue, with an emphasis on blue. Themes included the loss of a young boy ("Little Boy Blue"), the loss of a father ("How Far Is Heaven"), and the loss of eternal salvation ("Had It Not Been for You"). Two songs were about the sorrow and regret of a mistake-filled life, "If I Had My Life to Live Over" and the title song, the strikingly grief-filled "Wasted Years." The sadness and melancholy of these songs provided perfect material for the mournful and brooding harmonies of the trio.

Beasley and the Sons also included "Old Gospel Ship," the lively camp meeting tune that had already become a Sons of Song candy stick. "Old Gospel Ship" had been previously issued by Lowery's Fox label as a 45 rpm, but for some reason Sacred had not included the song on either of the group's two albums with the West Coast label. Another song on the album was the imaginative and avant-garde version of "Highway to Heaven," a song destined to become one of the group's most popular and crowd-pleasing tunes. Only a minute and fifteen seconds long, the song featured heavy syncopated rhythms, machine-gun-like staccato, and clever vocal nuances. "Highway to Heaven" would become perhaps their most distinctive song—a showpiece that demonstrated how strikingly different they were in their musical arrangements and vocal interpretations from the other gospel groups during that period.

The Sons had previously been singing "Highway to Heaven" onstage when Butler was still with the group, and the unusual and innovative arrangements came out of a rehearsal. "Our version of 'Highway to Heaven' was just three wild minds getting together and wanting to do something different. One of us would initiate something and the other two would fall right behind, just as if we had been doing it that way all along. It was amazing how we knew what the other was going to do," said Calvin.

Recitations would become a staple in the group's repertoire, and this album featured three by Calvin. Both Calvin and Robinson excelled at recitations because of the seemingly heartfelt sincerity with which they infused the lyrics. The late comedian George Burns is said to have remarked that once you learned how to fake sincerity, you had it made. The Sons excelled at faking or simulating sincerity, although on occasion their recitations were based on genuine feelings from an actual experience, such as Robinson's description of how he got saved as a youngster in "Amazing Grace." Calvin's recitations were almost always off-the-cuff ad-libbed lines that were occasionally based on some true experience.

The centerpiece of the album was, of course, the title tune, "Wasted Years." An Echoplex (a tape delay echo chamber) was used for the first time ever in Nashville, to create a fluttering sound on an electric guitar that produced a weepy-like musical effect. The poignant lyrics were particularly suited to the vocal stylings of Bob Robinson, and the song is highlighted by his extended solo. He imbued each phrase with heartrending emotion, and this may have been the song that earned him the sobriquet "the tenor with a tear in his voice." Robinson utilized his bag of vocal techniques, including ringing crescendos, words split in half ("way" becomes "way-hey"), and visceral passion—it was Robinson at his best.

"Wasted Years" was released as a single before the album was issued and was by far the biggest hit of all the Sons' records. The tune not only got extensive airplay on radio stations of all sizes, but also garnered a lot of jukebox play, a rarity for gospel songs. Ralph Emery, the popular all-night disc jockey on Nashville's WSM, the mother station of the Grand Ole Opry and a fifty-thousand-watt clear-channel powerhouse, was totally enamored with the Sons' rendition. Red Foley also recorded "Wasted Years." Emery would occasionally play Foley's version, then tell the audience, "Now, let's hear the good version of this song," and would flip the play switch on the turntable with the Sons' version. Although "Wasted Years" was the Sons' biggest hit, Calvin stated that it was never their most requested or popular song in concert. However, the popularity of the song, along with "Highway to Heaven" and other songs on the album, gave the Sons of Song a big career boost and rejuvenated their bookings.

Yet Calvin's drug abuse persisted. The trio began missing dates, and, when they appeared, Calvin's behavior on stage became increasingly erratic. Never a hypocrite, Calvin would sometimes tell an astonished audience that he had taken a pill to help himself give a good performance. Promoters became leery of Calvin's emcee work and then totally put off by the no-shows and by Calvin's and Robinson's frequent misbehavior in the community. After a while promoters fell into two groups: those who feared the group wouldn't show up and those who feared they would. The group that had taken gospel music by storm in 1957 was now faltering in 1961. When bookings dwindled, the group had little choice but to disband.

The world was closing in on Calvin. He had reached the point where it could be said that he had a great future behind him, having become a shell of his former self. The talented teenager who sang for the Blackwood Brothers and the handsome adult who set the gospel music world on fire in 1957 seemed part of a distant past and bore scarce resemblance to the dissipated person now consumed by pills. Little did he realize in those waning days that as he sang the sad lyrics to "Wasted Years," he was singing what would be the soundtrack of his life for the next three and a half decades.

Calvin clutching a Bible at age 11

Calvin at age 13, in Christopher, Illinois

The Newton family, taken in front of the Lavergne Avenue Church of God, Chicago, Illinois, circa 1945; Calvin and Leonard Newton with sisters Nora and Glatta and mother Irene

The Oak Ridge Quartet, 1953; (front row) Bob Weber and
Bobby Whitfield; (back row) Carlos Cook, Calvin, and
Joe Allred

The Sons of Song onstage

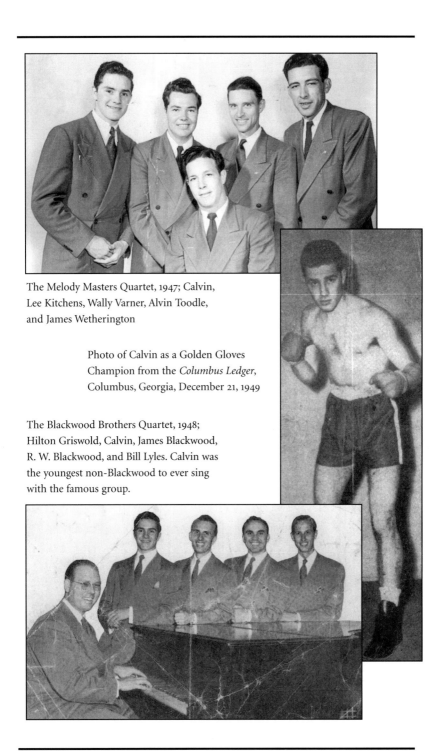

The Melody Masters Quartet, 1947; Calvin, Lee Kitchens, Wally Varner, Alvin Toodle, and James Wetherington

Photo of Calvin as a Golden Gloves Champion from the *Columbus Ledger*, Columbus, Georgia, December 21, 1949

The Blackwood Brothers Quartet, 1948; Hilton Griswold, Calvin, James Blackwood, R. W. Blackwood, and Bill Lyles. Calvin was the youngest non-Blackwood to ever sing with the famous group.

The Sons of Song, 1957.
Three young Atlantans about
to set southern gospel music
on its ear; Bob Robinson,
Don Butler (seated), and
Calvin

The Sons of Song at
Radio Recorder's Studio,
Hollywood, California,
1957; Bob Robinson,
Calvin, and Don Butler

Andy Town, Florida, June 1958; Calvin surveys his automobile that was demolished when Don Butler drove into the back of a truck loaded with watermelons.

Don Butler, Mahalia Jackson, Calvin, and Bob Robinson

Calvin and Joyce Wonder on their wedding Day, October 1963

Abernathy's All-Stars, Canton, Georgia, 1964; Jerry Redd, Bob Robinson, Calvin, and Paul Downing

Calvin, the 1969 employee of the year, and Colonel Sanders

Ambassadors for Christ, Atlanta Federal Prison, 1977; Luis Lopez, Dean "Sunshine" Powell, and Calvin

The Sons of Song, late 1980s; Charlie Burke, Calvin, and Bob Robinson

Gospel Music Hall of Fame induction of the Oak Ridge Boys, Nashville, Tennessee, October 2000; (front row) Tommy Fairchild, Calvin, Willie Wynn, Deacon Freeman, and Ron Page; (back row) Gary McSpadden, Joe Bonsall, Duane Allen, Bill Golden, Richard Sterban, Jim Hamill, and Noel Fox (© Alan Mayor; reprinted by permission)

Calvin and Bill
Gaither on the
cover of *Special
Homecoming
Moments*

Calvin and Joyce,
circa 2000

21. Searching

By the summer of 1961 Calvin was once more at loose ends, with no job, no plans, and a debilitating drug habit. Weighing what few options he had, he decided to go to Houston, Texas, and stay with a young couple who were big Sons of Song fans. The two claimed they could get him bookings. Since he hadn't been able to get any himself, he was desperate enough to allow two people whom he hardly knew the chance. He had no more than gotten settled in when he set out on foot one evening to buy a pack of cigarettes at a nearby market. On the way back, he decided to take a shortcut across someone's yard. Almost immediately he heard a man yell, "Hold it!" He looked up to see a burly, scowling Texan standing on the sidewalk a few feet away holding a shotgun. The man had thrown down on him because he didn't recognize Calvin and suspected he was a prowler, perhaps because Calvin was unshaven and dressed shabbily. In deference to the twelve-gauge, he raised both hands before attempting to explain anything.

Someone called the police, who asked Calvin who he was, where he lived, and what he did for a living. Because of his responses and perhaps his appearance, Calvin was charged with vagrancy, a misdemeanor crime that is lodged against people who are unemployed and without any visible means of support. The date of his arrest was June 30, 1961. Calvin was put in the back of the patrol car and taken downtown for booking and incarceration. (The crime of vagrancy is rarely enforced today, as evidenced by the proliferation of homeless people. Had it not been for his countless friends and supportive family, Calvin might have found himself living on the streets during this dark period of his life.)

Forty years later, Calvin recalled his brief period in the Harris County, Texas, jail. "I spent the night in jail and a funny thing happened. All the benches were full and I needed a place to sit. I wound up sitting on the end of the bench—barely—I mean I only had a couple of inches. Then, slowly I began nudging the guy sitting next to me to scoot down a little to give me enough room to have enough space to sit. I never looked up. I just kept my head bowed, but the other guys sitting on the bench—there must have been fifteen—realized I meant to have an adequate place to sit." The incident reveals that even at his lowest, Calvin still maintained a spirit of determination and defiance. These traits, which initially were responsible for both his success and his personal problems, were ultimately his salvation.

Calvin continued, "They let me make a phone call in the morning and I called the guy I was staying with to come get me. Another guy came instead, an older fellow who was also a big Sons of Song fan. He had recently gotten some insurance money from a wreck he had been in. He got me out and wanted me to go home with him. He said he wanted to take me to Las Vegas and get me some bookings there. The guy I had been living with was supposed to have gotten me some dates in Texas, but it hadn't worked out. So, me and the guy and his wife drove to Vegas, but when we got there he spent most of his time gambling. One night he lost sixteen thousand dollars, and while he was doing that he told me to 'entertain' his wife.

"He did take me to the Golden Nugget where I was supposed to audition. The Foggy River Boys were appearing there at the time, and, of course, they knew me and told the guy in charge that there was no need for me to audition; they would vouch for me." At that time, the Foggy River Boys consisted of Charlie Hodge, Warren Holmes, and brothers Bill and Monty Mathews. Hodge, of course, would go on to become Elvis Presley's onstage rhythm guitar player and close associate. Warren Holmes had sung bass with the Blackwood Gospel Quartet in Iowa when Calvin was with the Blackwood Brothers in 1948. Bill and Monty Mathews had sung previously with the Jordanaires when that group backed Red Foley in the 1940s on the Prince Albert part of the Grand Ole Opry radio show. The Foggy River Boys featured soft harmony in a style similar to that of the Sewanee River

Boys and the Mills Brothers. To a man, they were impressed with Calvin's vocal talents.

Calvin recalled, "Me and the guy I went out there with talked about it with the people at the Golden Nugget and we decided to hire two more guys, and the three of us would reprise the 'Sons' sound. I was to be paid fifteen hundred dollars a week but was told I needed a manager. The guy that took me out there found someone to serve in that capacity. But instead of looking after my interests, this new manager dealt me out and hired three guys and paid them a couple of hundred dollars a week and pocketed the difference. So, there I was; I had a job until my so-called manager gypped me out of it. I'm pretty sure the three he came up with to sing the Sons material didn't last long. I left Vegas after that."

It was yet another in a series of hard-luck stories. Calvin would have been a natural for Las Vegas. With his charm, sexual charisma, vocal talent, dynamic stage presence, and broad musical repertoire, he would have packed lounges up and down the strip and on Glitter Gulch, too. Instead, Calvin returned to Houston and auditioned at a huge, posh hotel as emcee for the renowned Ink Spots, who were performing there for an extended engagement. Calvin can't recall the name of the hotel, but it was probably the prestigious Hotel Rice.

"There were about thirty of us who auditioned, but I got the job. I opened three nights in a row with 'All of Me,' and the crowd encored me. So, after the third night, the owner fired me. A tenor opening up for a tenor main event is bad programming; they should have hired a comedian," said Calvin. But it was more than having a tenor open for a tenor main event. Having Calvin open for the Ink Spots was tantamount to having an Elvis imitator open for Elvis. Calvin's vocal techniques—crooning, slurring up to notes, and the frequent use of falsetto—were identical to the Ink Spots' vocal mannerisms. That he could sing this way as well as the Ink Spots didn't go unnoticed by them. "I later got a note from their tenor singer saying I was one of the best tenors he had ever heard and that he was sorry I got fired."

By now, it seemed that Calvin was experiencing failure and misfortune at every turn. He had been in a grinding automobile accident; his dynamic trio had disbanded; his record company had folded just as he was about to have a rock and roll hit; he got arrested for walking through someone's yard in Houston; he was bamboozled out of a job in Vegas; and he was fired as the opening act at a posh Houston night spot because he sounded too much like the main act. And all of the misfortune was occurring in the context of a growing dependence on drugs. Seeing no future in Texas, he moved back to the southern gospel circuit—the Southeast—where he would try once more to resurrect the Sons of Song.

Calvin contacted Bob Robinson and Lee Kitchens about re-forming the Sons of Song. Robinson was agreeable, but Kitchens lived in Tampa, several hundred miles out of the southern gospel music circuit. If he began singing gospel music again he would once more be gone for weeks at a time from his family, and he was reluctant to do it. Without Kitchens, the group lacked a baritone. Hoping to avoid having the baritone position become a permanently temporary position and in an attempt to please promoters and fans, Calvin and Robinson asked Don Butler to consider rejoining the group.

At that time, Butler was busy and fairly content with his lifestyle, which consisted of managing a restaurant and working at an Atlanta radio station. Butler also liked being home nights and weekends. Living out of a suitcase was drudgery, and he had firsthand knowledge that constant travel could be dangerous. There were many good reasons for him to say no. However, he knew the group had struggled ever since he left. Calvin and Robinson clearly needed him, and the truth was that he missed singing gospel music, especially with Calvin and Bob. Butler knew the Sons of Song had been special; after all, the group had been his idea. After a great deal of reflection and soul searching, Butler quit his two jobs and rejoined the trio. The Sons of Song became the *original* Sons of Song once more.

Lee Kitchens had been an excellent understudy and had done a competent job. However, with Butler returning, all the first-teamers were back in the lineup. In addition to having a great sound, the Sons of Song—with their good looks and expensive, flamboyant clothing—were a visual act, and, unlike Kitchens, Butler had a lot of stage presence. His gestures, body language, and towering stature brought a sparkle back to the group that had been missing since his departure. In describing Kitchens, Calvin stated, "He didn't go 'whammo' like Don did." Commenting on the differences, Butler said, "When he was with the Rebels, he was 'Mr. Proper,' a sweet guy, almost always on cue. His movements were mechanical." The original lineup—Calvin, Robinson, and Butler—had a cohesiveness and chemistry about them that neither they nor anyone else could explain. These qualities were what enabled them to solo in such divergent styles but then come together as one on their distinctive harmonies. It was what allowed any one of them to syncopate, slur, go double time, or move into some different and unrehearsed musical direction onstage and have the other two fall right in behind without missing a beat. Now, reunited, they would try to recapture the magic that had once captivated fans.

The Sons were extremely active in the recording studio after Butler's return. They began recording a new album for Songs of Faith that would be entitled *Unto Him*. This album was the follow-up to their first Songs of Faith album, *Wasted Years*, which, according to the liner notes on *Unto Him*, "was probably the fastest selling sacred and gospel LP to be released in years"—an impressive statement but probably exaggerated, although the 45 rpm version of "Wasted Years" was the most commercially successful of the Sons' recordings.

Bill Beasley was listed as the producer on all of the Sons' recordings on Songs of Faith. However, according to Butler, Beasley was basically just a businessman who relied upon the session engineers to run the sessions. The recording staff on the Sons' Songs of Faith albums have ties to Sam Phillips and Sun Records. Assistant producer Cecil Scaife, recording engineers Billy Sherrill and Scotty Moore, and arranger Bill Justis all worked at Sun Records during the mid-to-late 1950s.

Billy Sherrill had started out for Phillips as a recording engineer and songwriter. He was destined to become a legend as one of the creators of the so-called "Nashville sound" that would define country music in the 1960s and 1970s. As a producer, Sherrill launched the careers of beginners Tanya Tucker and Tammy Wynette and rejuvenated the stalled careers of Charlie Rich, George Jones, and later, Ray Charles. The other engineer on the Sons' Songs of Faith albums—Scotty Moore—had been the talented lead guitarist for Elvis Presley during his most productive years. Moore was equally adept behind a recording console. One of his early triumphs after he left Elvis was producing Thomas Wayne's pop hit "Tragedy" on Fernwood Records, a small Memphis label owned by Moore and others.

Unto Him features three medleys. On "Spiritual Medley," the Sons ingeniously string together snippets of six songs into a tight, coherent whole, with seamless segues bridging the different tunes. Collectively, the songs relate a minidrama, a story of salvation sought and obtained. "American Medley"— consisting of portions of "God Bless America" and "America"—begins with Robinson crescendoing "God Bless America," then features the superlative solo by Don Butler that would enthrall Elvis. The album's third medley, "Songs of the Cross," is just what the title proclaims: "The Old Rugged Cross," followed by a chorus of "He Was Nailed to the Cross for Me," "Must Jesus Bear the Cross Alone," and the chorus of "Haven of Rest."

Recitations had become a big part of the group's stock-in-trade, and *Unto Him* includes the unabashedly sentimental story of a little boy looking for his father—"Have You Seen My Daddy Here?"—featuring a heartfelt performance by Don Butler. "Into the Light" begins with a Bob Robinson solo with Elvis-like stylings, while Calvin solos on "Sweetest Mother," a song he recorded when he was with the Oak Ridge Quartet. Nashville session musicians were used and their musicianship was, as usual, superb, particularly that of Bill Purcell, the pianist. Four of the songs were written by the husband/wife team of John and Bonnie Smith, who had earlier contributed songs that were recorded by the Sons on the *Wasted Years* album. *Unto Him* was vintage Sons, three talented singers interpreting lyrics through individualistic vocal techniques while coming together with their brooding and melancholic harmonies. Although Calvin and Butler probably offered suggestions, the clever and innovative arrangements on the three sets of medleys were most likely done by the creative Robinson.

During this period—1961 to 1963—the Sons of Song made numerous appearances on Wally Fowler's television shows, which were aired in major markets throughout the South. Many of their performances were recorded, and in recent years, these tapes were assembled and transferred to videocassettes; they are now marketed by Calvin and by Larry McCoy, Wally Fowler's son-in-law.

The Sons had many high spots in their career, but both Calvin and Butler feel the group reached their summit when they appeared at East Tennessee State University with the undisputed queen of gospel music— Mahalia Jackson. By the time the Sons appeared with her, she had already achieved iconic status. When the name "Mahalia" was uttered, people automatically thought of a large black woman who sang straight from the heart with a fiery passion. It was said that Mahalia's big heart and gigantic spirit required a large vessel to contain them.

Like the Sons, she was an interpretive singer, combining the vocal styles of blues vocalists Bessie Smith and Ma Rainey with the emotional fervor of the Pentecostal church music she heard as a child in New Orleans.

"Our concert with Mahalia was the first and only time a southern gospel group appeared with her, and it was the first integrated gospel concert in Tennessee," Butler recalled. "We were booked at East Tennessee by Norton Urney, who was an automobile dealer. He booked Mahalia for that concert there at the college. He also booked Rosetta Tharpe there earlier and we appeared with her also. Norton had the ability to promote concerts because he had the money and was respected in the community. He would not book just a straight southern gospel concert. He liked the Sons of Song and he liked Mahalia, so he said, 'Let's put them together.' "

The Sons opened that night for the queen and came back on stage to join her in her encore number, "Amazing Grace," the old gospel standard written by a former slave trader named Newton—Calvin's ancestor John Newton. Butler recalled that, just as they were about to go on stage to sing the number, "She took my hand and said, 'Come on, big boy, let's go out there and show them how to sing.' That was a thrill."

Mahalia was likewise thrilled by the tight and passionate harmonies of the Sons of Song. "She asked if we would be open to doing a European tour and we said sure," said Butler. It is possible that Mahalia was so immersed in her singing and civil rights activities that getting back to the Sons with a formal invitation to do a European tour simply fell through the cracks.

None of the Sons followed up by trying to get a specific commitment, so another golden opportunity went by the wayside.

For a period after Butler returned, Calvin had his drug abuse problem under control, and bookings improved, to the extent that on at least one occasion they were double-booked on a Saturday night for both Pensacola, Florida, and the Birmingham all-night singing. Bookings were done primarily by Calvin, but occasionally by Butler. Neither can recall who was responsible for the snafu, but the Sons decided that rather than cancel one, they would sing at Pensacola, then fly to Birmingham and sing there later in the evening. Calvin recalled, "We chartered a plane and I don't know how many times the pilot went down the runway before he could even take off." Apparently, the small plane was overloaded. Butler said, in reply, "Well, if you remember, we didn't think we were gonna make it; we just barely cleared the trees. I don't know what was wrong with the plane. Anyway, when we got to Birmingham, there was no landing gear. We went down the runway with sparks flying and metal grinding. The pilot told us, 'When we stop, hit the ground and roll.' They turned off all the lights— 'cause there was a big jet coming in on top of us—to wave the jet off. I remember getting off of that plane in pitch dark and then we went on to the auditorium and performed that night like pros."

The last Songs of Faith album by the original group was entitled *Something Old, Something New* and was recorded in the early 1960s. The "something old" in the title referred to the songs selected for the album, which were classic hymns, such as "In the Garden," "Rock of Ages," "Precious Memories," "Never Grow Old," and the rollicking "Way Up Yonder." The "something new" was a reference to the string accompaniment, which consisted of perhaps a half-dozen violins playing the arrangements of Bill Justis, another Sam Phillips refugee. Justis had been musical director of Sun Records during the period when the tiny label made music history. Justis's contribution to the phenomenal success the Memphis label enjoyed was significant.

Justis formed a dance band in the early 1950s in Memphis and took up playing the saxophone just before rock and roll exploded. In 1957 he recorded "Raunchy," one of the all-time instrumental rock records. He and Jack Clement were both fired from Sun by Sam Phillips for "insubordination" in March 1959. After leaving Sun, he worked for a period in A and R for Bill Lowery. By 1961 he had moved to Nashville and become a freelance arranger. Arranging was what he did best; in fact, his wife recalled that in church everyone would sing the melody and Justis would hum an arrangement around it. In the seventies, Justis wrote the film scores to the *Smokey and the Bandit* movies.

Something Old, Something New was the last Songs of Faith album by the original trio. Any album or concert by the group featured solos and singing in unison, and *Something Old, Something New* had the usual blend. On the chorus, the Sons perform "Rock of Ages" just as if they were singing it out of a hymnal—all together, with no stylings nor interpretations, just good, straight-ahead singing. The interpretation occurs on the verses and features Calvin crooning and mixing falsetto. Of all the songs Don Butler recorded, there is perhaps none that showcases his unique vocal phrasing better than C. Austin Mile's evergreen "In the Garden." Words get caressed, stretched, compacted, slammed, and stroked as Butler's inspired performance reveals at least some of his musical influences. "That song probably shows the influence of Billy Eckstine and Al Hibbler on my singing," Butler stated. In addition to including it on *Something Old, Something New*, Songs of Faith issued a 45 rpm of "In the Garden."

Bob Robinson's solo on "Never Grow Old" is also stellar singing done by a true stylist. Robinson infuses his performance with soft yet passionate feelings that are both tender and moving. The album also featured what Calvin would come to consider his signature song—"When They Ring Those Golden Bells," a musical vehicle well suited to his vocal style. As he sings the title words, he climbs the note ladder, ending with the last three words, "those golden bells," sung in falsetto. One of the best songs on the album was "Jesus, Use Me." With the possible exception of "Wasted Years," "Jesus, Use Me," captures the brooding, melancholic harmonies of the Sons of Song as well as any song the original trio performed during their six-year period together. Justis's arrangements and the string section made this a superlative album.

At some point during 1962, the Sons of Song recorded a number of Lee Roy Abernathy songs at Abernathy's small recording studio in Canton, Georgia. According to Don Butler, the recordings were basically intended as demo tapes. "We went up to Lee Roy's every night for a week and just played around with it. The recordings weren't supposed to be released." And they weren't, for a long time. However, nine years later, in 1971, the songs were collected and issued on the White Church record label as an album entitled *The Sons of Song Sing 12 Lee Roy Abernathy Songs.* It was undoubtedly the poorest album ever recorded by the group.

Although innovative himself, Lee Roy Abernathy would often revert to the influence of an old-line orthodox singing-school music teacher, a knuckle-rapping autocrat who insisted on songs being sung his way. The problem was that the Sons of Song were the most unorthodox singing group in gospel music—three stylists who interpreted lyrics instead of singing the songs as they appeared on the page. As such, they were an absolute mismatch for Abernathy's musical ideas and values. Consequently, throughout the project, Abernathy would chastise Calvin, albeit mildly, for sliding or slurring up to notes, as well as "correcting" Butler and Robinson for what Abernathy perceived to be their musical mistakes. The Sons wanted to please Abernathy, and while Abernathy was a bit stubborn, he was no bear. "Lee Roy kind of chuckled and gave in after a while," Calvin recalled. As a result, both sides compromised their standards, and the outcome was a product representative neither of the Sons of Song nor of Abernathy. Not only is the performance lacking, but the sound quality is extremely poor. However, three of the songs on the album are first-rate: "You Can't Put a Price on Your Soul," the funky, bluesy "Hard Labor," and one later used on a television program about the civil rights movement— "I'm Building a Bridge."

Lee Roy Abernathy was an innovator, a visionary, and perhaps a musical genius. While on the one hand he had very pronounced orthodox views on how gospel music should be sung and performed, he also saw and explored connections between gospel music and blues. One of his compositions, "Sin Ain't Nothing But the Blues," recorded by the Statesmen, was considered sacrilegious by many and was banned by certain radio stations

and disc jockeys, including perhaps the biggest gospel jock at the time—
Atlanta's Warren Roberts, a huge fan of the Statesmen. Abernathy's most
popular and commercially successful composition—"Everybody's Gonna
Have a Wonderful Time Up There," also known as "Gospel Boogie"—was
a big pop hit for Pat Boone in the 1950s. It, too, was eschewed by many as
being too racy to be religious.

22. Wonder Woman

The first time Calvin saw Joyce was at the Ryman Auditorium at an all-night singing in the mid-1950s. In his typical flirtatious manner, he flattered her as he had countless other females. From behind the record table where he was working during intermission, he announced, "Little girl, if you'll hang around for ten more years, I'll marry you." Actually, it was to be more like eight years, although obviously no one realized it at the time. She was only twelve but was extremely pretty and was physically developed well beyond her years. Her appearance and demeanor impressed even a seasoned girl-watcher such as Calvin. Although Calvin's utterance was nothing more than an innocent, joking statement, Joyce was smitten for life. "I've always called it love at first sight, on my part, anyway; but I suppose at the beginning it was strong infatuation at first sight. I was just a schoolgirl, but when Cal walked out on that stage, I knew what I wanted out of life. I went up and talked to him during intermission, and that's when he told me he'd marry me in ten years. We stayed in contact through the years, and to be honest, I pursued him heavily. I had other boyfriends in high school, but at any point if Cal had said the word, I'd have dropped everything in my life and gone off with him."

Joyce June Wonder moved from Pennsylvania to Pulaski, Tennessee, with her parents and younger sister when she was eleven years old. She grew up in the small middle Tennessee town and absorbed many of the traits and values common to that area. Her parents were devoutly religious, and Joyce attended church with them twice on Sunday and once in the middle of the week. In her teens, she became the church organist at the Pulaski First Baptist Church. When they first moved to Pulaski from

Pennsylvania, the Wonder family wasn't familiar with southern gospel music, but they all liked music. So, when a neighbor, J. O. Scoggins, invited them to the all-night singing at Nashville's Ryman Auditorium, they eagerly accepted. That was the night Joyce met Calvin, when he was singing with the Oak Ridge Quartet. Over the next few years, the Wonders continued to drive up U.S. 31 from Pulaski to Nashville to hear the good gospel music that Wally Fowler brought to the Ryman the first Friday of every month. Calvin came to know the family, and he would sometimes take them out for breakfast in the early morning hours after the last notes were sung. By Joyce's senior year, she and Calvin had begun dating, although both went out with others; in fact, Joyce actually became engaged to someone else, but it was primarily a status thing—she got to wear a diamond engagement ring.

Joyce was intelligent and an excellent student. Her senior year she was valedictorian of her graduating class. She was also stunningly attractive, with eyes the color of the sky on a clear day. By her early teens she had a figure that was nothing less than voluptuous. When she walked down the street, males—young and old—stopped what they were doing to scrutinize her physical charms. A close friend, Shirley Hollis Cardwell, recalled, "Joyce was absolutely beautiful, one of the prettiest women I've ever seen."

In certain respects, she was the female counterpart of Calvin, although in others, she differed from him dramatically. Like Calvin, she had insecurities, which kept her from being conceited but also prevented her from competing in activities that would have made her the center of attention, such as cheerleading or entering beauty pageants that she could have probably won by just showing up. Like Calvin, Joyce Wonder was blessed with a warm, ingratiating personality that could brighten any room. Internally, she had a rock-hard constitution like that of her diminutive father, Frank Wonder. Her childhood socialization—what in the South is called "raising"—imbued her with certain fundamental values that would sustain her through the many turbulent years of her adult life. Above all, she believed in God, family, love, and loyalty.

"I was crazy about Calvin for a long time, but the exact moment I fell in love with him was before Lee Kitchens joined the group. I was at Ryman

Auditorium at the singing with my high-school boyfriend. In those days
the Ryman had a dingy hall that led to the bathrooms off to the right, facing the stage. I happened to look at that side door and saw Cal standing
there and I almost passed out. I hadn't seen or heard from him in a long
time, and he looked so haggard. I got up and walked out to him, and we just
put our arms around each other. He had lost so much weight and just had
a whipped, defeated air about him. I can't remember anything we said,
but I recall he had about given up. I knew from that point that man was
gonna be my life, and I'd do whatever needed to be done for him." Calvin
was then in his early thirties and a confirmed bachelor. He had witnessed
so much adultery among the southern gospel music entertainers that he
had adopted a cynical view towards the institution of marriage. (He had
himself enjoyed the company of some married women along the way.)
Seeing unfaithfulness in married men and women made him distrustful of
permanent intimate partnerships, and he wasn't going to marry anyone he
couldn't trust. He found in Joyce someone he could, in fact, trust.

Joyce had graduated from Pulaski High School in 1960 and was pursuing
a secretarial course at Falls' Business College in Nashville at night and working during the day for a local attorney. On weekends she usually traveled to
Wally Fowler's all-night singings, driving to Birmingham, Memphis, and
Atlanta, to see Calvin and to hear him and the other groups as well. At one
of the singings in Atlanta during the summer of 1962, Fowler brought back
the old Oak Ridge Quartet that had performed together before disbanding
in late 1956. Calvin did double duty that night, performing with Bob Weber
and some of the other old Oaks, and then with the Sons of Song.

That was the night that Joyce met Kathy South, an Atlanta legal secretary. Kathy lived with another legal secretary, Shirley Hollis, originally
from Birmingham but now living in Atlanta. Like Joyce, Shirley had at one
point had a crush on Calvin, back when she was in her early teens, but she
was over it. Shirley's family lived near Birmingham and used to come to
the monthly all-night singing at the Birmingham city auditorium.

Kathy South, however, did have a crush on Calvin, but she and Joyce
became friends nonetheless; in fact, Shirley, Kathy, and Joyce began sharing an apartment together near Atlanta when Joyce moved there from

Nashville. The three were not groupies, or "diesel sniffers," but were big gospel music fans who traveled all over the South attending all-night singings and other gospel music concerts, sometimes arriving back in Atlanta early on Monday morning and having to go to work after having slept only a few hours over the weekend. The three young women became friends with Sybil and Norris Graham and Arnold and Patsy Fulp, who were already good friends with the Sons of Song. Don Butler was living with Sybil and Norris Graham at the time, and Bob and Mary Robinson lived next door to the Fulps.

Bob had a piano and the Fulps and the Grahams would come over when the Sons rehearsed. The Grahams, the Fulps, and the three legal secretaries—Joyce, Shirley, and Kathy—became a tight circle of friends for the Sons of Song during this time, sharing their triumphs and tragedies and always offering support and encouragement, as well as, sometimes, hot meals and the use of their automobiles.

In the coming years, Calvin, in particular, was going to need all the help he could get, and Joyce would be there to give it to him—neither he nor she had any idea at the time just how much it would be.

23. Wedding Bells and Prison Cells

In the latter part of 1962 and on into 1963 the concert dates became increasingly random and infrequent. The Sons of Song had always been considered controversial, but now, with Calvin's mounting problems and their failure to show up for concerts, the big promoters had become very apprehensive about using them. Calvin's life continued on the amphetamine roller coaster, with peaks of boundless energy and false optimism, followed by black pits of depression and bone-wearying fatigue. During his few drug-free moments, Calvin was forced to accept a sobering reality: his life was on the rocks. His behavior, always on the edge, became increasingly erratic; in fact, he began to violate minimum standards of conduct—he began breaking the law. Butler and Robinson had begun to notice troubling signs when the trio performed out-of-town dates.

"It got to where when we'd finish a date and get ready to go home, Calvin would just hang in that town," said Butler. "Later on we found out that he would borrow or rent a car from someone and would rent a trailer, and then he would stop at hotels and motels along the road and rob people's cars." Calvin's descent into crime was initially awkward and ineffective, but over time he made the transition from being a bumbling thief who ransacked vacant cars in parking lots to being a fairly proficient, skilled burglar who stole sizable quantities of valuables wherever he could, although automobiles remained his favorite prey. Calvin got lots of tips on how to commit crime from his cousin, Bill Whitlow, said to be a mob associate in Chicago.

Bill Whitlow had such an engaging personality that Calvin's dad used to remark that Bill could have sold refrigerators to Eskimos. If he had, he probably would have stolen them back, because Bill preferred stealing to selling. For him, it wasn't just a profitable hobby; it was a lifestyle and career choice. A charming rascal and consummate high roller, Bill Whitlow was undoubtedly a negative influence on Calvin.

As Butler observed, if the Sons played an out-of-town date, Calvin would obtain a trailer from a rental agency, attach it to an automobile, and then literally steal his way back to Atlanta. At one point, Calvin had a rental trailer full of stolen articles that he had appropriated on a seek-and-steal mission in Florida. He asked Arnold and Pat Fulp if he could park the trailer in their driveway, just for a little while, until things cooled off. They said okay, but when Atlanta burglary detectives came snooping around, Pat sent word to Calvin that if he didn't come get the trailer, she was going to push it off a nearby bluff. A retired Atlanta detective stated that another trailer full of swag was traced to Norris Graham's house. Calvin must have been U-Haul's best customer.

In separate interviews, Don Butler and Jimi Hall related a burglary/theft that Calvin carried out while on tour. The only difference in their accounts was the location. Hall thought it was in West Virginia; Butler is certain it was in Marion, Illinois. Butler stated, "We stopped for dinner. When Jimi and I were sitting at the table finishing up our meal, Calvin got up and said he'd be back in just a minute. I didn't know but what he'd gone to the restroom." Hall and Butler finished their desserts and concluded that Calvin wasn't coming back to the table. "When we went to get in the car, Calvin had something in his hand in the back seat looking at it. He said that a friend met him there and gave it to him," said Butler. On the way back, without explaining why, Calvin instructed Butler to take back roads. "When we got back to Atlanta, we found that he had loaded all this luggage he had stolen in the trunk. It was the last time he ever rode in my car," said Butler.

Calvin and Joyce Wonder began dating regularly after she moved to Atlanta in 1962. A romance soon blossomed. They decided to live together, so they rented a tri-level home and shared the expenses, although Joyce assumed the role of primary wage earner, a distinction she has maintained throughout their relationship. Joyce recalled, "It devastated my parents when I moved in with Calvin. Living with someone out of wedlock totally violated their personal and religious values. I had always been the perfect daughter—valedictorian of my class, church organist—never gave them a minute's trouble. Mother and Daddy came down to see us and tried to talk me into coming home with them, but I said, no, I was staying with Cal. They left, and pretty soon a policeman knocked on the door. He told me my parents were outside in their car and would like for me to come talk with them. I told him no, that they could come to the house to talk to me. I figured if I went to the car, they'd pull me in and make me leave. The policeman asked me how old I was, and then asked to see my ID to verify that I was twenty-one. Then he went out and told Mother and Daddy there was nothing he could do, since I was of age. It really tears my heart out now to realize how badly I hurt them, but all I knew was that Cal and I belonged together. I've never changed my mind about that, and I've never regretted my decisions— I just wish they could have been less traumatic to the ones I loved."

She continued, "The amphetamine abuse was real bad then. He was taking as many as six at a time that he was getting in Birmingham. After taking them, he'd be so optimistic; nothing could stop him; he'd go off and I wouldn't know where. I knew things were spinning out of control, but I didn't know any way to fix it. What made things even more difficult was that I was only seeing the present moment—not the broad picture nor the long-term effects. I begged and cried many times for him to stop what he was doing, but I lacked the wisdom at that point to know how to make him get help. It reached the point that I would just pray—sometimes all night long—that he'd get back alive. Sometimes I wouldn't hear from him or know where he was for several days at a time."

During the period of Joyce's all-night prayer vigils, Calvin had gotten hooked up with a sleazy Atlanta character named Jacky, who was fencing some of Calvin's stolen property. Joyce knew Jacky because he managed the parking garage where she parked her car when she worked for a law firm. "One night Calvin and Jacky went out together and I was concerned, but Cal said not to worry, that he'd be back before midnight. He didn't get home and it got later and later. Finally I was about to climb the walls, so, in desperation, I called one of Calvin's friends to see if Calvin might be there. The friend said he hadn't seen him that night and asked me where he was supposed to be. I told him I didn't know, but he'd said he was going by Jacky's. He said, 'Well, honey, I hate to tell you this, but you might not ever see him alive again.' Talk about a horrible night; that one was about the worst."

Joyce was extremely deferential to Calvin, for two reasons. First, there was a fairly significant age difference: Joyce was an innocent twenty-one-year-old; Calvin was extremely worldly at thirty-three. The second reason was philosophical. Despite the fact that she is a strong person, Joyce feels that the role of the woman in an intimate partnership is that of subservience to the man. These factors rendered her virtually powerless to change the tide of dark events unfolding in their lives.

Butler, Robinson, and others attempted to counsel Calvin about the stealing, but to no avail. Butler noted, "We talked to him about it, but Calvin knew better than anyone. He'd laugh at you; he thought it was a cute thing to do. He was just like a preacher's kid: all the way for the Lord or all the way the opposite way. He was always rebelling. He rebelled against his upbringing and all the traditional things of the church. Calvin had that anger and he had to have an outlet for it, yet he had a tender heart. He always wanted to live like the others who were successful and he wasn't able to do so. He always lived above his means. He found the quickest way to do that was just steal some things and sell them and make money, and that was going on a long time before Bob and I found out about it."

In 1963, when the Sons were almost totally inactive, Calvin began traveling all over the southeastern United States plundering automobiles, motel rooms, businesses—anywhere he might be able to score. He soon filled up the first floor of his tri-level home with stolen goods, causing those in the know to name it the "bargain basement," because Calvin would give you a good deal on a stolen television, stereo, or whatever else might be available. While Calvin may have been good at stealing, selling the stolen property, or "fencing," as it is called, was another matter. He wound up giving a lot of what he had stolen to friends, and made very little on what he sold.

One night he broke into an automobile that was filled with all types of guns—that was one of his best scores. He did some "smash and grabs," too, throwing a brick through a jewelry store window, scooping the contents up quickly and then making a run for it. Once he broke into a salesman's car and stole a huge trunk, thinking it was full of men's overcoats. However, when he pried it open, he found it filled with what appeared to be frilly, expensive lingerie. Calvin showed the garments to a strip club owner and the man wound up buying all of them as Christmas presents for his girls, except for two items Calvin kept to give to his mom and Joyce. As Calvin's mom opened up her present and held out the garment for viewing, a piece of paper fell to the floor. She picked it up and read aloud, "This has been selected for your loved one by your funeral director." The garment was a shroud, meant to be used in a burial. Everyone had a big laugh and the two presents went to the trash without Calvin's mom ever knowing where they came from.

Calvin's dysfunctional, self-destructive behavior of crime and drug abuse intensified during the summer of 1963. In mid-August, he made a theft run up to Kentucky where he ransacked the Bluegrass State thoroughly before driving south to Springfield, Tennessee, near Nashville. There he checked into a mom-and-pop motel and began swiping guests' luggage. By then he was running low on pills, so he called Arnold Fulp, and Fulp agreed to bring him a fresh supply. Fulp wasn't into drugs, so Calvin gave him detailed directions on where to obtain them. Unfortunately for them, a motel desk clerk was listening in on the call and then reported to authorities that he had overheard in a conversation that a bunch of "bennies" would be brought to the motel.

Local law enforcement mobilized quickly. At the direction of the local district attorney's office, members of the Springfield police department and sheriff's department and Tennessee Bureau of Investigation agent Bill Whitehurst set up surveillance on the motel. Then, around 2:30 A.M. on August 28, 1963, Fulp drove slowly onto the motel property and parked next to a Chevy II convertible bearing Georgia license plates. Fulp got out of the car carrying a paper sack with a fruit jar containing 150 dextroamphetamine sulfate tablets, or "dexies." He located Calvin's room, knocked gently, and was greeted by Calvin. Moments later, the police banged loudly on the door and demanded that it be opened. Calvin complied and was immediately arrested. The police were astounded by what they saw. Crammed full of stolen property, Calvin's room resembled a well-stocked pawnshop.

In a front-page article entitled "Dope, Jewelry Seized Here," the *Robertson County Times* reported the following day: "Jewelry and appliances worth several thousand dollars and a small quantity of narcotics were seized early yesterday . . . One of the men, Wesley Calvin Newton, who gave his address as Atlanta, was charged with illegal possession of legend drugs, possession of burglary tools and grand larceny . . . Among the items found in the motel room and Newton's car, Whitehurst said, included: two suitcases full of jewelry, some of it termed 'very expensive,' three almost new television sets, an expensive camera, a set of binoculars and a pistol and shoulder holster. The officers . . . did not know where most of the loot came from . . . Whitehurst quoted Fulp as saying that Newton had been stealing items from tourists for about eight months and disposing of the loot in Atlanta."

Calvin had obtained a private investigator's license from the Atlanta police department so that he could carry the gun, but, license or not, authorities—particularly prosecutors and judges—have always taken a dim view of an armed thief. His possession of a handgun made a bad situation worse, as he would discover at sentencing. The newspaper article ended by saying that the owner of the automobile Newton was driving was Joyce Wonder, who was from Pulaski. It mentioned that no charges had been placed against her, and that she had previously been employed as a secretary for a Nashville attorney who described her as a "high-type person."

Fulp was also arrested and charged with illegal possession of drugs. Both Calvin and Fulp posted bond immediately and returned to Atlanta. The next issue of the *Robertson County Times* featured another front-page story about the arrest, highlighted by a four-by-six-inch photo of a sheriff's deputy and TBI agent Whitehurst inspecting the large array of Calvin's contraband, which included uncut diamonds. The worth of the haul was estimated at twenty thousand dollars. Law enforcement had also seized glass-cutting equipment and other tools commonly used in the burglary trade. A few of the items seized by police, including a diamond ring, were Calvin's personal property.

The paper quoted Jim Porter, the district attorney, saying, "Some of the luggage was taken from the Key Motel here a few days before the arrest. One suitcase belonged to an Australian racing driver who had stayed in a motel in Hopkinsville, Kentucky." The article also stated that Porter was uncertain whether his office and law enforcement would be able to trace all of the stolen property. They ultimately couldn't, but their efforts resulted in more trouble for Calvin and in Joyce Wonder's first and only brush with the law. Joyce recalled, "After Calvin got out on bond and came back to Atlanta a few days later, the Atlanta police came to search our house. Of course, they'd gotten the information from Springfield. Cal had all sorts of contraband in the house, including amphetamines and stolen property, so they took us to jail in Atlanta. Before leaving, the police let me call my boss to tell him what was happening. He said he'd be down in the morning to get me out. They were kind enough to put me in a little cell by myself. The matron was very nice and told me I wasn't the type that should be in a situation like this, and she didn't want me to be in a cell with criminals.

"Cal had told me there were bedbugs in the Springfield jail, so I was afraid there were bedbugs in the Atlanta jail, also. I remember spending the night literally sitting on the iron edge of the bed, as I figured the bugs would be in the mattress. They had taken my watch, so I had no idea of how long I was there. But I do remember worrying about what Cal was going through, as I knew they would not be as gentle with him as they were with me. Two detectives took me into a room, gave me some coffee, and asked me a lot of questions. I honestly didn't know anything they wanted me to know, so I wasn't much help. Later, someone came to the door with breakfast, but I told them I didn't want it. As I recall, lunch was brought around, too. I know this: I was there a long, long time, and I wondered if Mr. Hall, my boss, had simply decided to abandon me there.

"Finally, they came to get me; they said someone was there to bail me out. I walked out expecting to see Mr. Hall, but instead it was my daddy and our youth minister at church. Daddy drove my car home, and the youth minister and I rode together. Of course he tried to 'talk some sense' into me. He told me how much I was hurting my family and myself and throwing my life away. He told me the Lord had put him and his wife together, and the Lord would have someone for me, too. I told him the Lord had already chosen someone for me, whether he believed it or not, and I wasn't leaving Calvin. When we got home Mother came to the door and hugged me. It still breaks my heart to remember how frail she felt in my arms—she's a little lady, anyway, but she must have lost ten or fifteen pounds during those few weeks. It was extremely difficult for both my parents because they had never had to deal with anything like this before.

"They begged me not to go back to Atlanta, but I told them there was no way I would leave Cal in that situation, that I belonged with him. They finally agreed to let me go back but wouldn't let me take my car—Daddy had paid for a lot of the car for my graduation gift. Cal's folks came and got me, and I made arrangements to stay with the other girl that worked in my office."

Calvin was both amazed and gratified that anyone could be as loyal, supportive, and loving as Joyce had been under such dire circumstances. He told her that he loved her for it, and, to show he meant it, he promised that if she still loved him when he got out of prison, he'd marry her. Sensing a golden opportunity, she replied that, as his girlfriend, she couldn't do anything to help him when he went to prison, and probably wouldn't get to see him, at least not as much as if they were married. Calvin couldn't believe anybody would want to marry someone for whom prison was a certainty. However, as they talked it over, he quickly warmed to the idea. They decided to run off to Georgia in search of a marriage license and a preacher, and wound up getting married on the day before Calvin had to be in criminal court in Springfield.

On October 3, 1963, Calvin pled guilty to larceny, possession of burglary tools, and possession of illegal legend drugs, and was sentenced to three years at hard labor, to be served in a Tennessee penitentiary. The three counts ran concurrently and were also concurrent with his theft-related charges in Atlanta, to which he copped a plea in a separate hearing. Arnold Fulp got off with a suspended sentence.

"Mr. Ziegler, the attorney I worked for in Nashville, represented Calvin," said Joyce. "He found out at the hearing that we had gotten married and he called my parents and told them. Daddy was upset and was trying to think of some way to undo it, but Mother said, 'No, they're married now. Joyce would never be happy if she wasn't with Cal, and we're not doing anything to try and break up a marriage.' From that day on, you couldn't ask for any parents to be more supportive and helpful. After Cal's sentencing, they called us and told us to come home to them. We went back to Atlanta, where I worked a notice, and we packed what little we had and went to Pulaski."

Calvin had made many mistakes during his life, particularly in the five-year period from the Sons of Song's automobile accident up until his incarceration in 1963. Most were due to his faulty decision making, which was usually done in a shoot-from-the-hip manner and often based on emotion rather than intellect. A lot of his problems stemmed from his being both impulsive and compulsive. His impulsiveness kept him from weighing the consequences of his acts. He often charged off blindly on a thoughtless path of self-destructive hedonism, believing that if it felt good he should do it. His compulsiveness was at the core of his amphetamine abuse. He had realized for some time that pills were his enemy, yet he was psychologically addicted and continued to take them. His criminal activity was probably the result of a combination of the two traits, along with other factors.

Years later Calvin learned that he had an addictive personality. He confessed, "If I eat chocolate, I want an entire box. If I eat ice cream, I want a quart. If I eat cake, I want the whole thing." Dr. Robert Ossof of the Vanderbilt Voice Center treated singer Carl Perkins for throat cancer. Perkins had smoked cigarettes and abused alcohol his entire adult life, and had an extremely hard time quitting smoking, even when he discovered he had cancer. Dr. Ossof remarked, "People who are . . . artistic . . . are far more addictive, far more emotional, and the more emotional you are, the more addictive you are." With Calvin, there was also a strong correlation between his amphetamine abuse and his stealing. Amphetamines do not cause a person to steal, but in Calvin's case they pushed someone over the edge who might otherwise have continued to live right on it.

While Calvin's amphetamine abuse may have stemmed from an addictive personality, Don Butler's assessment of Calvin's criminal behavior being part of his rebelliousness also has merit. Calvin explained, "My folks were Pentecostals. They had set such rigid rules on me, and when I got out in the world and found out I didn't have to go by those rules, I guess somewhere—when trouble came along—I figured I didn't have to live by anybody's rules."

Without a doubt, marrying Joyce Wonder was the wisest decision he ever made, and she was certainly the best thing that ever happened to him. Joyce was to give Calvin all her love, devotion, loyalty, and support. She was smart, attractive, personable, and strong, and could have married a doctor, lawyer, or businessman and enjoyed a life of material comfort. Instead, she chose the man she loved, and consequently endured decades of hardship, emotional pain, and frequent deprivation. But there were also a lot of laughs, plus the enjoyment and contentment that come from sharing your life with the person that you love. Not once did Joyce ever second-guess her decision to marry Calvin. She became his stabilizing force and was always there to pick up the pieces of his life, which would be continually shattered in the years to come. Calvin didn't go into prison alone; he took Joyce's spirit with him, which comforted him and gave him a reason to hang on.

He needed something, for he was about to enter one of the biggest hellholes on earth. Calvin is unequivocal about what Joyce meant to him during this period. "Joyce was my salvation; I couldn't have made it without her."

24. If I Had Wings

And when he had spent all, there arose a mighty famine in that land, and he began to be in want.

—Luke 15:14

After sentence was pronounced, Calvin was shackled and led to the dank, grungy Robertson County Jail, where he remained for three stressful days before being taken to Tennessee State Prison, thirty miles away in west Nashville. In jail, the bedbugs kept him awake at night, crawling on him and his bunk. In the daytime he had inmates to contend with. Within hours he got into a dispute with an inmate who threatened him with serious bodily injury. Shortly thereafter, Calvin was offered a straight razor by another inmate for protection. Calvin thanked the man but told him he would take his chances without it. In jail, there are always those who test the new inmates immediately, probing for weakness. Calvin was used to the drill. In his youth, the Catholics and neighborhood ruffians had done the same thing, and he had withstood their challenges. The criminals might be bigger and tougher than his childhood bullies, but so was he. At this point in his turbulent life, if someone came to Calvin looking for trouble, he had come to the right place.

After his short stay in the bug-infested jail, he was put in the back of a sheriff department's patrol car, and he and the deputy began their journey to Nashville, down Highway 41 South. After they had traveled about five miles, they passed through Ridgetop, where Willie Nelson's pig farm was located. Nelson's musical career was foundering at the time, and he had decided to quit the music business and raise pigs. (As it turned out, his luck raising swine was not much better, so he returned to entertaining and soon thereafter found fame and fortune.)

As they rode, Calvin gazed at the countryside and reflected on his future. Technically it would be a year before he would be eligible for parole, but with good-time credits for exemplary behavior he could possibly be out in six months or less. Six months wasn't all that long. Time would pass, and when he got out, he and Joyce could sit down and plan their future. Calvin had yet to learn that the clock ticks a lot slower in prison. Deprivation, boredom, loneliness, and isolation can almost stop a clock dead in its tracks, making minutes seem like hours, days like weeks, and months like years. Yet running counterpoint to the mind-numbing boredom was the ever-present fear of violence, which, in prison, is simply part of the dynamic.

Calvin wasn't the only entertainer who had wrecked his life and career with amphetamines. As the cruiser reached Nashville and made its way down familiar streets, he looked in the direction of the illustrious Ryman Auditorium, where he had thrilled audiences for a decade. Don Gibson, a member of the Grand Ole Opry, had been popular there, too, since 1958, when he burst on the country music scene with his huge two-sided hit, "Oh, Lonesome Me," and "I Can't Stop Loving You." Unlike gospel singers, people like Gibson who sang country made big bucks, particularly those who wrote the songs they sang, and Gibson did.

Although a star, Gibson was a somewhat retiring individual, and he had a tendency to put on weight. He discovered that his shyness, weight gain, and lack of rest were all problems that could be alleviated by amphetamines. He began using them and rapidly succumbed to their evil spell. By 1963, he was taking twenty-five at a time. Like others hooked on speed, he took tranquilizers, too, which made him even more disoriented. When he showed up two hours late for the Opry one Saturday night, he was fired on the spot—they didn't care whether he was a star or not. Gibson's life went downhill after that for a number of years. His marriage broke up and he stopped performing. He did enjoy mild success in the 1970s but nothing compared to what it could have been. Preoccupied with his own worries, Calvin wasn't aware of Gibson's problems at the time.

A few minutes after the drive through downtown Nashville, the deputy pulled into the parking lot of the biggest building in west Nashville.

In 1963 there were only three prisons in Tennessee. Ft. Pillow was located in west Tennessee and the internationally infamous Brushy Mountain State Prison in east Tennessee. Serving middle Tennessee was Tennessee State Prison, also known as the "main" prison, or TSP, but referred to by guards and inmates alike as "the walls," because of the huge thirty-foot-high concrete barrier that enclosed the compound. The aging prison had been completed in 1898 and by 1963 was decrepit and outdated. In 1992, the prison was closed and subsequently became the site of many prison movies, including *The Green Mile*, based on a Stephen King story, and *The Last Castle*, starring Robert Redford. When Calvin was there, some of the lifers and long-timers called TSP "Swafford's graveyard," after a notorious prison warden who had overseen the prison in the 1940s. By whatever name, it was no place for the faint of heart. The main prison housed death row and the state's electric chair, which had been utilized as recently as 1961. It also provided room and board for murderers, rapists, child molesters, thieves, perverts, wife beaters, drug dealers, and various other felony offenders, of whom a few were musically talented.

About twenty years before Calvin arrived, a black male named Johnny Bragg had been sent there for a long stretch—six life sentences. To help pass the time, he and other black inmates formed a musical group. After a few rehearsal sessions they decided to call themselves the Prisonaires. Their close harmony singing drew the inevitable comparisons to the Ink Spots. They subsequently became well known in the Nashville area, performing for the governor and other dignitaries from time to time.

One wet, dreary day, while walking in a light rain to their prison jobs, Bragg and another member of the Prisonaires, Robert Riley, began chatting lightheartedly about females, probably in an attempt to take their minds off the grim reality of their lives. "I wonder what all the little girls are doing right about now," Bragg wondered aloud. It was a simple, rhetorical remark, made to pass time, but from it came musical history. As they continued their way to the prison laundry where they worked, Bragg and Riley began playing around with lyrics that dealt with what they were doing at that moment: walking in the rain, reflecting on romance. Within minutes they composed a tune that became one of torch singer Johnny Ray's biggest hits, and also one of the biggest pop hits of the fifties—"Just Walkin' in the Rain." It was first recorded by the Prisonaires in 1953 at Sun Records, after the group had been escorted there by prison guards. The Prisonaires' version did fairly well, selling around fifty thousand copies. Then, in 1956, Don Law, head of Columbia Records, pitched the song to Johnny Ray's producer, Mitch Miller. Ray recorded it, and "Just Walkin' in the Rain" peaked at number two on the pop charts during the fall of 1956. In *Good Rockin' Tonight*, writers Colin Escott and Martin Hawkins noted, "The first writer's check Bragg received was for fourteen hundred dollars. Bragg, who had never seen such a sum on a check or anywhere, mistook it for fourteen dollars and asked the warden to deposit it in the commissary cash register so that he could get some cigarettes and candy."

In 1963 blacks and whites didn't interact socially in prison, so Calvin never met Bragg or any of the other Prisonaires while he was there.

Inmates at the main prison were housed two to a six-by-nine-foot cell, an area that corresponds to the size of small walk-in closet. With the iron beds jutting out three feet into the precious space available for moving about, it was practically impossible for two inmates to be standing at the same time. Each cell had a metal toilet without a lid, a sink, and two metal beds. The floor, ceiling, and walls were concrete, except for the door, which was grated steel. A dim bulb provided illumination sufficient to make reading nearly impossible but sleep difficult. New inmates were issued a thin mattress along with clothing. They were also given a number: Calvin became inmate #58119.

Like most prisons of that era, this one housed its prisoners in a tier system that featured rows of cells stacked on top of one another, back to back—a tier of cells on one side and a tier on the other. At the main prison there were five tiers. In such an environment there is absolutely no privacy or quiet; an inmate is bombarded by a never-ending cacophony of screaming, cursing, crying, screeching, laughing, shouting, blaspheming, Tarzan yells, and all other sounds of which a human is capable. Competing with other noise, small, tinny-sounding radios blared country music or rhythm and blues. In their tiny cells, inmates sweltered during the hot Tennessee summers and shivered under a smelly woolen blanket in the winter. Upon arrival, all inmates were photographed, fingerprinted, examined by a doctor, and given a battery of tests as part of the prison classification program. Calvin's photo shows him looking scruffy and bewhiskered; he had recently put on weight, bulking up to 180 pounds on a frame that measured a couple of inches short of six feet. He was thirty-four, considered old for a new inmate—crime is a young man's game. As he submitted to the process, he was apprehensive but not fearful. He had grown up fighting in tough, southern Illinois coal-mining communities, and he brought his rebellious, defiant attitude with him. Yet Calvin's tough-guy attitude was more posturing than reality, for despite his youth of fighting and young adulthood of boxing, he was not a violent person. However, the prison administration apparently recognized his troublesome attitude during the classification period. In reviewing test scores, interviews with professionals, and personal observations, someone wrote in a psychological evaluation, "Prognosis for prison and civil adjustment is guarded."

November 1963 stands out as a historical bookmark because of President John Kennedy's assassination on the twenty-second of that month, a Friday. Calvin recalled that he was in the prison yard when news reached the inmates that the president had been killed. Like most, Calvin was shocked and saddened by the senseless act of violence. Not everyone around him felt that way, however—especially one inmate, who probably hated all forms of authority and viewed the assassination as a cause for celebration. The inmate began saying how happy he was that the president had been murdered, that he was nothing but a "pimp" for the wealthy and powerful. He kept on, enraging Calvin more with each successive remark. The inmate persisted, until finally Calvin exploded in anger and went after him, but was restrained by other inmates before blows could be exchanged. Looking back, Calvin said, "I'm a diehard Republican, myself, but there was no cause for that—he was our president."

Relations with his cellmate weren't much better. He had been confined in his tiny living area with a lifer, a man who had killed his wife by stabbing her multiple times with an ice pick. Calvin had no more than settled in when the man began dictating rules for the cell and what he expected Calvin to do and not do. Calvin listened for a few minutes and then told the guy to stuff it. It was bad enough having every second of your life regimented by prison officials, but no inmate was going to tell him what to do, ice pick killer or not. According to Calvin, the man snitched him out to prison officials, portraying Calvin as a defiant troublemaker. Word had probably already leaked out about the incident in the prison yard, and this new story only reinforced the perception that the department of correction apparently had not gotten inmate Newton's attention, at least not yet.

Calvin had just completed his classification period and would have probably done the remainder of his short sentence at the main prison. But he was perceived as a troublemaker and the Tennessee Department of Correction had a place for people like that. This was the chain of events: those who messed up on the outside got sent to prison; those who messed up on the inside got sent to Brushy Mountain State Prison, known in prison circles as "the end of the line." Calvin had heard all about Brushy, and he recoiled in horror when he learned he was being sent there. At Brushy, inmates had to work in the coal mines, and men who didn't make their quota, or "tonnage," as it was called, would either get whipped or put in "the hole"—solitary confinement. The hole was a place of eternal darkness, where prisoners were given bread and water during their period of confinement. There was no indoor plumbing; inmates were given two buckets—one for drinking water, the other for the emptying of bladder and bowels. When they let someone out of the hole, the inmate was temporarily blind. Another inmate would be assigned to lead him around until he could see again.

Years ago a Tennessee ex-convict wrote, "The Brushy Mountain coal mining prison, near Petros, is to the state what the salt mines are to Red Russia—and with a history just as sordid. Over the years scores of men have been killed and crippled in those mines and starved and brutally beaten." The comparison with the Siberian salt mines had been made previously. A booklet issued to visitors at the prison in 1998 stated, "The prison became known world-wide when it was likened to 'conditions which prevailed in the Siberian prisons under the Russian regime.' " The statement originated with Episcopal bishop James M. Maxon in 1931, when he spoke in Athens, Greece, and later in Memphis, Tennessee, about the prison's reprehensible conditions.

As recently as 1997, a Nashville newspaper, the *Nashville Tennessean*, in an article entitled "Tennessee's Alcatraz," observed, "The Rock is a hard place. Brushy Mountain State Penitentiary remains Tennessee's Alcatraz. Isolated and virtually escape proof. Every man who ever escaped Brushy has been caught. But what went on within the walls was just as unforgiving. Violence and vengeance lace its rich and rugged history."

Brushy Mountain State Prison is located in the harsh, rugged, mountainous terrain of east Tennessee, near the tiny town of Petros. Unlike the towering majestic Smokies, a few hours away, the squat mountains surrounding Brushy are visually forbidding and laced with a dense undergrowth of prickly briars and sharp rocks. The site was selected by the state for one reason: the rich deposits of coal found in the region. Those who lived in Petros, or, for that matter, Morgan County, either worked at Brushy or mined coal—there were no other jobs.

The prison was built flush against a mountain; in fact, the back (north) wall isn't a wall at all but a vertical rock bluff. This architectural anomaly earned Brushy a spot in the Guinness Book of World Records; it is the only prison in the United States that has a natural bluff as part of its prison wall. The bluff and three stone walls, ranging in height from eighteen to twenty-two feet, enclose the prison. The wall was constructed from rock hand-quarried by the prisoners.

Entering the prison in handcuffs and leg irons, Calvin noticed gun towers atop the wall in each corner, just as in the main prison, manned twenty-four hours a day by impassive sharpshooters who would have shot someone trying to breech the wall as quickly as they would have gunned down a jackrabbit while hunting. In addition, there were ten gun ports inside the prison, including one aimed directly into the main dining room, a place of frequent violence in prison because of the proximity of the inmates to each other. The prison dining hall is where the term "watch my back" originated.

On June 10, 1977, Brushy Mountain's most famous inmate, James Earl Ray, who had assassinated Martin Luther King, Jr., escaped from there with six others by scaling the prison wall where it joined together with the bluff in the northeast corner of the prison yard. The escapees used pieces of metal conduit that they accumulated over a period of time and then secreted in the yard. At the appointed hour they screwed the pieces together, creating a makeshift ladder. Then they put the ladder against the wall and shimmied over it. All were captured nearby within four days, as the entire world followed the search through extensive media coverage. Ray, the last one captured, had been cut to ribbons by the briars, rocks, and sharp thorny underbrush that permeate the inhospitable hillsides surrounding the prison. Fatigued, defeated, and wearied by the unforgiving landscape, he was all but whimpering when found, offering no resistance whatever to his captors when they discovered him lying under some leaves.

When Calvin was at Brushy, over 60 percent of the inmates worked in either the coal or the slate mines. Even under optimum conditions mining is one of the most dangerous occupations in the world. Obviously, mining conditions at Brushy were not optimum, and the work there involved dangers not found in free-world mines. A former employee recalled that in the 1930s, when as many as five hundred inmates worked in the ground, there would usually be at least one death a week. "They'd put 'em in a place like a rock fell on 'em but they'd put a knife to 'em. There was fights going on all the time." Calvin was assigned to work in the slate mines. Slate has greater density than coal and is consequently much heavier, making the work harder and even more dangerous. The mines operated around the clock, and Calvin worked the graveyard shift, miles down in the ground. For a while he was made to pull a coal car with a heavy rope; it was backbreaking work, and he eventually got "Rat," a huge black inmate, to help by paying him a nickel.

Calvin's father, uncles, and other relatives had all toiled in the mines years before and were aware of the risks. Accordingly, Leonard Newton was absolutely aghast when he learned of Calvin's work assignment, particularly when Calvin informed him that he was losing his voice because of the constant temperature changes above and below the ground. Leonard Newton immediately wrote Marshall Roberson of the Tennessee Parole Board beseeching him to get his boy out of the mines before he lost his voice. Both Calvin and his father knew Roberson, who had been the dean of men at Bible Training School when Calvin was a student there.

Marshall Roberson was touched by Leonard Newton's heartfelt letter. Roberson knew firsthand about Calvin's talent, having heard him at Bible Training School. To him, the request seemed both reasonable and legitimate. Roberson conferred with other correction officials and it was agreed that Calvin's voice—his future livelihood—shouldn't be jeopardized by his working in the mines. Through Roberson's efforts, Calvin was brought back to the main prison in Nashville shortly after Christmas 1963 to serve the remainder of his sentence. He had been at Brushy a little more than a month. He would be eligible for parole in March 1964, after he had served five months of his three-year sentence. With Marshall Roberson on the parole board Calvin figured he'd be a cinch for parole at his first hearing.

Administration at the main prison felt strongly that prisoners needed religion for reformation and rehabilitation. To help achieve such an objective, a new chapel was built at the main prison in 1963. The prisoners built the furnishings, and the wall murals were also the product of inmate creativity and talent. On February 16, 1964, the *Nashville Tennessean* Sunday magazine did a cover story on religion at the state prison. Entitled "Pen Stripes and Prayers," the article stated, "Music is an important part of worship services at the prison. Deputy Chaplain L. H. Hardwick, Jr., a Pentecostal minister, conducts the prison choir. He has plenty of excellent singers to choose from. *One of his soloists sang with one of the country's top gospel quartets before he was arrested for stealing goods from parked automobiles*" [emphasis added].

The soloist was, of course, Calvin. In addition, it was Calvin who was pictured on the cover of the magazine, wearing a prison-issue striped shirt, mouth open wide in song. Even in prison, his great singing talent was noticed by others. Legendary gospel songwriter Vep Ellis came to see Calvin while he was at the main prison, to offer his prayers and encouragement. Two of the most performed tunes by the Sons of Song were Ellis's

"Heavenly Love" and the highly inspirational "Jesus, Use Me." Ellis had been a music instructor at Bible Training School, and thus had known Calvin since he was a teenager. Ellis was in Nashville to perform a concert and had Jimi Hall with him. According to Hall, Ellis told him, "Calvin Newton is in prison here and we need to go see him." Hall was still irritated at Calvin for stealing luggage on the Illinois trip. However, he apparently didn't mention this to Ellis and acquiesced with Ellis's suggestion. Ellis and Calvin had a good visit. Calvin was touched to know that Ellis cared enough about him to come see him.

Finally, Calvin's date with the parole board arrived in March 1964. He came before them and was respectful and properly contrite, making all the right sounds, letting them know that he was sorry about the problems that caused his incarceration. Marshall Roberson—Calvin's presumed ally on the board—listened to what Calvin had to say with a frown and furrowed brow. Roberson stated that after having listened to Calvin for a few minutes, he asked him, "What's this I hear about you having some sort of stolen goods warehouse in Atlanta before you were arrested?" Calvin's eyes grew wide with surprise at Roberson being privy to such information. Although the so-called bargain basement of misappropriated merchandise had been common knowledge among certain gospel singers, not many others knew about it. Caught between a rock and a hard place, Calvin admitted that, yes, he had stolen to the extent that a large area was needed to contain the items.

Roberson said he told Calvin that as far as he was concerned, Calvin had been much deeper into crime than he had been representing to the parole board and that he, for one, was going to vote to deny parole. The other members joined suit, and parole was officially denied. Roberson has said that a former member of the Sons of Song gave him the information that led to his voting to deny Calvin parole. The informant was most likely Jimi Hall, who probably related the information to Roberson when he visited the prison with Vep Ellis.

According to Roberson, Joyce Newton and her parents waited for him after the hearing and verbally accosted him for having voted to keep Calvin in prison. The warden came out to the parking lot and acted as peacemaker, telling Joyce that she could visit with Calvin for a few minutes before leaving. The warden also reminded her that Roberson was just doing his job.

With Calvin's parole denial, Joyce was mobilized into action. She and her father prepared a petition to Governor Frank Clement, asking him to commute the remainder of Calvin's sentence. The petition stated that Calvin would soon be a father, and he desperately wanted to be out of prison by the time his child was born. Joyce pointed out that Calvin had participated in religious services in prison and was rehabilitated. She persuaded many prominent citizens in the middle Tennessee area to draft letters in support of commutation. The petition list grew and among the names was that of Jake Hess, who had been the first person to sign it. Near full term with her pregnancy, Joyce drove to Nashville to deliver the petition and to seek a conference with the governor.

Clement was impressed by Joyce and by the large and prominent list of names on the petition. It certainly didn't hurt that he liked gospel music. In fact, an issue of the 1954 *Gospel Music World* had proclaimed that "gospel music has no greater friend than Frank Clement," after the governor appeared at the Ryman Auditorium at a singing where Calvin and the Oak Ridge Quartet performed on the same evening. Moreover, Clement was a good man who strongly believed in prison rehabilitation. He was persuaded that Calvin needed to be with his expectant wife.

Thus, with the power of a pen and the authority of his office, Governor Clement commuted the remainder of Calvin's sentence on May 26, 1964. Calvin was lounging in his cell when he received knowledge of the governor's act; at the same time he was informed that Joyce's water had broken. Frank Wonder, Calvin's father-in-law, picked up Calvin and the two of them raced back to Pulaski, where at that very minute Joyce was giving birth to Wesley Calvin Newton, Jr. Calvin had beaten the stork by hours; he became a free man and a father on the same day. Although the birth made everyone happy, Wes had been born prematurely, which was much more problematic in the sixties than now. For several days it was touch and go. Then, as his tiny body developed, the baby slowly began to thrive. "I remember one of the happiest days of my life was when I learned he had

gained an ounce," said Calvin. After three-and-a-half weeks, baby Wes
was discharged from the hospital. Now that Calvin was a married man
with a family, everyone hoped that the days of crime and drug abuse were
behind him.

Calvin and Joyce lived with her parents for the next few months as they
struggled to get their feet on the ground. It was during this period that
Joyce learned how hard her father had fought to get Calvin paroled.
Without her knowledge, Frank Wonder had made trips to the parole
board, the sentencing judge, and even the district attorney who had pros-
ecuted Calvin, attempting to persuade them to give him a break. He
became one of Calvin's strongest supporters, but still, there were times
when he wanted to tell Calvin that he wasn't all that impressed with him—
big gospel singer or not.

On one occasion he did, getting into Calvin's face, verbally taking him to
the woodshed about his past lifestyle of diamond rings, unborn-calf shoes,
expensive automobiles, and other fancy things that Frank didn't have any
use for. Calvin took issue with the criticism, and the discussion escalated
rapidly into a heated argument that raged for several minutes. Then, their
chests heaving from expended emotion, things grew quiet as they glowered
at one another with disdain. After a few moments of tense silence, Frank—
a little banty rooster of a guy—took a step forward, tapped Calvin's chest
with his index finger, and said menacingly, "I'll tell you something else,
Calvin. I don't think you were ever a Golden Gloves fighter either." Having
painted Calvin into a corner, Frank just stood there, as did Joyce and her
mother, waiting to see what Calvin's response would be.

Joyce was wild with fear that her father and husband were about to
fight; her heart was beating so hard she thought it was going to explode.
Calvin looked at Frank for what seemed like an eternity, then replied gently, "Well, Frank, just let somebody try and start something with you and
you'll see." When Frank heard this, his face softened; he looked down, then
nodded and slowly walked away. "I was as proud of Calvin then as I ever
have been," recalled Joyce.

25. Musical Chairs

Calvin has always thought that Jerry Redd was the finest first tenor in southern gospel music. Redd's pure, high tenor voice is both unique and captivating. He and Redd crossed paths in the fall of 1964, and their meeting led to Calvin's return to gospel music. At that time, Jerry Redd, though young, was an established southern gospel music singer. Born in Etowah County, Alabama, he began singing with the Senators, then sang with the Plainsmen Quartet during the period when they sang backup to Johnny Horton on some of his big hits on Columbia Records, including "North to Alaska." He had also sung with the Stamps Quartet. In the late 1960s he sang with the Speer Family.

Redd recalled, "By 1964 Lee Roy Abernathy had just about retired from gospel music, as far as a fulltime basis. But some of us were over at his house one day—I think it was Ed Dodson, Phil Brammlett, and Wally Fowler—and we got to jamming—singing. Then Calvin walked in and we started talking. Calvin said something about Bob [Robinson] would be interested in singing, and Lee Roy, I think, all that talk kind of honed his interest. Paul Downing and I happened to go to Lee Roy's again, and we finally decided to get together."

Out of the jam session and talks came one of the greatest, albeit short-lived, groups in southern gospel music—Abernathy's All-Stars—consisting of Lee Roy Abernathy, manager, pianist, and arranger; Jerry Redd, first tenor; Calvin Newton, second tenor; Bob Robinson, baritone; and the foghorn-voiced Paul Downing, bass. Of the group, Redd commented, "It was the most different thing I ever sung with. It was absolutely miraculous; it was a happening. Lee Roy worked out some terrific arrangements, and you know, Calvin has a very unusual voice and is the greatest interpretive singer I've ever heard."

The group only lasted about three months and unfortunately never got into a recording studio. The only audio artifact that documents their existence is a rehearsal that was taped on a cheap recorder. The few copies circulating today are collector's items. The tape reveals that Redd's declarations have merit. The group had a different sound, due in part to the four talented vocalists, the blend of their voices, and Abernathy's blues-inspired arrangements. Although innovative, the group had a prototypical heavyweight southern gospel quartet sound that featured the stratospheric high tenor voice of Redd balanced by the huge, deep, booming bass of Downing. Calvin and Robinson sang the inside parts and Robinson's baritone work is more than adequate. Robinson normally sang both first and second tenor.

The group traveled in style. "Lee Roy was not what you would call a pauper," said Redd. "He had acres of pianos in the Atlanta area. He sold pianos and that's the way they were advertised. Lee Roy wanted a bus to travel in, and me and Paul went over to airport transit and bought one for him—paid cash for it, too," with Abernathy's money. Bob Robinson's son, Dan, then ten years old, remembered getting to sweep the bus out one day while the group rehearsed. "The bus had these five stars on each side with 'All-Stars' written underneath. It was impressive." In addition to providing the fancy bus, Lee Roy sprang for some fancy threads for the group, clothing similar to what the Sons of Song had worn. Calvin was excited again. The All-Stars had so much talent that they might experience instant success, just as the Sons did in 1957.

"The first date was Albertville, Alabama," stated Redd. "Before we went out, Lee Roy told me to take my mandolin out on stage with me—I could play mandolin. I did, and the crowd went wild. Lee Roy was one wise old bird." Albertville is located on Alabama's Sand Mountain, home of great gospel first tenors, including "Cat" Freeman and Bobby Strickland. However, the most famous gospel singer to come off Sand Mountain was a bluegrass gospel performer who played the mandolin and sang high tenor—the inimitable Ira Louvin. Abernathy undoubtedly sensed that the Albertville audience would react enthusiastically about a mandolin being used to accompany gospel music, and would perhaps associate the All-Stars and their music with Louvin and his.

The dogmatic Abernathy normally had very fixed ideas about how a song should be performed, but he relaxed his views with the talented All-Stars. "Lee Roy was used to teaching people how to sing, but all of us knew how, and knew how to do it well," said Calvin. Redd agreed, adding, "Lee Roy usually had a certain style that his groups sang, but he abandoned all that with the All-Stars."

The tape-recorded rehearsal includes the group's most performed numbers and begins with "Jesus Is the Greatest Friend." Abernathy's arrangement gives the song a bluesy feel, and begins with Redd and Downing trading high and low notes. Abernathy took the old song "Rock-a My Soul" and put in some unorthodox key changes and chord progressions to give it a new flavor. On "He's a Personal Savior," Redd sounds remarkably similar to Denver Crumpler, who used to sing the number with the Statesmen.

Despite their promise, the group folded in early 1965, after about four months. Redd said he was to blame for the group disbanding. "I had been in law enforcement before, and I had a chance to join the Cobb County [Georgia] sheriff's office. Had we stayed together, I believe we would have hit the tip-top in gospel music because it was that different." Calvin, Joyce, and Wes moved to Chattanooga, where Calvin's parents were living. There, Joyce got a job working in Mayor Ralph Kelly's office. They remained there briefly until Jake Hess presented Calvin with a great opportunity—an invitation to revive the Sons of Song, who would then tour with his new group, the Imperials.

Calvin wasted no time in getting the Sons back together. On the one hand, he wanted to re-form the group and do what he dearly loved; on the other hand, he really had no other option. In 1964, he was thirty-five years old, and had no job skills or work experience other than in gospel music, which he had performed professionally since he was sixteen. For their part, Bob Robinson and Lee Kitchens were eager to try and rekindle the magic that the trio had created so many times on stage and in the recording studio. But the three were apprehensive about how audiences and other performers would respond to the group, knowing that Calvin had just gotten out of prison. For instance, would anyone book them? They knew this could be a problem, but Jake was offering them a salary and regular work. As long as they worked with Jake, they wouldn't have to worry about bookings. In addition, Jake had a touring bus and the Sons could travel with the Imperials. And Jake had a weekday gospel music television show on one of the big Nashville stations. The Sons could get some great exposure singing on Jake's show.

At the time, Jake Hess was perhaps the biggest superstar in southern gospel music. Elvis Presley idolized the man; he was Elvis's favorite singer. The Sons could just hitch their wagon to Jake's star and go back to cleaning the other groups' plates like in the old days. It was almost too good to be true.

Jake wanted all of the Imperials and all of the Sons of Song to move to Nashville for convenience and logistics. The two groups would be gone a lot, and the families could remain behind and be close-knit and supportive. Everyone readily agreed, and as the men sought rental trailers to haul the belongings, the wives and children gathered up clothes, toys, and cooking utensils—they were headed to Nashville! It was an exciting time for both groups and their families. Dan Robinson recalled, "Nine families moved from Atlanta to Nashville, which was the base of operations for the two groups." Calvin and Joyce found a little pink house off Harding Road and set up housekeeping, and Joyce got a job working for a Nashville attorney after finding a babysitter for Wes.

Jake had left the Statesmen Quartet earlier to start his own group—the Imperials. He wanted a regal-sounding name for his new quartet, so he contacted Marion Snider and received permission to use the name "Imperials," since Snider had a group by the same name in the 1940s. Jake could have spent his entire career with the legendary Statesmen, but he wanted the freedom to try out some musical ideas and to get out from under Hovie Lister's micromanagement. He had gotten tired of closing every show by watching Hovie jump up on a piano bench and sing "Get Away, Jordan." With the Statesman, everything was formulaic and tightly scripted by Hovie.

Although the ideas and changes that Hess wanted to incorporate into his new group were relatively modest, they were nonetheless considered controversial to the staid and unimaginative southern gospel music groups. Hess wanted a different sound and a different look. No whooping and hopping around on stage, just four talented guys standing in one place, singing. Musically, he wanted to press the envelope, just as the Sons had in 1958. It is likely that he was influenced by what the Sons of Song had done in the late fifties.

Pianist Henry Slaughter left the Weatherfords in 1963 to join the Imperials. Slaughter shared Jake Hess's musical ideas and vision. Said Slaughter, "The Imperials had a desire to make a break with what was known as gospel at the time. It had become sort of stagnant or was going country. The Rambos and the Goodmans were sort of country gospel. The all-night singings were getting boring and the crowds were diminishing. The Imperials came along to bring some fresh air into the thing." Slaughter agreed to go with Jake's proposed new group several months before the group actually started. Slaughter recalled, "I had about forty arrangements before the guys ever sung." With Jake's marquee name, his new group had instant acceptance with gospel music fans.

However, the big-name gospel groups disliked, resented, and were fearful of what Jake was doing. Although they failed, they did everything they could to undermine him and his group, including extortion. All of the major promoters were warned that if they booked Jake and the Imperials, the other big-name gospel music acts wouldn't appear at the same concert with them. But their extortion attempts failed because Jake was just too popular and too talented; in fact, Jake Hess was the biggest name in gospel music. In his book, *Nothin' But Fine*, Hess wrote that things came to a head in Winston-Salem, North Carolina, where promoter C. R. McClain begged Jake not to go on stage after McClain had been told by the other groups that they wouldn't sing that night if the Imperials did. Jake told McClain that if the Imperials weren't allowed to sing, they would be out in the audience telling everyone the reason. With that, the fearful McClain allowed them to perform. The other groups caved in and sang, also. Jake and the Imperials never had a problem after that; however, it wasn't that way for the Sons of Song.

Jake recalled the plight of the Sons during the mid-sixties. "Wouldn't nobody hire them. So I put 'em on salary and put 'em on my bus." It was a great stroke of fortune for the Sons. The Imperials traveled extensively, performing several times a week all over the United States. Although Hess never said so, his signing on the Sons may have been more than just altruism, for what the Imperials were doing in the 1960s was actually just a continuation of what the Sons had done in the 1950s. Having the Sons on the same venue with the Imperials would reinforce the notion that Hess was trying to convey: gospel music doesn't have to always look and sound the same. In fact, Henry Slaughter confirmed that that was one of the reasons for Jake Hess hiring the Sons. "At that time, we were trying to find somebody to work with and not just do concerts by ourselves, that we felt like we could make some new trends with, and two groups would make a good program, and the program was working fine." Slaughter remembered the two groups making a far west tour in 1965. "We played Long Beach [California]. Polly Grimes was promoting us on the West Coast. That was the main reason for the trip." Just as the tour began to unfold, word of the joint venture reached the movers and shakers in gospel music. There was a predictable outcry.

Jake Hess said, "About five or six of the leading people in the business got together and had a meeting and said that they would never sing on the same stage with them [Sons of Song]. Lee Roy Abernathy called me and said these people in Atlanta were meeting and that they definitely would not sing on the same program with them or us, if they were gonna do that type thing. That rubbed me wrong, so I bowed my neck and I was just gonna forget it and the Sons of Song and the Imperials, we were just gonna do our little thing, but Lee Kitchens overheard the conversation [with Abernathy] and they [the Sons] decided to leave; they didn't want to cause me any trouble, and it might have been good for both of us, I don't know, but I sure didn't think so at the time."

Thus, in one fell swoop the hopes the Sons had of reclaiming their lofty status were dashed upon the rock of a sobering reality: southern gospel music was a cutthroat business. It seems highly unlikely that the "leading people" in gospel music objected to Calvin and the Sons on purely moral grounds; they had no moral claims to raise with the squeaky-clean Hess, yet had nonetheless tried to blackball him. Their concerns centered more on having to contend with a group that, as Don Butler stated, "cleaned their plates every night."

Looking back at what happened, the gentlemanly Lee Kitchens, who almost never swears, stated, "It was just plain old dirty-assed jealousy. God wasn't in gospel music back then." Bob Weber, Carlos Cook, Billy Warren, and others echoed Kitchens's assertion that God wasn't in the music during the mid-twentieth century. The refusal of other groups to sing on the same program with the Sons of Song filled Calvin with a bitterness that lingered for years. By announcing that they would refuse to appear on stage with the Sons, this powerful group of gospel music insiders poisoned the well with all promoters and made it impossible for the group to get any bookings. Yet their threat went beyond that: they warned that if *any* group appeared onstage with the Sons of Song, they would never sing with that group again.

Singing gospel music had been a livelihood for Calvin Newton, Bob Robinson, and Lee Kitchens since all three were teenagers. Yet now, in 1965, they were totally shut out of the business. No promoter would risk incurring the wrath of the "leading people in the business" by booking the trio. The promoters had been put under the gun by the so-called leading people before; they knew the threat was serious and would have been carried out—"Book them and you'll never book us again."

In the early 1990s a tearful W. B. Nowlin apologized to Calvin for having capitulated to the demands of those who had blackballed the Sons. Nowlin was one of southern gospel music's biggest promoters during the mid-twentieth century.

Hess didn't identify who the people were at the Atlanta meeting, but it would have certainly included Hovie Lister and James Blackwood, and most likely Brock Speer, who let it be known he didn't want Calvin Newton anywhere near the Speer Family bus, because "there's women and money on it." The remark crushed Calvin, who had never done anything against anyone in gospel music, or for that matter against anyone that he knew.

The Sons were in California with the Imperials when these events occurred. They decided to stay and got Polly Grimes to book them at some California churches and other small venues. Thousands of miles out of the southern gospel music circuit, Grimes was insulated from the threats of the movers and shakers. The Sons of Song also looked up the legendary African-American songwriter Doris Akers, and began a short association with her. Among Akers's standards are "Lead Me, Guide Me," and "Sweet, Sweet Spirit." Her songs were known for elegant and sophisticated lyrics and for melodies that were more European art and American popular than African American.

At the time, she was director of the Sky Pilot Choir, one of the first racially mixed choirs in Los Angeles. Calvin recalled that the choir would make an impressive entrance into the auditorium, walking down the aisles singing. "When we were in California, Doris Akers heard us sing, and we went to her house for a few days. She thought the Sons of Song were great. She had recently made an album with the Statesmen, but she called Tim Spencer of the Sons of the Pioneers, who had recorded her with the Statesmen, and told him, 'Here's the people I want to record with,' but it never happened," said Calvin.

Why it never happened and why their association with her ended is part of a national tragedy. The Sons were working with Doris Akers in August 1965. On August 11, 1965, a California highway patrolman stopped a young black man in Watts, a predominantly black section of Los Angeles. An argument ensued, then escalated and led to rioting, pillaging, and property damage of forty million dollars. Thirty-four people were killed. Doris Akers lived in Watts. When trouble began brewing, she called the Sons at their motel and warned them not to come into the area, saying that they were the wrong skin color and that people were getting hurt, even killed.

After Doris Akers's telephone call, the Sons packed and went back to Nashville. Continuing to be victimized by hard luck and misfortune, the Sons had no choice but to take day jobs so that they could eat and pay rent. Bob and Mary Robinson worked at a dry cleaning company, washing and pressing other people's clothes.

Calvin decided to produce records. He formed a company—Justice Recording—and then put out word that he was in business. By 1965, Calvin had spent hundreds of hours in recording studios, although he had never sat on the other side of the glass as a producer. Nonetheless, he was familiar enough with the process to produce a session competently. At the time, Ralph Davis sang with an Athens, Tennessee, group called the Gospelaires. "We had been singing together for a couple of years and had put out a couple of 45s and wanted to do an album. Quentin Goins put me in touch with Calvin, who agreed to produce us. We were young and a little apprehensive, but Calvin made us feel comfortable in the studio. He gave us ideas, suggested endings to certain numbers, and if we had trouble with a certain part, he would help us out. We were pleased with the album," said Davis.

He should have been, for it was a fine album. The Gospelaires' nineteen-year-old bass singer, Carlin Crabtree, was a featured soloist throughout the album, and deservedly so—he was a fine vocalist. On one number, the upbeat "Roll On, Jordan," Crabtree, laying down a heavy rhythm line, sounds like a young Jim Wetherington. However, it is the outstanding alto singing of Ralph Davis's wife, Alvilee, that really makes the album shine. The Gospelaires' rendition of the old Cleavant Derricks gem "Have a Little Talk with Jesus," features innovative key and tempo changes plus a strong ending. The arrangement has Sons of Song written all over it, so Calvin must have had a hand in that number, although he cannot recall now whether he did or not. Calvin remembers that the session was done at a downstairs studio near Vanderbilt University. He hired an engineer and musicians and completed the album in two sessions of three hours. Veteran sideman Ernie Newton played bass and Dick Cotton played guitar. Someone played a snare drum with brushes on several numbers but wasn't credited.

Unfortunately, there weren't enough groups to produce for Calvin to make a living at it. To make things worse, he was taking amphetamines again, and was hooked. With Calvin, when the drugs began, crime often followed. Blackballed out of gospel music and unable to latch on to anything else, he went back to stealing. During this desperate period of the mid-to-late 1960s, there were times when he would check Joyce and little Wes into a motel somewhere while he went out searching for a score.

He had to find one, because he didn't have money to pay the motel bill. Whereas greed may have motivated his past crimes, now he was stealing to survive and to provide food and shelter for his family.

Needless to say, the constant drug abuse produced a great deal of marital discord. Joyce yelled, pleaded, threatened, cajoled, and used every other ploy to try and get Calvin to quit the amphetamines. Nothing worked. Sometimes she would find his pill bottle and flush the contents down the toilet. "When he was out at night, and I never knew when he was coming home, I'd be so distraught—could never sleep, but would lay there and pray for hours and hours. Then, when I'd hear his car come into the driveway, I would experience this overwhelming sense of relief; I'd rush to the door and unlock it, but then when he got there, all that emotion turned into anger and I'd call him every name in the book for not calling me and letting me know something. He told me later that he often delayed coming home because he knew when he got there I'd be furious," said Joyce. One time when they were in a car and Calvin was driving, she got so mad she actually jumped out of it while the car was still moving. She wasn't hurt, but she surprised herself; normally she was the most levelheaded person she knew.

On other occasions, when he couldn't sleep, Joyce would sit up with Calvin and talk. Sometimes they would even have a pajama party and bake some of Joyce's delicious homemade bread that was served up piping hot with butter. "To me, the really bad times were when the singing opportunities weren't there; he didn't have any dream to follow, and was trying to get something going on in his life—that's when the pills really exacerbated the problem. He totally lost perspective on what was and wasn't acceptable, feasible, or possible," she recalled.

One of her worst memories was Christmas Eve 1964 when Calvin didn't come home. Joyce had only a rough idea where he might be, possibly singing at a faith-healing crusade or maybe with relatives in Illinois that she couldn't contact because they had no phone. Snatching the curtain back every few minutes, she eventually saw the dawn chase the stars out of the sky. It was Christmas Day, and there she was, with a seven-month-old baby, no groceries, and no presents. Nearby, she could hear car doors slamming, people laughing, firecrackers popping, and the delightful shrieks of children, as she sat glumly in a darkened room with the curtains drawn. Her Christmas Day meal was a frozen turkey TV dinner that she ate while pondering the whereabouts of her husband. The only thing she could be sure of was that, wherever he was, he was undoubtedly whacked out on pills. In a funk, she thought, Well, one thing about it—Christmases couldn't get any worse than this. Perhaps her present was that she couldn't see into the future.

"Cal got home in the middle of the night Christmas night. He had stopped by Pulaski, and had a little bitty red wagon for Wes, plus some gifts from my parents. He said we would have our Christmas dinner a day late; so all was right in my world again for a little while," said Joyce.

The most desperate and foolhardy crime Calvin ever committed was in 1965 in broad daylight in the busy Green Hills Shopping Center, in a fashionable section of Nashville. Loaded on drugs, he noticed several cops at a nearby donut shop. Thinking they would be distracted, he drove up to a jewelry store and threw a brick through the window. He scooped up a few rings and watches and roared out of the shopping center with the store's burglar alarm clanging. The owner ran out and jotted the tag number down, and the police traced the vehicle to Joyce Newton. Joyce was contacted, but she told them she honestly didn't know where Calvin was or what he had been up to. Calvin drove down to Mississippi to stay with two old friends, the Reverend Hank Story and his wife. The Storys managed to talk some sense into him, so he called the authorities and agreed to turn himself in. Fortunately, the store owner was reasonable. An agreement was worked out: Calvin would return the jewelry, pay for the damages, and then enter a Madison, Tennessee, hospital for detoxification. In return, the charges would be dropped; it was one of the few times Calvin caught a break. Exhausted from lack of sleep and malnourished from not eating, Calvin benefited enormously from his period of rest and recuperation in the hospital.

Calvin moved his family to Winston-Salem, North Carolina, in early 1966 where his good friend and the former Oak Ridge Quartet bassist and owner, Bob Weber, lived. There, Joyce obtained a job as a legal secretary and Calvin started up Justice Records again, producing custom recordings of local country, gospel, and what would now be called "garage rock" bands, although "beach music" was the term back then. The most famous beach music group out of the Carolinas during the sixties—actually the most popular ever—was the Swinging Medallions, with their big hit "Double Shot of My Baby's Love."

Calvin stated, "I met a guy named Bennette Simpson, who was a local musician and had a recording studio. I started using his studio to sell custom jobs. I would record these little rock and roll bands—the Thunderbirds, the Ladies Men, the Mercedes and others." The British music invasion was in full stride in 1966 and there were a few copycat bands recording at Justice, including a group of Bridgewater College kids who called themselves the English Muffins.

Jay Thompson, a local disc jockey, worked with Calvin. "I had known Calvin since I was a kid; I used to go to the concerts of the Sons of Song and the Oak Ridge Quartet when he was with them. I worked for him part-time, getting groups and finding groups. Cal did most of the production. I did some PR work and sold the contracts. Things were booming; we couldn't keep up with the demand. The Arthur Smith studio in Charlotte was the main studio in the state but next to it, we were the busiest. We had great staff musicians. One of the best was Phil Blythe, who had played with some big names and was a fantastic guitarist." Bennette Simpson was also an outstanding trumpet player who at one time had played with Lawrence Welk and had his own quintet, which was popular locally.

Although Calvin was busy for a while, there wasn't much money in custom producing, and when things slowed down, Justice shut its doors. However, years later, in the 1990s, Calvin learned that the old records of beach music had become a hot item and that there was a big demand for anything that was on the Justice label. A man contacted Calvin, and, after some negotiations, Calvin sold the rights to the Justice recordings for six thousand dollars.

Unable to eke out a living with his record company, Calvin decided to move his family back to Pulaski to undertake an endeavor that had nothing to do with music. He would wind up devoting several years to the profession, and would even win an award.

26. Gospel Fried Chicken

Around 1968 the Newtons moved back to Pulaski, Tennessee, where Joyce's family lived, and opened up a restaurant that catered to workers at a factory across the street from her parents. Their restaurant—the Horn o' Plenty—was located in the basement of Joyce's parents' home, and featured lunch and dinner meals. Joyce recalled, "Cal did much of the cooking. I prepared the vegetables and the chicken and dumplings—one of our specialties—but he did most of the other meats, made the slaw, and fried the chicken, which was our *big* specialty. He had a way of frying chicken that was the best I've ever tasted; our customers said so, too." Even though it was a popular little eating establishment, with Calvin's fried chicken the talk of the town, the Horn o' Plenty didn't last long—the Newtons weren't making enough money to justify its continued existence. However, the unlikely combination of a Kentucky colonel and two former Blackwood Brothers piano players resulted in Calvin's cooking and selling a lot more fried chicken for the next couple of years.

Jackie Marshall and Wally Varner were cut from the same mold. Each had played piano for the Blackwood Brothers in the fifties; both were showy, flamboyant, and tremendously talented. In concert, James Blackwood always allowed the two to showcase their keyboard skills. Their musical hijinks never failed to enliven an audience. Marshall and Varner had more in common than musical talent and showmanship; both had an entrepreneurial spirit that resulted in their becoming Kentucky Fried

Chicken franchisers. Varner invested in KFC with two of his brothers, whereas Marshall proceeded on his own. Eventually both sold enough chicken to make them millionaires. Calvin recalled, "Jack had a handshake deal with Colonel Sanders. The colonel told him, 'Give me a nickel for every chicken you sell.'"

In the late 1960s Varner offered Calvin a job in one of his KFC locations in Chattanooga. Actually, it was Wally Varner's wife, Ginny, who was responsible for the offer. Wally didn't want to hire Calvin because he was an ex-con. It was an entry-level position and Calvin's first few days were spent cleaning out the grease traps—the most difficult and unpleasant job in the fried chicken business. Early on, Ginny Varner stopped by the store where Calvin was training. While there, she insisted that Calvin stop working and come to lunch with her, Wally, and others. Calvin told her that he thought Wally probably wanted him to keep cleaning the grease traps, and, besides, he was covered in grime from head to foot. "Nonsense," she replied. "You look just fine. Wash up and come on. I'll take care of Wally." Calvin enjoyed his luncheon respite and visited amiably with Ginny, while Wally fumed but didn't make a scene.

Calvin completed his training in Birmingham and was sent to Chattanooga to run an area store in that city. Soon he prepared boxes and buckets of chicken, worked the cash register, greeted customers, mopped floors, hosed the parking lot, filed reports, and continued to clean out grease traps. Unless his short stints as a record producer and at the Horn o' Plenty restaurant are considered, his job at Kentucky Fried Chicken was the first one with regular hours and fixed responsibilities he had ever had, and he was almost forty years old. As a singer, he was accustomed to sleeping until noon and then goofing off until it was time to dress for wherever he was singing that night. Sometimes, the groups he sang with only performed three times a week, two hours or less each time. Except for the travel, singing was a fairly leisurely pursuit, especially compared to working in the hectic fast food industry.

He worked for Varner for a short period, then accepted a job from Marshall, who at that point had stopped calling himself Jackie. Jack Marshall made a manager out of Calvin and had him running his KFC outlet in East Ridge, a Chattanooga suburb. Calvin excelled at his job as manager of the East Ridge KFC store, to the extent that he was named KFC employee of the year. Colonel Sanders himself made the award, and the two had their picture taken together. Calvin succeeded because he put everything he had into it—just as he had when the Sons of Song were starting out and had their grueling daily twelve-hour rehearsals. Joyce Newton observed, "Whenever Cal takes on a job, he gets into it gung ho and wants to do it better than it's ever been done before. Of course, this puts some people off, but it's his way."

Shortly thereafter, Jack Marshall asked Calvin to take over Marshall's KFC outlets in Murray and Mayfield, Kentucky. "When I got to Murray, the KFC inspectors were going to shut the store down because it didn't meet their sanitation standards. I asked them to give me two weeks and by that time if it wasn't the cleanest store in the chain they could shut it down," said Calvin. He rolled his sleeves up and gave it his all, working long hours—sweeping, scrubbing, mopping—bringing the premises up to an acceptable sanitation level. After the store passed its inspection, he painted red and white stripes on his car and adorned it with a chicken bucket. The highly distinctive car stood out as much as Calvin's Thunderbird had in the 1950s. Children would throw up their hands and yell at the chickenmobile; Calvin would honk and wave.

A typical workday was thirteen hours long, from 9 A.M. to 11 P.M. "When I closed, I had to balance the cash register and prepare the night deposit. I also had to make sure that the kitchen was cleaned and the floors were scrubbed; many times I did that myself, plus sweeping and hosing the parking lot off."

Joyce was pregnant with their second child and couldn't work, so their finances were stretched to the limit. They lived initially in a tiny mobile home, then a cramped apartment. When the local drive-in would have dollar night, Calvin, Joyce, and Wes would go to see a double feature. Joyce would pop some popcorn and make a gallon of Kool-Aid, and they would have a great family night.

Calvin's friend Bill Cooley noted, "Marshall would hire all of these down-and-out gospel singers to run his stores. He had Calvin in Tennessee and Bill Shaw running one in Mississippi." (Shaw had been what many consider the finest first tenor in southern gospel music, a reputation he acquired when he sang with the Blackwood Brothers Quartet in the 1950s.)

Marshall visited the store from time to time, as did the colonel himself. "We had a Colonel Sanders day at Murray State University. He came and rode around in his convertible and then came over to our tiny little apartment and took a nap. He gave me the keys to his house and told me that if I was in the area and he wasn't home, to just go on in and eat, sleep, whatever, and when I was through to lock the door," said Calvin.

Just as Calvin put a thousand dollars down on a farm in the Murray area, Marshall told him he wanted him to go to Marshall's KFC store at Fort Campbell and work under Marshall's uncle. Questioning Marshall's motives, Calvin quit instead, but the two remained good friends. Calvin's work ethic as a fast-food manager was exemplary, as was his integrity—he never took a penny that he didn't earn.

While the Newtons were in Murray, Kentucky, in 1969, a second child was born, and she came on her father's birthday, October 28. The child was named Jackie in honor of Jack Marshall. Her full name was Jackie Sue Newton. Doctors and nurses alike were amazed at the spunky little baby girl who could seemingly cry on pitch.

When Calvin was working at KFC, he didn't so much as sing in the shower. Even on those frequent occasions when he socialized with Jack Marshall, a great gospel pianist, he and Marshall never played and sang. It wasn't that he didn't want to—he loved singing. But he was always busy, and, besides that, no one ever asked—until 1970.

27. Still Magic after All These Years

By 1970 the Sons of Song had been inactive for five years, and it had been that long since Calvin had seen Bob Robinson and Lee Kitchens, much less sung with them. After the Sons disbanded in 1965, Robinson sang for a stint with the Foggy River Boys, and then joined Billy Graham's Asheville, North Carolina, radio station as an announcer. Kitchens had been in and out of gospel music, too, but by 1970 had quit singing and was working full-time tuning pianos.

However, in April 1970 the Sons were invited to perform at an all-night singing at Birmingham's Boutwell Auditorium. No one recalls exactly why, but it could have been J. G. Whitfield's idea—he had taken over the all-night singings from Wally Fowler. For their part, the Sons didn't care why or whose idea it had been; they were excited at the prospect of singing together once more, especially at Boutwell. Boutwell had always been their hot spot. Don Butler is fond of saying that the Sons owned Boutwell "lock, stock, and barrel."

Calvin, Robinson, and Kitchens met the day before the concert, had a quick rehearsal and pronounced themselves ready to go. Although all three were seasoned entertainers and had performed hundreds of times, they were nonetheless nervous about how they would be received. Would anyone remember them? Would they still be able to spellbind crowds as in the old days? They would be glad to get just a good, polite response.

Whatever anxiety the three experienced as they made their way to the spacious auditorium was soon dispelled. The return of the Sons of Song generated an electricity in the building that had thousands buzzing with breathless anticipation.

Gospel music journalist Jan Cain memorialized that momentous evening. Writing in *The Singing News*, Cain observed: "April 11th was a night Birmingham fans will remember for all time. It was homecoming for the Sons of Song . . . While I chatted with friends in the lobby, I kept hearing questions: 'Are they here?' 'Where are they?' 'Have you seen them?' There was no doubt 'they' were the Sons of Song . . . One could feel the aura of excitement rippling like waves through the audience as J. G. Whitfield came on stage to introduce the Sons of Song . . . The audience was electrified . . . All too quickly it was over . . . Three of the most talented men that ever walked on a stage—Bob Robinson, Cal Newton, and Lee Kitchens—had given one of the greatest performances of their lives."

Perhaps as well as anything that has ever been written about them, Jan Cain's article captures the sheer magnetism and charisma of the trio. Calvin's friend Billy Warren, a gospel music singer himself, stated, "When they walked on that stage, you expected to hear something. They were class. Bob and Calvin could switch parts and you'd never even know it. One would hit a note and the other would grab that note and keep going. I think the main thing about the Sons of Song, along with their talent, was their stage ability or presence." Whatever it was, they still had it after years of inactivity.

Although they were received as if it were a reunion of the Beatles, the 1970 homecoming singing was a one-shot deal. After it was over, Calvin, Robinson, and Kitchens went their separate ways and the Sons of Song went back into mothballs.

Calvin moved his family to Huntsville, Alabama, where he began a calendar company. The idea was to publish a calendar that had important events and birthdays listed and sell advertising to area businesses. He got a couple of other gospel music singers involved—Roy Carter of the Chuck Wagon Gang and Ron Page, who had sung with the Oak Ridge Quartet immediately after the group was re-formed in 1957. The idea pretty much fizzled, and Carter and Page dropped out quickly, but Calvin persisted, eking out a living, staying one step ahead of the creditors, something he was good at by then.

In October 1973, the Sons received another invitation to perform—this time at the highly touted National Quartet Convention, considered the keystone event of southern gospel music. The convention—held that year in Nashville's new municipal auditorium—lasted an entire week and featured nonstop activities, especially gospel music performed by the top acts. Thousands of fans and gospel music industry figures attended the yearly event. On this occasion Don Butler, the original baritone singer, would appear with Bob Robinson and Calvin.

Calvin and Robinson met with Butler at Butler's Brentwood, Tennessee, home the night before their performance to rehearse. It had been ten years since the original Sons of Song had performed together, yet when they gathered around the piano, Robinson struck an arpeggio and the three came together instantly and began singing the same song on key and in harmony. After the song they laughed and looked at one another in amazement. The following night it was the audience's turn to be amazed.

The Gospel Music Association's newspaper, *Good News*, reported: "Tuesday's program opened with more than 20 persons participating in an old fashioned convention singing school with Connor Hall, Brock Speer, James Blackwood, Mr. and Mrs. Oliver Jennings, Howard Goodman and Jim (Big Chief) Wetherington leading the 'class' in singing. But the group that stole the show was the Sons of Song made up of Calvin Newton, Bob Robertson [*sic*] and Don Butler. The group had not sung together in more than 10 years . . . Others . . . included the LeFevre Trio, Hovie Lister and the Statesmen Quartet and the Speer Family."

As Don Butler commented about the group in 1958, when the Sons of Song finished, you knew the fat lady had sung. The statement was obviously still true fifteen years later. Butler stated, "Afterwards, people were saying, 'They sounded like they had never stopped singing.'" Vestal Goodman was so taken by the Sons' performance that, uninvited, she got up on stage at the convention and began singing with them.

The two great shows in Birmingham and Nashville brought rays of sunshine into Calvin's life. From them he got a jolt of happiness. It was a good feeling, knowing that he could still do so well what he had obviously been put on earth to do. As he and Joyce drove back to Huntsville after the show, he thought to himself that maybe things were going to get better. He became buoyant with hope and optimism. One thing was certain—he hadn't seen many face cards in the past ten years. Maybe the performance at the National Quartet Convention had been an omen, he thought—a sign that things were about to take a turn for the better.

In fact, his life was about to change, but it would be from bad to worse. Straight ahead, ugly, sinister clouds loomed on the horizon, concealing the angry storm within. He was about to enter a period of darkness in his life that he couldn't have imagined in his wildest nightmare—the most horrific part of his wasted years.

28. Making Money

In December 1974, Calvin and a few ad hoc business partners figured out a way to make a half-million dollars in a month: it
involved a printing press and green ink. The plan was set in motion when
an old friend of Calvin's, who was a big fan of gospel music, contacted him.
"This guy knew a banker and a lawyer who wanted some [counterfeit]
money to take to the Cayman Islands, and he asked me if I knew a printer.
I spent a few days and then it occurred to me, 'Well, I know a printer—
Bennette Simpson—who had everything in the world you would need.'
I wasn't making any money at the time and Simpson was in severe financial straits. I called the guy in Atlanta back and said, 'What's the deal?'"
The man informed Calvin that the banker and the lawyer wanted a quarter
million in twenty-dollar bills first, and, then, if all went well, they would
subsequently want three million more. Calvin approached Simpson with
the offer and it was eagerly accepted; Simpson needed money desperately
because of a failed business and medical expenses.

Nowadays, authentic-looking counterfeit bills can be turned out effortlessly by a teenager with desktop publishing software, but in the 1970s it
was an intricate operation that required knowledge and skill, plus printing
and photography equipment. A likeness of the bill would have to be prepared from a photo negative and then the likeness would have to be transferred to a metallic plate. Two plates would obviously be required to print
both sides of the bill. To assist in the process, Simpson employed a former
police dispatcher, Vernon Winfrey Newell, who had been fired for
misconduct. Newell, who was known as "Duke," was considered a good
"doodler"; that is, he possessed a modicum of artistic skill. Duke was

recruited to prepare a printing plate from the photo negative made by Simpson. Calvin was the facilitator and bagman; his job was to transport the money back to Atlanta for shipment to the Caymans.

According to authorities, it was on or about December 15, 1974, that Calvin, Simpson, and Newell met at Simpson Printing Company, 401 Dean Street, S. E., Winston-Salem, North Carolina, where they discussed and subsequently agreed to print the counterfeit money.

Unfortunately for everyone involved, Newell had two serious flaws: a drinking problem and a big mouth, which resulted in authorities finding out about the plan almost immediately. Calvin recalled, "Duke went into a bar and said, 'Hey, fellas, I need a drink, but I don't have any money. But if you'll take care of me tonight, I'll take care of you next week.'" It turned out that in the bar Newell had chosen there was an FBI informant monitoring conversations, hoping to find a tidbit of information that he could sell. The informant immediately ingratiated himself to Newell, plied him with drinks, and coaxed from him all the details of the plan. He then demanded to be let in as a partner, which would enable him to obtain more information and therefore get more money from the FBI.

Calvin, Simpson, and Newell accepted the informant, in all probability an underworld character who played both ends against the middle, into the group. The informant immediately tipped off the FBI, and they contacted the Secret Service, the agency with primary jurisdiction over counterfeiting. The Secret Service wanted to question the informant, but the FBI refused, citing policy: they don't reveal their informants, not even to another law enforcement agency. The Secret Service gained access to the informant only after two United States attorneys insisted on it.

With an informant on the inside, the Secret Service got immediate briefings on all the counterfeiters' activities. Secret Service Special Agent Ronald House, now retired, stated that every Secret Service agent in North Carolina was assigned to work the case once it was determined that the group planned initially to print close to a half-million dollars. The FBI also committed a number of agents to the investigation.

Government documents revealed that on December 18, 1974, Calvin, Simpson, Newell and the informant met at Steak 'n Eggs restaurant, near the print shop, to work out the final details, blissfully unaware that they were under surveillance by FBI Special Agent Morris Eller. FBI Special Agent Zach Lowe already had the print shop staked out, along with Secret Service special agents Willie Oliphant and T. J. Bondurant. The meeting at Steak 'n Eggs broke up after about forty minutes, and Bondurant and Oliphant observed a 1974 Thunderbird bearing Tennessee license plate 44-K688 enter the print shop parking lot at 12:15 A.M. FBI Special Agent Claude Davis, assigned to run the tag, determined that it belonged to Calvin Newton. The other conspirators arrived a few minutes later, and Simpson and Newell went to work.

Simpson photographed and made negatives of the back side of a twenty-dollar Federal Reserve note. From that, Newell prepared a plate. Special Agent Lowe, who had been able to see clearly into the business at midnight, found that by 4 A.M. the previously unobstructed view through the windows had been blacked out to the extent that light could not be seen shining through.

Having prepared the plate, Newell and Simpson then printed up fake bills worth $426,000. However, making money is a two-step process. They had only printed one side, the obverse side. Special Agent Lowe, by now unable to see through the windows, began snooping around the premises. Either Newell or Simpson carelessly put four sheets of paper in the outside trash that had the likeness of twenty-dollar bills printed on them, and these were discovered and retrieved by the enterprising Lowe.

Despite their carelessness with the discarded sheet, the group decided that it wouldn't be a good idea to keep the money at the print shop. Calvin then came up with an idea that he deeply regrets to this day. Bobby Whitfield, the Oak Ridge Quartet piano player, had become a barber and had a shop in Winston-Salem, where he lived. Calvin packed up the $426,000 in two cardboard boxes, took them to Whitfield's barbershop, and asked if he could store them there, saying they were a Christmas present for his wife, Joyce. Happy to see Calvin, Whitfield readily agreed, and he subsequently had a lot of questions to answer before authorities were satisfied that he had nothing to do with the scheme. He was subpoenaed as a witness in the government's case against Calvin and the others. In 1955,

Whitfield had been a character witness for Calvin in his first-degree burglary trial in Charlotte. This time he would have been compelled to testify against him had the matter gone to trial.

Having corroborated the information provided by the paid informant, the federal agents had probable cause to obtain and execute a search warrant and to make arrests. House said it bothered the agents that they were going to have to pull the plug on the case on Christmas Eve. Although not sympathetic with the counterfeiters, they either knew or assumed that there were families whose Christmas would be ruined when the men were arrested. However, based on developments of the investigation, the agents felt they had no choice; if they didn't intervene, the money would be moved to Atlanta, then out of the country.

Accordingly, Calvin and Newell were arrested at Simpson's print shop at approximately 3 P.M. on December 24. At that point, Newell had a twenty-dollar bill mounted on a photographic camera machine placed in position to have negatives taken. A plate would then have been made and the other side of the bills printed.

Special Agent Ronald House recalled Simpson's subsequent arrest. "It was very embarrassing the way that things went down. We had to hit the print shop quicker than we wanted to, and the guy that owned the print shop [Simpson] came in with his two daughters, and we arrested him and his bladder broke. It broke bad right in front of his daughters; it was an embarrassing thing."

Joyce and the two children were in Winston-Salem at the time, and as Calvin was being put in a police cruiser to be taken to jail, his four-year-old daughter, Jackie, cried, "Please don't take my daddy away, it's Christmas." As the car pulled out, those words reverberated in Calvin's ears. His arrest made 1974 the worst Christmas of his life, more so than the one he had spent in Brushy Mountain prison years earlier. Calvin was now forty-five years old, much too old to be still committing crime; how could he have been so foolish? He had, once again, been totally impulsive and shown extremely poor judgment and, of course, he was full of pills. His associates, Simpson and Newell, possessed the expertise to carry out counterfeiting successfully, yet they had no savvy or street smarts, and were anything but cunning.

Newell had disclosed the entire plan to a complete stranger, who turned out to be an FBI informant. But Simpson had been every bit as indiscreet. Simpson occasionally allowed a North Carolina highway patrolman, James Helms, to use his printing equipment during Helms's off-hours. On December 14, 1974, Simpson confided to Helms that he was on the verge of bankruptcy, and he was of a mind to go in the shop and print up enough money to pay off his loans—not the sort of statement a prudent person would make to a cop. Although Newell and Simpson were bunglers, the scheme would have worked if they had only kept their mouths shut. Talmadge Bailey, head of the Secret Service Agency in Charlotte, North Carolina, stated that the bills were of fair quality and would probably have passed if they had hit the streets.

The arrest and subsequent stories received front-page treatment from the Winston-Salem *Journal*. The story broke the day after Christmas, and on December 27, 1974, a *Journal* staff writer reported: "Three men of oddly different backgrounds—a musician turned printer, an ex-policeman fired because of a lottery operation and a Tennessean with a criminal record—were released from jail yesterday after arraignment on counterfeiting charges."

The story was a sad commentary on what Calvin's life had become, because it revealed that his primary identity by then was that of a criminal "well known to Tennessee authorities," according to one news story. It was Simpson, not Calvin, who was considered an entertainer. At the conclusion of arraignment, Simpson and Calvin were released to the custody of their wives. Simpson, Newell, and Calvin were each subsequently indicted by a federal grand jury on April 11, 1975, and charged with four counts of counterfeiting and one count of conspiracy to commit counterfeiting.

Counterfeiting is a serious crime, and Calvin's situation was more dire than either Simpson's or Newell's, for several reasons. With a whopping six felony convictions that spanned twenty years, Calvin was considered a career criminal. In addition, he had a .357 magnum pistol under the seat of his car when he was arrested, a circumstance that makes sentencing judges very unhappy, something he should have learned in Springfield eleven years earlier when he had been apprehended with a gun by Tennessee authorities. Finally, he was considered the instigator and ringleader of the counterfeiters. Calvin was familiar enough with the criminal justice system to anticipate that, with these factors, he was going to receive a heavy prison sentence.

Consequently, he wasn't surprised when on May 7, 1975, he was sentenced to eight years of imprisonment pursuant to a plea-bargained agreement. In return for his pleading guilty to one count of counterfeiting, the remaining four counts were dismissed. The judge informed him that he was to serve his sentence at the federal prison at Maxwell Air Force Base in Montgomery, Alabama. The Maxwell facility was considered a lightweight prison primarily for white-collar criminals. Life is not a piece of cake in any prison, but, compared to other institutions, Maxwell was easy time. Violence was rare there because violent offenders were sent elsewhere.

However, Calvin stunned the judge and others in the courtroom when he asked if he could instead be sent to the federal prison at Atlanta, so that he could be closer to his family. Atlanta is one of the three original federal prisons. Constructed around the turn of the century, it has always been a maximum-security prison, and in the 1970s was considered the most dangerous prison in America. When the super-maximum-security prison Alcatraz was closed in 1963, the dangerous inmates who resided there were sent to Atlanta.

In the mid-1970s the Atlanta federal prison was out of control, with violence, murder, and corruption so pervasive that two Georgia congressmen, Senator Sam Nunn and Representative Wyche Fowler, called for congressional hearings to investigate the matter. An ex-con himself, Calvin knew that he would be exposing himself to danger at Atlanta, when he could have pulled easy time at Maxwell. He never gave it a second thought; he wanted to go to Atlanta so that Joyce and the kids could visit more frequently. The judge furrowed his brow but nonetheless granted the unusual request. It wasn't every day a man was willing to risk danger so that he could be closer to his family.

Calvin had an additional request. He asked to be allowed to build a fence around his family's home and attend to other family matters before entering prison. Calvin had moved his family to Chattanooga where they would be living next door to Calvin's dad. Since, in the judge's opinion, Calvin posed no threat to society, he acceded to Calvin's request and decreed that Calvin could voluntarily surrender to the Atlanta federal prison authorities on June 6, 1975, to begin serving his eight-year sentence. In the thirty days that Calvin had to prepare for prison, he built the fence, sought assurances from his dad that he would look out for his family, and tried not to think about the awful burden he had placed on his wife, Joyce, who stood by him firmly. After he was gone, she sat Wes and Jackie down and explained to them, "Your daddy did something wrong and he's being punished for it. But he isn't a bad person and he loves both of you very much and hates he can't be with you." The children nodded and continued to think what they always had: that their dad had hung the moon.

It was going to be a hard period for Joyce, but with her fierce commitment to her husband and children, she was determined to keep things together. As always, she would attend church weekly, pray daily, and enjoy the Christian fellowship of the members of her church. She was also blessed with a blissful ignorance of the horrid conditions at the Atlanta federal prison.

The day before he was to report, Calvin hugged and kissed Joyce and the kids and said goodbye as he boarded the Greyhound bus for Atlanta. Calvin's dad, Leonard, was with them at the bus station, too, and as he shook hands with his son, Joyce noticed the older man's sorrowful expression, which he attempted to hide behind a steely reserve. "Where did I go wrong?" was undoubtedly a question that Calvin's father posed countless times.

The drone of the big Greyhound engine had a soothing hypnotic effect on Calvin as he traveled south on Interstate 75. He drifted in and out of thoughtful reflection as the bus rolled past Dalton and Cartersville. He had pretty much come to terms with what he had done and what he had ahead of him. Don't do the crime if you can't do the time—that's what he had always heard. He knew he could do prison time, even in a tough joint like Atlanta. That wasn't the hard part. The hard part was leaving a wife and two small children to fend for themselves. Over and over, during the bus ride and for years thereafter, he was tortured relentlessly by a single thought: What if something happens to my family while I'm in prison— something that I could have prevented had I been there? Like a pesky gnat that won't be shooed, the thought of not being able to take care of his family was an unwelcome guest in his life, hovering nearby the entire time he was in the Atlanta federal prison.

29. Awakening

Often what seems to be a living death becomes the very situation that awakens the human soul to the deep knowing that a better life is possible.

—Gloria Gaither

The federal prison at Atlanta, or "the big A," as some call it, is a maximum-security institution housing the most dangerous types of offenders. When Calvin was sent there, half of the inmates in Atlanta were serving sentences of twenty years or more; many were lifers. Built at the beginning of the twentieth century by inmates using granite quarried from nearby Stone Mountain, the facility consists of massive, grim, gray buildings contained on 162 acres. By 1975 it was old, nasty, broken down, and dangerously overcrowded, housing over two thousand inmates in an area designed for twelve hundred.

The prison is shut off from the outside world by a huge concrete wall that measures thirty-nine feet high, four feet thick, and four thousand feet long. Seven long, hard years of inmate labor were required to finish the huge barrier. When it was completed in 1910, it was the largest cement masonry structure in the world. In keeping with prison design and philosophy of the period, the structures and walls were built on a gigantic scale in an effort to overwhelm the inmate, just as Tennessee State Prison had been.

Because of the effectiveness of the powerful RICO racketeering laws enacted in the late 1960s designed to combat organized crime, Atlanta was teeming with New York City mobsters when Calvin arrived. In fact, the list of Mafia wise guys in Atlanta read like an organized crime *Who's Who* for that period. The most prominent was Colombo crime family chieftain Carmine Persico, Jr., aka "Jr." or "the Snake." To gain insight into organized crime, actor James Caan, preparing for his role as Sonny Corleone in the blockbuster movie *The Godfather*, hung out with Persico so much that the FBI agents who monitored Persico initially mistook Caan for an aspiring mobster.

Several other inmates who were in Atlanta with Calvin were featured in a popular movie of the early 1980s, *GoodFellas*, which included the story of the multimillion-dollar Lufthansa airline heist in the late 1970s. In his book *The Ten Million Dollar Getaway*, author Doug Feiden stated that the Lufthansa robbery was planned in the prison yard at Atlanta. Lucchese crime family captain Paul Vario and two Lucchese family associates, Jimmy (the Gent) Burke and Tommy DeSimone, were all serving time in Atlanta during the mid-seventies. Other tough upper-echelon cons who had pulled time in Atlanta included 1960s Mafia godfather Vito Genovese and Atlanta's most prominent inmate—Al Capone—who was there four years before being sent to Alcatraz.

Because of lax policies, corrupt and incompetent prison officials, and the presence of numerous wealthy mobsters, the Atlanta federal prison in the early-to-mid-1970s was a cauldron of violence, corruption, and wrongdoing. Tales of mob hits, drug trafficking, and cozy treatment for crime chieftains became so flagrant and pervasive that in September 1978 the United States Senate Permanent Subcommittee on Investigations conducted hearings. In their published report they wrote: "The inquiry found that the Atlanta Penitentiary has become the setting for violent inmate murders, extensive narcotics trafficking, and various other criminal activities . . . there were distinctions in the nature of incarceration of known organized crime figures at the penitentiary, compared to the less desirable status of ordinary inmates."

The "distinctions in the nature of incarceration" referred to the steaks, lobster, wine, liquor, drugs, color televisions, females, and other amenities enjoyed by the mobsters, while Calvin and the others suffered the "less desirable status," a category that entitled one to a tiny, cramped cell where temperatures resembled those of the Arctic or the Sahara, depending on the time of year.

The report noted further that Atlanta had the largest prison industry in the United States, a circumstance that inmates took advantage of to manufacture homemade knives used in acts of violence, particularly by mob assassins. Early on, Calvin stumbled upon a stabbing victim lying in a pool of blood. As he kneeled down to render assistance to the gravely injured man, a voice behind him hissed threateningly, "Get away from him, Newton." He did as he was told, leaving the victim to bleed to death. New York City Mafioso Vincent Papa was stabbed to death in Atlanta while Calvin was there. One area of the prison had so many killings that the inmates named it "Death Valley."

Homosexual violence was rampant also. His first night in Atlanta Calvin listened in horror as one inmate brutally raped a smaller man in a nearby cell. Locked in his own cell, he had no choice but to listen to the piercing screams and pitiful cries of the young inmate as he pleaded for someone to help him. The sad, sordid episode made Calvin determined to do something about the young, naive inmates who most often fell prey to such activity. To that end, he joined the Yokefellow Prison Ministry and spearheaded a group of inmates who advised new arrivals on how to avoid homosexual entanglements. "One thing we told them was, 'Don't ever accept money, cigarettes, or gifts from anyone; that will make you indebted to that person, and if you don't have the money to repay them, they will demand sex in exchange.'"

This was the world that Calvin Newton entered on June 6, 1975. He would be forced to associate with the top organized gangsters in the world, who issued hits on inmates as casually as when they were free and on the streets. Eighteen inmates were murdered there during Calvin's period of incarceration, a record that will likely never be broken in prison circles. In addition to the organized-crime figures in the prison, a large number of violent psychotic inmates were also housed there. While there was some predictability regarding the mobsters' mayhem, that was not the case with the insane prisoners. One night in the chow hall, a vacant-eyed inmate advanced zombie-like upon Calvin with his dinner knife drawn. When Calvin stood up with his own knife to prepare for the attack, the crazy man abruptly veered off in another direction.

Furthermore, empirical studies indicate that one out of every three inmates in prison is a sociopath, a person without a conscience or moral scruples. With a population that contained a preponderance of inmates serving long sentences, sociopaths in the Atlanta federal prison were undoubtedly commonplace.

The chaplain of Atlanta during the mid-seventies was veteran corrections employee Charles Riggs. Riggs came to know Calvin well during his incarceration in Atlanta. Riggs recalled, "At the time it [Atlanta] had the reputation of a pretty tough place to be. It was really a bit surprising to have a person like Calvin in that setting." Riggs was unaware that Calvin had actually requested to be sent there.

While on the one hand Calvin was out of his depth with the vicious criminals in Atlanta, he entered the prison an ex-con himself. Consequently, he knew how to steer clear of trouble and "do his own time," as inmates are advised to do. Calvin was also adept at getting on the good side of big, powerful inmates, the kind you wanted for friends rather than enemies. He hadn't been there long when he made friends with a New York City wise guy named Maurice, whom everyone called "Big Mo." Big Mo was a lifer, having been convicted of murder on a government reservation. In Atlanta, Big Mo was as tough as they came. Jake Hess once went to Atlanta as part of a prison ministry to pass out religious material. Jake hadn't gone far before he was stopped by Big Mo, who asked him who he was and what was he doing there. When Jake answered, Big Mo told him to go ahead, and not to be worried about being around dangerous people, because Jake wouldn't have any problems while he was in Atlanta—Big Mo guaranteed it, and he was true to his word.

Calvin and Big Mo frequently played handball together during their yard time, spending many an afternoon huffing and puffing on the asphalt, laughing and kidding one another as they slapped a tiny black ball against the huge gray wall that ringed the prison. Big Mo also loved to hear Calvin sing. Not everyone else did, however. One day when Calvin was working as an electrician, he was atop a ladder rewiring a light fixture, and he unconsciously broke into a gospel song. Down below an Italian who pre-ferred opera told him, using colorful language, to shut up. Calvin shrugged and stopped singing, but being verbally abused that way put him in a funk. Later that day, Big Mo asked Calvin why he was so subdued. Calvin related the story to the burly mobster, who listened in stony silence and had no comment at the story's conclusion, other than the hardening features of his face.

A few days later, Calvin noticed that his heckler was never around any-more. He asked Big Mo if he had seen him, only to be told, "Oh, you don't have to worry about that guy. You won't be seeing him again." The man's body was found a short time later at the bottom of an elevator shaft. His throat had been slashed. The killing had all the earmarks of a mob hit. Whether Big Mo had anything to do with it is anybody's guess, but one thing was clear: Calvin could now sing anytime he wanted. Not long after that, while in a mischievous mood, Calvin warned his cellmate, Billy Fender, that when he started singing he was getting ready to kill somebody. Fender nodded fearfully and made a mental note. The next weekend, when Fender was visiting with his folks, Calvin turned in their direction, gave them an icy stare, and then began humming "Amazing Grace." The family bolted in different directions while Fender took cover under a dining table. Eventually, Fender chuckled when reminded of the incident.

All inmates entering prison undergo classification, a process in which the person is given a battery of physical, mental, psychological, and apti-tude tests to determine his needs, for purposes of treatment and rehabili-tation. The potential for violence and troublemaking are also assessed. A program is then established for the inmate. He might be put in the class-room to get his GED or given some type of vocational training along with a job in prison industries that would allow him to make some money. Like all other new inmates Calvin underwent this assessment period when he first entered Atlanta. As part of the process, new inmates, or "fish," as they were known by guards and the other inmates, were required to fill out questionnaires that would provide background information and help in determining vocational interests.

Unaware that his criminal convictions precluded a career in law, Calvin wrote that he wanted to study law and become an attorney. Chances are he would have made a fine attorney, had he made such a decision earlier in life. He had all the qualities: he was bright, articulate, and charismatic (it is easy to picture Calvin dominating a courtroom with his dynamic presence, particularly if women were on the jury). However, hedging his bets, he added on the questionnaire, "If I can't get the above, please allow me electrical rehabilitation work and heating and air conditioning. I could do very well at this."

Calvin brought two things with him when he entered prison: genuine remorse for what he had done and a steely resolve to change his life. He was sorry for having messed up not only his own life, but also the lives of his wife and two children. He knew they would struggle, not so much from the loss of his income as from his absence. He wouldn't be there for them when they needed him, and all three needed him tremendously. Despite all of his problems, he was the unquestioned leader of a very close-knit family, and he had let them down.

Many nights in Atlanta he lay awake, tormented by the thought that something bad might happen to one of them and he wouldn't be there, because he was in prison for having committed a foolish crime while high on speed. Besides the remorse he had over putting his family in a bind, he was sorry that he had broken the law. He knew that some of the property he had stolen in the 1960s probably had strong sentimental value for those from whom he had taken it, in addition to being worth a lot of money. As he lay there those sleepless nights in his bunk, while others around him snored, he thought about how much he wished he could return all the property he had stolen from so many people.

He also knew that the government, and by extension, the taxpayers, were out thousands of dollars from investigating and prosecuting his crimes, plus the expense of incarcerating him afterwards. What a waste, he thought. All that money that the government had spent on him could have been used for a much nobler purpose. He vowed it would never happen again—none of it—the crimes or the drugs. He set about putting his life in order. He soon made the acquaintance of another inmate with the same type of resolve.

It was during classification that Calvin met a young Viet Nam veteran, Dean Powell. Powell had served two tours of duty in the jungles of Southeast Asia in reconnaissance. "I didn't want to serve that second tour in Viet Nam," he said. "That was when I got involved in drugs—heroin, opium derivatives, stuff that would take you up and down." Powell brought his drug habit back to the states with him and before long he began dealing to support his habit. Soon thereafter, his criminal activities escalated to involve interstate transportation of huge amounts of drugs and eventually included stolen property as well. After an informant ratted him out to the DEA, he was arrested and subsequently sentenced to seven years in prison.

Although a high school graduate, Powell was functionally illiterate when he entered Atlanta. He knew he was going to a dangerous place, but following his arrest and a series of heartfelt discussions with a preacher, he was saved and surrendered his heart to the Lord. Determined to begin life anew, Powell developed an attitude imbued with a commitment to better himself in every respect—spiritually, mentally, and physically. He also felt an obligation to witness to others about his newfound religious convictions. Powell recalls, "I would give testimony to my case worker or anyone else that would listen to me." Calvin met Dean Powell during a game of pinochle. Noting Powell's pleasant disposition, Calvin dubbed him "Sunshine." Soon, that was what everybody called him. "Calvin was about twenty years older and had so much wisdom and was such a joy to be around," said Powell. Calvin and Powell became close during their initial period of confinement and have remained friends throughout the years.

Prison records indicate that Calvin completed the classification process on July 31, 1975, and was formally assigned to vocational heating and air-conditioning training. In addition, he received a medium custody rating, which meant that he had more freedom to move about the prison than some inmates but less than others. Considering that he was new, medium custody was probably the best that he could have hoped for.

Prisons have much greater accountability than other governmental agencies; therefore prison personnel are required to file frequent reports, especially summaries regarding an inmate's attitude, adjustment, and progress. From records obtained through the Freedom of Information

Act, more documentation can be found about Calvin during the thirty-two months he was at Atlanta than any other period in his life. It is fortunate that such an account exists, because it lends credibility to this remarkable period of personal growth, maturity, and expiation. By sheer force of will, and perhaps aided by divine intervention, he made the darkest moments of his life his most shining hour.

For instance, on August 25, 1975, E. R. Young, chief electrician in the facility, composed the following "to whom it may concern" memo: "Newton knew nothing about electricity when he came here, but is rapidly learning to be a qualified electrician. He wants to learn, and he bugs all of us constantly to show him how to do any job we are working on. I'm with this man several hours a day, five days a week, and I find him to be cooperative, willing to work and dependable."

Then Young added: "When you are around a man a lot, you get to know him pretty well. Newton, in my opinion, does not possess a criminal mind. In here the inmates refer to a man like Newton as a 'square.' He never talks about breaking the law, only about how he wants to be a worthwhile husband and father to his two children."

E. R. Young wasn't the only prison staffer to observe Calvin's exemplary effort and behavior. On August 27, 1975, vocational training instructor R. H. Evans verified Calvin's enrollment in the heating and air-conditioning class and then added a few personal observations: "Newton is assigned to the afternoon class. But, through his own determination he has additionally attended class in the morning and during his lunch hours. He has an outstanding attendance record . . . Very seldom does an instructor get a student with Newton's determination and persistence. Speaking as his instructor, I am proud to have inmate Newton in my class. His work and grades are outstanding."

Calvin stayed busy. He worked, attended classes, and played handball with Big Mo and pinochle with Dean Powell. Then, in his cell at night after lockup, he spent a great deal of time in silent contemplation, often composing songs with a message, sometimes venting his feelings in candid, emotional letters, most of which were never mailed. The poet Robinson Jeffers once wrote that people would rather confront a tiger in the road than face their feelings, and Calvin experienced this predicament in Atlanta. During his nightly confinement in his tiny, cramped cell, he was forced to confront his thoughts and feelings. Reflecting on his past was often unpleasant, but ultimately therapeutic. Sometimes he got angry at himself and sometimes he got angry at others. A few times after the lights were extinguished and his feelings got the best of him, he cried. Before he left, he had forgiven everyone who had ever wronged him, and prayed for forgiveness from all those he had wronged.

The high point of the week was always Saturday, because that was when Joyce and the kids came to see him, without fail, every time, not a single weekend missed.

Joyce recalled, "The kids were always excited about getting to go spend time with Daddy. For the first few months we usually stayed overnight. That way, we got to spend two days with him. But after I started playing piano at the Cedar Hill Church, we had to get back every Saturday night." There were breakfasts at McDonald's, and at prison they would get snacks out of the vending machines. Sometimes they would stop and eat on the way home, although Joyce had them on a tight budget.

Joyce had no idea how dangerous prison really was. She thought misbehavior was unlikely because of the guards and because it could delay an inmate's parole. Not long after Calvin had gone to Atlanta, she found out otherwise. One weekend as she and the kids were lined up to go through the metal detector, Wes noticed that a woman ahead of them somehow got through without being checked. He mentioned this omission to Joyce, who thought it was inconsequential. The woman and the three Newtons proceeded to the visitors' area where Calvin met his family and the woman met her husband. Joyce, Wes, and Jackie got into a spirited conversation with Calvin and forgot about the woman who had come in just ahead of them until the woman suddenly screamed angrily, jumped up, and pulled out a long kitchen knife that she was going to use to stab her husband. Calvin stood in front of his family while guards rushed to the scene to disarm the woman.

After this incident, Joyce developed a different perspective on Atlanta. She realized that the inmates weren't choirboys and that some of the women visitors weren't Girl Scouts. Even so, she never fully realized how danger-ous things were, primarily because Calvin didn't tell her what it was like, and because she felt that Calvin could take care of himself.

Initially, when Calvin was going through classification, he wasn't allowed any visitors. During that period, Joyce, stressed by his absence and the addi-tional responsibilities thrust upon her, began to eat more. She never took tranquilizers to calm herself, but a chocolate bar every now and then hit the spot and seemed to have the same effect. By the time she and the kids were allowed to visit, she had gained weight. Calvin noticed and right off the bat said, good-naturedly, "Look's like you've put on a few pounds." Upset by what she considered an insensitive remark by her father, little six-year-old Jackie scolded him, saying, "Oh, yeah? Well, she's not a bit fat at home."

Calvin had other visitors in addition to his wife and children. Bob and Mary Robinson came to see him, as did Bob and June Weber. One day three young Texans who were tearing up the pop and country music charts with their soaring, seamless melodies dropped by. Rudy, Steve, and Larry Gatlin came to see Calvin to offer support and let him know how much they had been influenced by the Sons of Song when the three were kids and just beginning to sing. Calvin was touched.

Through the week Calvin began spending more time with Dean Powell. Consumed with the need to share his religious convictions, Powell stayed after Calvin to start going to church. Powell recalled, "We were walking on the yard one day and I was trying to get him to come to church services. By then I realized he had a lot of guilt for what he had done with his life. Calvin made the comment, 'Well, the Lord's got enough people up there; he doesn't need me.' I told him, 'Yes, but he doesn't have Calvin Newton.'" Soon Powell's perseverance paid off and Calvin began attending church services regularly. Powell still recalls one of Calvin's first prayers. "God, just help us to be ourselves and not pretend to be anyone else. That prayer has stayed with me all these years," recalled Powell. Calvin's prayer may have affected Powell, but it was his singing that touched countless others at the Atlanta prison.

In 1974 the tune "One Day at a Time" became a popular gospel song. Six years later, it was a smash hit for country singer Christy Lane. The lyrics are nothing less than a mantra for anyone in dire straits, be it grinding poverty, chronic illness, drug or alcohol addiction, or incarceration. The writer, Marijohn Wilkins, called the song "a cry for help"; she composed it during a dark period of her life when she was struggling with alcohol and with marital and financial problems. In the song, the Lord is asked to provide strength to get through today, without regard to what happened yesterday or what might happen tomorrow.

In the harsh confines of the federal penitentiary at Atlanta, this musical prayer became Calvin's signature song and most requested number. Over and over, to receptive and responsive inmates, Calvin's melodious voice became a source of comfort as he sang Wilkins's song of inspiration. Wally Fowler's daughter, Faith Fowler McCoy, stated, "When Calvin sings, God anoints his voice. Through God, he has the ability to touch and heal people. I've seen him do it."

Not long after he began attending and participating in church services, he was approached by the prison chaplain, Charlie Riggs, who mixed compassion with a no-nonsense approach to his dealings with inmates. "I never tried to figure out people's crimes and sentences. I simply focused on trying to help them cope with life in prison." Riggs had noticed Calvin's electrifying presence on stage, and also Calvin's understanding of the dynamics of a church service. Riggs recalled, "Cal had a lot of talent and did good solo work, plus he was more of a showman than many of the others. Onstage, he had presence, but he was also savvy about organized church work. He had a lot of sense of the universal, what worked and wouldn't work. In other words, Cal had an understanding that went beyond one denomination."

According to Calvin, attendance at inmate services was lagging when he began participating in church services there. Calvin stated that Riggs approached him with a straightforward proposition: you help me build up church attendance and I'll help you when you come up for parole. It was a tempting offer but one that really wasn't necessary. Calvin's interest and devotion to religion had already been rekindled at that point, and he would have been a part of church services regardless. Nevertheless, Calvin eagerly accepted the carrot Riggs dangled.

As further proof of Calvin's religious sincerity, he became involved in the Yokefellow Ministry, a Christian organization with a mission of ministering to the needs of prison inmates. Calvin became Yokefellow's inside coordinator of prison activities. He then joined a third prison ministry— a brand new one.

The new ministry had been started by an ex-con, who until recently had been a well-known inmate in the federal system. Moreover, his was one of the most recognizable names and faces in the entire world. He had been on the cover of *Time* magazine; he had appeared as the featured guest on numerous Sunday morning television news programs devoted to political issues, including *Meet the Press*; Mike Wallace and *Sixty Minutes* had devoted a portion of one of their broadcasts to him. Yet on the inside he had merely been inmate 23226.

He spent most of his relatively short period of confinement in the prison at Maxwell Air Force Base, performing chores such as cutting grass, raking leaves, and working in the prison laundry, which became his permanent job. Fellow inmates snickered that inmate 23226—Mr. Big Shot— who was accustomed to being chauffeured around in a huge, black, shiny limousine, was now washing their smelly socks and dirty drawers. The new demeaning lifestyle was initially hard on inmate 23226.

In addition to being subjected to humiliation, he sometimes actually feared for his life; he'd received death threats. After years of wearing expensive tailor-made suits and fashionable silk shirts, he wore what amounted to hand-me-down rags for clothing: cheap drab cotton shirts with buttons missing and old cloth pants that barely reached the tops of his socks. But clothing wasn't that important to inmate 23226 anymore because he wasn't the man he used to be—he had changed. Soon, he would have an enormous impact on the life of Calvin Newton and other inmates as well. The man's Christian name was Charles, but his friends, family, and associates— which included President Richard Nixon—called him Chuck.

30. Colson and Parole

Charles W. "Chuck" Colson was so devoted to his boss and believed so strongly in the man's political philosophies that he once wrote in a memo to his subordinates that he would "walk over [his] grandmother for Richard Nixon." He became known as Nixon's "hatchet man," a truly dubious distinction considering that Nixon's inner circle included some of the most ruthless and misguided zealots ever to serve a president. As revelations unfolded during this period, the public learned about the Nixon administration's duplicity, which included the "dirty tricks" campaign, the White House "plumbers," the so-called "enemies" list, the misuse of the IRS, and other unsavory practices and events, including the most prominent—the Watergate burglary and cover-up.

During the early 1970s, H. R. Haldeman, John Erlichman, John Mitchell, and others were so strongly associated with malfeasance and wrongdoing that the mere mention of their names was enough to trigger contempt and hostility in the minds of many Americans. However, it was Chuck Colson, special counsel to the president, who inspired more scorn and loathing than any of the others; indeed, he became the lightning rod for the storm of protest that gripped the presidency during this period. Incredibly, it was a role he relished. The former ex-marine was a team player who would eagerly fall on a grenade for the commander-in-chief. He took great pride in being the president's go-to guy when there was an unpleasant or difficult task that needed to be carried out.

However, as the unfortunate saga that came to be known as Watergate played itself out, Colson became increasingly disillusioned with the president as well as with his own role in the gross misconduct of the administration. He became introspective and depressed. In his biography, *Born Again*, he stated that he began to feel a terrible emptiness in his life during this trying period. In searching for answers, he sought out a friend, Tom Phillips, the CEO of Raytheon, New England's largest employer. Phillips told Colson that he had recently become a Christian. Phillips counseled Colson, prayed with him, and provided him a copy of C. S. Lewis's *Mere Christianity*. As Colson began reading the book, he was swayed by Lewis's towering intellect. Extremely bright and well educated, Colson needed more than dogma to convince him of Phillips's representations. Lewis's reasoning, which Colson found both subtle and profound, provided the impetus.

Colson became a Christian, accepting Christ during the turbulent period when his name and face were appearing nightly on television and in the paper. With a criminal indictment and possible jail time looming, many were skeptical of his conversion. Newspaper columnists and editorial cartoonists had a field day lampooning his dramatic lifestyle change. However, his new Christian friends, including former archenemy Harold Hughes, stood steadfastly by him. Although he swore he wasn't guilty of what he had been charged with—obstruction of justice—he nonetheless pled guilty to the crime. He did so despite his attorney's protests, who felt that Colson's chances of acquittal were excellent. With the flood of negative publicity and overwhelming public sentiment for punishment, Colson knew he would be receiving jail time. He hoped it would be six months or less. Instead, he received a one-to-three year sentence.

He spent most of his sentence at the federal prison at Maxwell Air Force Base in Montgomery, Alabama, a minimum custody facility whose inmate population primarily consisted of white-collar criminals, bootleggers, car thieves, and other nonviolent offenders. At Maxwell, Colson found himself among the dregs of society. A Washington blueblood who had an Ivy League education and was a senior partner in a prestigious Washington, D. C., law firm, Colson was suddenly thrust into a forced association with illiterate hillbillies, low-level big-city wise guys, and small-time scam artists. Nonetheless, he resolved to immerse himself in the culture, in part for self-preservation and in part because he felt a genuine need to minister to lost souls in need of compassion, mercy, and understanding. His feelings that he was doing something important and purposeful were reinforced as he searched the scriptures and read Luke 4:18: "The Spirit of the Lord is on me: therefore he anointed me to preach good news to the poor. He has sent me to proclaim freedom for the prisoners and recovery of sight for the blind, to release the oppressed, to proclaim the year of the Lord's favor."

Colson became part of an informal prison ministry that consisted of a few inmates getting together to pray, read the Bible, and witness for the Lord. Upon his release from federal prison, inspired by the scriptures in Luke, he felt a calling to form a full-time prison ministry. In 1975 he and Harold Hughes, the ex-senator and ex-governor of Iowa, petitioned the Federal Bureau of Prisons to furlough men and women from selected federal institutions to attend a fourteen-day religious retreat in Washington, D. C. Inmates were rigorously screened by Colson's organization, which made selections after being convinced of the applicant's promise and sincerity. The first group of inmates met in Washington in November 1975.

Other groups of inmates quickly followed. Calvin, along with fellow Atlanta inmates Dean Powell and Luis Lopez, were in the eighth cohort that traveled to Washington, D. C., where for two weeks—July 10, 1977, to July 24, 1977—they underwent intensive prison fellowship training in peer relationships at Holy Name College. Calvin was immensely gratified to have been chosen to leave the high, gray walls of a maximum-security prison and travel unescorted to a destination hundreds of miles away. Naturally, Joyce and the kids tagged along behind, hoping to visit with him, and were overcome with joy when they were told that it would be okay for Calvin to stay at the motel with his family, instead of on the college campus where the other inmates were housed.

The September 1977 edition of *Jubilee, The Newsletter of Prison Fellowship* observed: "It was July 23, the 'graduation' of Prison Fellowship's eighth Disciples Class. The men were completing two weeks of intensive Bible study, preparing to return to their six penitentiaries, no longer just inmates, but ambassadors for Christ."

The class and the visit with his family energized Calvin, and he returned to Atlanta renewed in spirit and purpose. He knew there was a parole date in the not-too-distant future and that he would be a strong candidate. He also knew that Atlanta was about to have a special visitor.

Just as Colson had played host to Luis Lopez, Dean Powell, and Calvin, shortly thereafter it was their turn to host him, for Colson had decided it was time to bring his ministry to the toughest prison in America: the Atlanta federal penitentiary. It was a visit Colson would never forget, and one in which Calvin was to figure prominently. It was during the scorching dog days of August 1977 that Chuck Colson chose to go to Atlanta and try to reach lost souls. Colson had been in many tough prisons by then. He had suffered severe anxiety at New York's infamous Attica and at ancient McNeil Island, off the coast of California. He had endured treacherous icy conditions to travel to Sandstone Prison in Minnesota. He saw and heard things at these institutions and others that both frightened and saddened him, but the horror of those institutions paled compared to the hell on earth at the Atlanta federal penitentiary.

In his second book, *Life Sentence*, Colson recalled seeing, smelling, and being appalled at the "paint chipped concrete, slimy latrines, and slow-moving gates" that greeted him upon arrival at the large Georgia federal prison. He noted, "For two years the agony of the Atlanta Federal Prison spilled out of its rock wall confines into grisly headlines, congressional hearings and TV specials. The grip of organized crime reached through the prison's iron gates and clutched the very innards of life inside. Death struck swiftly, often and with impunity." Continuing, he observed, "Over a period of 16 months, 10 men were brutally murdered, gangland style. One was burned alive in his sleep; others savagely slashed or beaten. Prison officials tried to clamp down, but the terror continued as 2,000 inmates lived in fear for their lives. Guards recoiled at the prospect of walking along cellblock corridors; visitors were banned."

As Colson and his associates made their way into the prison they were met by the new warden, Jack Hanberry, and by Chaplain Charlie Riggs.

Both were corrections veterans who were labeled by the inmates as "tough but fair." Riggs had rounded up 150 inmates to attend the service, but Hanberry, a former chaplain, decided to allow the entire general population—2,000 inmates—to be there. Riggs informed Colson that there were eight "brothers" waiting to have prayer with Colson before the service began. Colson described the meeting as a "joyous reunion" with warmth and happiness. He did not mention Dean Powell by name, referring to him instead as "Sunshine," the name given to him by Calvin. He mentioned "Cal," who was described as a square-jawed ex-gospel music singer. Colson briefly mentioned two others and stated that after embracing the men they sat in circled chairs. Colson listened while the men briefed him about the tense conditions in the prison.

Colson recalled, "Cal, who was the official leader for the group, spoke first. 'We're glad you're here, Chuck. The betting was two to one you wouldn't show.'" Colson stated that Calvin then warned, "Look, Chuck, things are bad. The men are very tense. I don't want to alarm you, but some dudes are expecting a little trouble here tonight." According to Colson, Calvin warned him against preaching or even mentioning the name "Jesus." Colson added that Calvin's warning was accompanied "by a chorus of 'right, man' and 'amen.'" Inmate Don Taylor suggested that he speak of prison reform instead. Amazingly, Chaplain Riggs, standing against the wall, nodded agreement. The atmosphere was so volatile that even the chaplain thought a religious message would be a bad idea.

Sunshine explained, "The trouble is, Chuck, that the men feel you're out to con them," adding that the warden had been saying good things about Colson, enough to make the inmates suspicious in and of itself. To the inmates, Colson was just another authority figure running a scam. Colson wrote that, not since he feared for his life in his early days of confinement in Maxwell, had he known fear in prison, but he began experiencing it again with his eight "disciples" in the sweltering room. They ended their meeting in prayer.

As Colson took the podium in the packed, sweltering auditorium, he initially intended to speak of prison reform but quickly abandoned the idea and instead began tracing the origins of his Prison Fellowship ministry.

His stern, skeptical audience began to loosen up when he told them of the time in Washington when neighbors around the Fellowship House confused congressmen with convicts. The heat in the room was overpowering—his clothing was drenched with perspiration—but he persisted in his message that Jesus had changed his life and could do the same for those in the audience.

When he realized that the inmates were becoming receptive to what he was telling them, Colson bore down with his simple message of truth—Christ loves everyone, including all of you, every single one of you, especially every one of you. Nothing that any of you have said or done is beyond his forgiveness. Just give him a chance, Colson admonished, and he'll change your life like he did mine. They listened intently, becoming responsive and then demonstrative. Soon, inmates were standing; some of them even stood on the seats of chairs. There was clapping, shouting, singing, and rejoicing, all inspired by the excitement and joy of what they were hearing. A remarkable transformation occurred. A feeling of hope had bloomed among what had been a disconsolate and cynical group of bitter, angry men.

Colson wrote, "The change in the faces was awesome." A spirit of harmony and jubilee swept away the distrust and hatred that had greeted him when he began his sermon. After he finished, inmates of all stripes, including a Mafia chieftain, came forward to shake his hand, praise him, and let him know what his words had meant to them. One black inmate simply put his head softly on Colson's shoulder and wept. The earthly heat that had almost melted Colson earlier had turned into a refreshing heavenly warmth, and he and the others basked in it. Colson wrote that after the service he made his way back to Chaplain Riggs's office, where he and his eight disciples bowed and gave thanks to the Lord for the blessed evening. Colson wrote, "Cal stuck out his hand for a last farewell. 'I wish I could stay with you guys,' I said as tears filled Cal's eyes. Funny thing is, I meant it. I didn't want to leave these men behind."

Colson's visit had been uplifting for Calvin, and he took the experience and added it to the other positive things that were occurring in his life. Then he went back to the treadmill-like monotony of regimented activities that he didn't like but to which he had become accustomed. At Atlanta, time passed slowly, but it passed. By February 1978, Calvin had spent three Christmases inside the gray cavernous walls. During that time, he completed a course in welding and another for electricians. He received a prison merit award and a cash gift of fifty dollars for repairing the prison bus, which saved the institution over a thousand dollars. He also worked in prison industries, having signed an agreement for all but fifteen dollars of his earnings each month to go directly to his wife. The amount— almost $150—was enough to make a car payment, which pleased him enormously.

His dad passed away with cancer while he was in Atlanta, and he was allowed to attend the funeral. Cat Freeman came up from Alabama to sing. Calvin was saddened by the fact that hardly anyone was there. At the cemetery he said goodbye to his dad, and then Joyce drove him back to Atlanta. A few weeks later he had accumulated thirty-two months of prison time, a special plateau in his incarceration—his parole hearing date. It was February 15, 1978.

Dressed in his "power suit," Charlie Riggs, the chaplain, was waiting in the hallway outside the Spartan room where the parole hearing would take place. He shook Calvin's hand as Calvin made his way before the men who would determine whether he would be conditionally released from prison or remain and serve more time.

Calvin was hopeful that he would be granted parole; after all, his conduct and attitude could have served as a model for inmate behavior. He had worked in the prison, learned two new trades, and obtained a state license as a welder. In addition, he had devoted himself to three religious organizations: Chaplain Riggs's prison ministry, the Yokefellow Ministry, and Colson's new Prison Fellowship. He had sent money home every month, he had glowing reports from work supervisors, and there were flattering letters in his file from outside sources that included preachers and politicians. To top it off, Calvin hadn't been written up a single time for having done anything against the prison rules.

In addition, he had a job waiting for him, an extremely important factor in parole determination. He also had a strong, viable marriage and two small children, another weighty consideration. Calvin was obviously devoted to them. Hadn't one of his supervisors mentioned that they were all he talked about? Another element in his favor was his age. Calvin was forty-eight years old, pretty long in the tooth for a criminal. Parole board members knew that teenagers and those in their early twenties commit most crime. These factors were all in his favor.

Unfortunately, his negatives tended to offset all of the positives. For one thing, Calvin had a criminal record spanning twenty years. Parole board members, leafing through his application and prison records, also noted that he had served a term in Tennessee prisons for drugs and burglary, which had run concurrently with a Georgia sentence for breaking into automobiles. Parole board members realized that the so-called clearance rate for burglary was a paltry 13 percent, meaning that the perpetrator gets by eighty-seven times out of a hundred without being arrested. There was no telling how many crimes this guy Newton had committed, hundreds probably.

It was true that he had been a model inmate, living at the foot of the cross, saying and doing all the right things. But what would happen when he got back in the free world? Most likely, he would stay on the straight and narrow for a few months, reporting to a parole officer and working at some dreary job. But sooner or later, he would start back popping pills and stealing; you could count on it. The parole board members had been seeing Calvin Newton types for years. No, as far as they were concerned, thirty-two months on an eight-year sentence wasn't exactly a pound of flesh. When the parole board finished talking to Calvin, the consensus seemed to be that he would have to cool his heels and build some more time before they would cut him loose.

Then it was time for Chaplain Riggs to testify. Riggs related how the prison ministry had shrunk to thirty to forty people per service before Calvin came along and infused it with his dynamic qualities. Newton had been a positive influence on the lives and souls of many inmates; he'd done a lot of good for the institution. Riggs told the board that he knew when an inmate was running a con, when someone was merely talking the talk; Newton was different.

Riggs's comments were met with skepticism, even derision. This guy Newton had really done a number on old Charlie. You would think Riggs would know better by now, they snickered. With that, the grizzled veteran exploded. His voice thundered beyond the room and down the hallway where Calvin anxiously awaited. If the parole board didn't believe in any of the programs inside the institution, then they should abolish them and just let the inmates sit inside their cells. Newton had done everything anybody could ask of an inmate. He didn't have any business being in Atlanta in the first place; he wasn't violent and he wasn't a threat to society.

Riggs really laid into them, but they didn't take it lying down. Calvin soon heard the voices of parole board members returning Riggs's verbal volley. A heated disagreement ensued for several minutes; then, their voices grew softer. At that point, Calvin didn't know what to make of the meeting. He surmised that they had reached accord but wasn't sure whether it was to grant or deny parole. Shortly thereafter, Riggs left the room and found Calvin. His face beaming, Riggs shook Calvin's hand vigorously and remarked, "You got it! It took some doing, but you're gonna walk." Riggs had been true to his word.

Thus on February 15, 1978, after having served thirty-two months in the most dangerous, violent, corrupt prison in America, Calvin was paroled. His incarceration had been spent productively, for now he had marketable job skills. He had also matured and had gained insight and understanding. He came out of prison a better person. His stay there had been a period of personal growth and spiritual redemption. Moreover, he had paid his debt to society. Now, it was time to go home. He picked up his meager belongings and his mustering-out pay and never looked back, except in somber reflection years later, when he observed, "They busted me—totally and completely. After Atlanta, I wouldn't have spit on the sidewalk." The federal government had gotten his attention—no more crime for Calvin Newton.

31. **Out of the Depths**

The descent to hell is easy.
The gates stand open night and day.
But to reclimb the slope
and escape to the upper air:
this is labor.

—*Virgil*, The Aeneid, *Book 6*

Calvin met Joyce, Wes, and Jackie at the prison gates, where
they had a joyous reunion, complete with tears, hugging, and laughter.
After thirty-two long months in the worst prison in America, he was going
home to start his life over. He got behind the wheel in the family car,
and headed north up the congested concrete ribbon of Interstate 75 to
Chattanooga, the same stretch of road that Joyce and the kids had traveled
over a hundred and twenty-five times in the previous three years.

When they pulled into the driveway, Calvin saw trees in his front yard
decorated with shiny yellow ribbons, in keeping with the bouncy, popular
1970s song "Tie a Yellow Ribbon." The lyrics relate the true story of a man
who, like Calvin, has been released from a Georgia prison after three years.
Uncertain whether he will be welcome, he has written his wife and asked
her to tie a yellow ribbon around an old oak tree on the city square of their
hometown—White Oak, Georgia—as a sign, to let him know if she will
take him back. If not, he'll "stay on the bus [and] forget about us . . ." By
the time the bus reaches the square, everyone on it is aware of the man's
situation and is holding his or her breath in suspense. The bus driver slows,

and then someone yells, "There it is"—the yellow ribbon. The occupants of the bus cheer wildly while the man cries tears of joy. For Calvin, there was no suspense. He knew he was welcome but was nonetheless pleased and flattered to see the bright yellow bows waving hello. His sisters, Glatta and Nora, had thought of the idea.

His homecoming following the thirty-two month banishment was truly one of the happiest periods in Calvin's life. He had earned his freedom back, and he had paid his debt to society. Activities that people in the free world took for granted were great treats for him. He could stay up as late as he wanted and then sleep until noon. He could raid the refrigerator whenever he felt like it, play with the kids, go to the movies, or spend some time with his wife alone.

He had forgotten what privacy was like. Also, he didn't have to worry every moment that some mobster or sociopath might try to cut him. He no longer had to stand in place five times a day to be counted, either. He would miss Big Mo and the handball, and Dean and Luis Lopez and the prison ministries, but prison was behind him.

His family had been and would always be the most important part of his life, and now he could begin to repay them for the sacrifices they had made because of his foolish mistakes. His resolve to do the right thing was perhaps heightened by the knowledge that any further legal transgressions on his part would result in the revocation of his parole: he still owed the United States government over five years on his sentence. If he screwed up, he would be right back in prison; his release was conditional upon his obeying not only the law but the rules of parole.

Realizing that crime and gospel music were no longer career options, Calvin, utilizing his newly obtained skills as a welder, found employment with the TVA at the construction site of the proposed Bellefont nuclear power plant near Scottsboro, Alabama. The pay was good, but it was a grimy blue-collar job that required him to wear brogans and cloth uniforms, a far cry from the days of the custom-tailored tuxedos and unborn-calf shoes that he had worn as a member of the Sons of Song. He rose each day before sunup to splash water on his face, gulp down a quick cup of coffee, and trudge to his car carrying a sack of bologna sandwiches for lunch. He would dutifully arrive at the job site, punch the clock, put on his leather work gloves and heavily shaded goggles, fire up his torch, and then weld for eight monotonous hours.

He did his job and he did it well, but there was never any applause, and he was never called back for an encore; there were no stages or spotlights. Instead, he toiled in grim anonymity. The messages he carried in his shirt pockets were not enticing invitations from "diesel sniffers" but mundane reminders from his wife to pick up bread, milk, and toilet paper on the way home, or a note to himself to get gasoline so he could cut the grass. Although he tried not to show it, he was in some ways deeply unhappy. Billy Warren stated, "Calvin had a hard time latching on to anything after he got out of prison 'cause his real love was gospel music, and he was trying to get away from that and be a normal husband and father."

But Calvin remained upbeat, energetic, and helpful to others. Young Mark Waits worked alongside Calvin during the Bellefont construction days and recalled Calvin's personal warmth and kindness. "I was only twenty-one when I began working at Bellefonte, and some of the older welders tried to give me a hard time. Calvin always took up for me and would help me out when I was stuck on a difficult weld or had some problem. One time the guy who ran the tool shack wouldn't give me the tools I needed, so Calvin went in there and told the guy he didn't want to catch him giving me a hard time again, and I never had a problem getting tools after that." Reflecting on that period, Waits observed, "God sends you people at different times in your life to help you get through that period, and I truly believe that Cal was one of my guardian angels." The statement is remarkably similar to one made by Dean "Sunshine" Powell about what Calvin meant to him when they were in the Atlanta federal prison together.

Welding may not have been as glamorous as singing gospel music, but it paid a lot more money. Most weeks Calvin racked up overtime, and with Joyce's good job, they were better off financially than they ever had been. Calvin missed the stage and the spotlight, but he had to admit that it was great not having to worry about the creditors the first of every month.

By 1979, Wes was in his mid-teens and Jackie Sue was a rambunctious nine-year-old. Calvin and Joyce decided it was time for their children to begin studying music. Jean Bradford, a long-time friend, lived in nearby Fort Oglethorpe, Georgia. Jean taught music in her home, both voice and piano. She was the widow of "Shorty" Bradford, a well-known gospel singer who had sung with the Homeland Harmony Quartet and later with the Happy Two, a duo consisting of Bradford and the renowned Lee Roy Abernathy. With a phenomenal four-octave range, Shorty Bradford had also taught voice before his death in the 1960s. Of course his partner, Lee Roy Abernathy, taught voice and had a popular correspondence piano course. Jean Bradford not only taught music but had also achieved prominence as a songwriter whose compositions are found in Protestant hymnals everywhere. With her own knowledge and talent, plus her decades-long association with her husband, Shorty, and his partner, Lee Roy Abernathy, Jean Bradford had impeccable credentials for teaching anyone how to sing.

Jean recalled those days. "Cal had just gotten out of prison and I got a call one day from Joyce—they wanted to know if I'd work with their children and teach them how to sing harmony. Jackie was nine and Wes was sixteen. So, they started bringing them to my house, and one day Calvin came in and the three of us were singing as a trio and he was so pleased." The Newton children were both talented and had good voices. Wes had a soft lyric tenor voice, while Jackie sang with more sass and punch, in keeping with her spirited personality. Jean Bradford soon discovered that Jackie was a natural. "The first day she came, Jackie could do whatever I told her; then she started doing it on her own." With nearly perfect pitch, Jackie could sing the alto, soprano, or tenor part on key. She had her dad's talent, and with formal training was to become more technically proficient than he was.

Jean had two daughters. Carolyn, the younger, had sung with her mother around the house. Soon, Carolyn was joining Jean, Wes, and Jackie as they sang in the Bradford living room. Calvin suggested that he join them and form a group: thus the Cal Newton Family evolved. After about six months of singing on weekends in area churches, he decided they were good enough to do an album. The group rehearsed diligently for the project and then booked time at the Sound Room in Fort Oglethorpe to cut the tracks. Jean asked the Goss brothers—Lari, Ronnie, and James—to produce the tape. "We grew up in Cartersville together. They're my personal friends; that's why they agreed to come and do that." At that point Lari Goss hadn't achieved the prominence as a producer that he presently enjoys, but he was nonetheless extremely skilled at producing and arranging. Like Ralph Carmichael, he could jot down the string arrangements while a rhythm track was being played back.

Entitled *Collector's Edition*, the album featured a fine song written by Calvin—his first—entitled "Momma, Can't You Hear the Music," and a great solo by Jackie Newton on "Jesus Loves Me." Calvin was so excited about little Jackie's rendition of "Jesus Loves Me" that he entered her in the talent competition at the 1980 National Quartet Convention, where she surprised everyone by winning second place.

In the early 1980s, perhaps heartened by his pleasant experience with the Cal Newton Family, Calvin tried once more to revitalize the dormant Sons of Song. He contacted Bob Robinson and Lee Kitchens and both were amenable to giving it another shot. Like Calvin, they loved singing, and they knew they sounded good together. The Sons decided they needed some fresh product, so they booked a recording session in Kingsport, Tennessee, in Tilford Salyer's studio, Tri-State Recording. Calvin had a double agenda. Salyers recalls, "Calvin wanted to know if I would do two albums: one on the Sons of Song; the other on his daughter, Jackie. He asked if he could finance it, and I agreed. I even took the cover photo of Jackie."

Salyers added, "They didn't want a lot of production because they just operated with a piano. When you do a lot of fancy singing like they did you don't want to drown it out with all the music." Accordingly, the only instrumentation heard on the album is Bob Robinson's piano work and that of two young men from the Kingsport area who each went on to prominence as gospel music producers: Bobby All, who played bass, and Russell Mauldin, who played drums.

Salyers reflects on the 1982 session rather fatalistically. "It wasn't a sensational thing. We gave it our best. They pretty much had the sound [of the original Sons of Song] but they were older, and they just didn't have that drive, that determination that they had back in the fifties." Tilford Salyers had been a promoter during the heyday of the original Sons of

Song in the late 1950s and had booked them many times in Kingsport, Roanoke, and Raleigh. Of the original group and sound, he remarked, "It was new, original, and different. I loved it." Salyers had been particularly enamoured with the booming baritone voice of Don Butler. "Kitchens could do the job, but nobody could take Butler's place."

The album was called *Encore*, and included old Sons of Song hits such as "Wasted Years," "Sorry, I Never Knew You," "Sometimes I Cry," and "Jesus, Use Me." Despite Salyer's gloominess, the album was a fine effort by the trio. Mauldin's and All's spare picking, coupled with Robinson's piano work, provided the right touch, and Salyer's production was quality work. Lee Kitchens recalls that the strategy was to give the group a new album to support their proposed touring. But the bookings were sporadic and infrequent, too much so to justify the giving up of other sources of income and pursuing of gospel singing on a full-time basis. However, the trio appeared from time to time at big singings, often preceded by a picture and article in a newspaper or periodical mentioning that the legendary group would be performing.

The album cover photo revealed three middle-aged men aging gracefully. By this point the Sons of Song were an oldies act, not unlike their rock and roll counterparts, such as the Coasters, the Drifters, and others who were trying to make a living with personal appearances while singing decades-old hits. Robinson's locks were longer than his neatly coiffed 1960s hairstyle, and he now had a thick, dark mustache and a goatee flecked with gray. The otherwise conservative Lee Kitchens had also gone modish, with a beard trimmed closely and almost totally gray. Ever the rebel, Calvin had the same hairstyle he had had in the 1950s, and he never sported facial hair.

The high point during this period was a reunion appearance at a New Year's Eve all-night singing at Birmingham's Boutwell Auditorium in 1983. The fans reacted to them enthusiastically, just as they had decades earlier when the Sons played their favorite venue. Marring this otherwise upbeat occasion was a remark made by a member of one of the other groups performing that night. As the Sons were leaving the stage, one of the Kingsmen got right in Bob Robinson's face and spewed, "Why don't you go back home!" The sensitive Robinson was crushed by the heckler's boorishness. After a quarter century, it was obvious that the Sons of Song were still the black sheep of southern gospel music. Moreover, the responses of the audience and the performers followed the same old pattern—wild acceptance by the former and jealous rejection from the latter.

Calvin's job as a welder ended after he got into a dispute with a union boss, who, according to Calvin, wanted a kickback in exchange for Calvin getting a union card. He went into business for himself and worked in home remodeling. Wes helped out and business was good for a while, but, like almost all of Calvin's endeavors, the venture was ultimately ill-fated. In 1983, he was forced to take bankruptcy after an employee cheated him out of forty thousand dollars by diverting money to his own use that should have been spent on construction projects. By now, misfortune and bad luck had become a lifelong pattern for Calvin.

However, hardened by years of adversity, the Newtons responded to their financial situation with equanimity and stoicism. Joyce took a second job with the post office. The pay was good but the long, hard hours tested the strength of the durable woman. Nonetheless, she maintained a sixteen-hour workday for four years. Calvin was willing and able but just couldn't seem to latch onto anything. His life had stablized into an unglamorous, ordinary existence of working at boring blue-collar jobs, helping raise two kids, and struggling to pay the bills. It appeared to him and others that his glory days were behind him. If life was a card game, he was just breaking even.

Fortunately, there were a few occasional perks that helped sustain him through this bleak period. During a sold-out 1979 concert in Chattanooga, country music superstar Larry Gatlin gratified Calvin by telling the packed audience about the enormous impact that Calvin and the Sons of Song had had on the Gatlin Brothers' music. Gatlin's remarks were memorialized by Chattanooga *Times* reporter Nikki Hasden, who wrote: "Commenting on the three-part harmony that he and his brothers do so well, Gatlin paid tribute to the Sons of Song, who had greatly influenced them, and to one of the group's members, Calvin Newton, who sat in the audience."

In 1984 two feature stories on Calvin and his daughter, Jackie Sue, accompanied by color photographs, appeared in a Sunday edition of the Chattanooga *Times*. The article, entitled "Jackie Sue Newton Patterns Her Singing on Style of Her Dad," said that young Jackie had been influenced by her father in the same way the Gatlins and Elvis Presley had been. It also mentioned that Jackie had dropped out of ninth grade in order to pursue a singing career, although she continued her education at home. The other article focused on an extremely ambitious project undertaken by Calvin and his friend, Billy Warren, that involved a movie called *The Gospel Singer*. Warren, had filmed two small projects in the past: one was coproduced with Atlanta singer Tommy Roe and the other was a made-for-television movie.

In the article, Calvin stated, "The story line deals with the two personalities, the two sides of Cal Newton. Why I did those things comes in later in the picture. I was a preacher's son. My granddad was a preacher, and I saw the church do them wrong. I was searching for the truth." Staff writer Taylor Brooke added that the movie was being produced by a California company and that the movie would be Warren's third film. However, Warren couldn't raise the money to go forward with the project, and it never got past the talking stage.

Although now in his fifties, Calvin still had dreams of a career comeback. However, by then, he was considered a has-been in gospel music, which over the years had undergone a metamorphosis and had no identifiable center as in the old days. In the 1980s southern gospel music had taken a back seat to Christian music, of which one variation—Christian rock—featured long-haired kids singing ambiguous lyrics about a higher power while knocking out deafening power chords on Stratocaster guitars. Groups like the Statesmen and the Blackwood Brothers—four white men singing barbershop harmonies while backed by a piano—were dinosaurs. Even so, a few of the southern gospel groups persisted, including the Masters V, consisting of former members of the Blackwood Brothers and Statesmen quartets.

But even in the face of all the changes, Calvin desperately wanted to make a comeback, to show the world that he was as talented as ever. To that end, he made phone calls that went unreturned, wrote letters that went unanswered, and went to concerts and shook hands with people who said they would help, but didn't.

Consequently, Calvin decided to try something on his own. He and Billy Warren scaled back their Hollywood aspirations and instead collaborated on a recording project that culminated in Calvin's first solo album. The album's title said it all—*Cal Newton: Great Songs My Way*. The project consisted mainly of Calvin's unique stylistic interpretations of gospel standards. To help imbue the album with a black gospel feel, Calvin and Warren recruited a couple of young Chattanooga African Americans to sing backup vocals on the project, along with Calvin's daughter, Jackie Sue. The interplay between Calvin and the backup singers produced a delightful synergy on several of the cuts and illustrated the ease with which Calvin could traverse the various musical genres. Rock, country, white gospel, or black gospel—he was comfortable and adept with all of them.

What would otherwise be a fine album is marred by shoddy instrumental work and uneven production. The musicians frequently play wrong notes, but more irritating is their insistence on including flourishes that almost seem like deliberate acts of sabotage. Nowhere is this musical mayhem more abundant than in the opening strains of "Precious Lord, Take My Hand," in which the piano player literally attacks the keyboard in a maniacal frenzy for a few tortured moments. Calvin somehow salvages this song with a touching autobiographical recitation about his father, who labored in coal mines during the day and took a Bible study correspondence course at night so that he might be a preacher.

Creating pictures with well-chosen words and a subdued mood with his soft inflection, Calvin utters a truly memorable line: "Many times I'd come in late at night and his eyes would be closed, but his Bible would be open." The story continues with his dad eventually dying a miner's death of black lung disease and nobody attending his funeral, except Calvin and a few others. His voice now quivering with emotion both feigned and heartfelt, Calvin intoned, "One of these days there won't be any black lung and there won't be any dirt under his fingernails. He'll sit on the porch like he used to, saying, 'Listen, everyone, that's my boy singing. Listen to my boy.' " Then the boy sings the remainder of the great old song. Released as a cassette, *Cal Newton: Great Songs My Way* didn't make a ripple in gospel music record sales but nonetheless serves as strong testimony to Calvin's incredible musical versatility.

In the fall of 1988, Calvin dropped by to see a North Carolina business-man named Charlie Burke who also promoted gospel music. They remi-nisced about the good old days in the 1950s when Burke's semipro quartet, The Southerners, opened for the Sons of Song at a Sons' appearance in a nearby baseball park. The concert was memorable because it was the first time Bob Robinson appeared on stage after the wreck that nearly killed him. Calvin told Burke that he and Bob Robinson still wanted to do some Sons of Song appearances. "He thought that because I promoted music maybe I could help 'em, but he didn't realize I could sing much. He hadn't heard me in years," said Burke.

By that point Lee Kitchens was no longer making the long trek from Tampa to sing with Calvin and Robinson. The Sons had no baritone for those increasingly infrequent occasions when they sang somewhere. Burke told Calvin that he thought he could handle the baritone part. "I pulled out a couple of old records I had of the Sons of Song, kinda brushed myself up on them and we got together, the first night at the funeral home, if I remember correctly, and started singing some of them songs. Calvin got tore all to pieces, and he said, 'Man, you fit this thing.' "

And he did. Burke has a big, deep baritone voice, in the same vein as Don Butler. His voice blended well with the two other distinctive voices and anchored the sound as well. Calvin and Robinson picked up a complete package with Burke: they got not only a fine singer but also a promoter and a wealthy businessman, who later bankrolled a first-rate recording session for them. Burke immediately began using his contacts to secure bookings for the group.

"We drove out to Fort Worth and sang for W. B. Nowlin, on his pro-gram with the Stamps, the Singing Americans, and seems like one more group," Burke recalled. W. B. Nowlin's Fort Worth singings had become legendary over the years in southern gospel music. It was Nowlin (he is now in the Southern Gospel Music Hall of Fame) who originated the popular Battle of Songs, which fueled competitive zeal among all the groups who performed in that huge Texas arena. The newly re-formed Sons of Song were being well received by audiences, which usually contained a sizable number of hard-core Sons of Song fans. Burly and bespectacled, Burke didn't look like a member of the Sons, but his singing was excellent. With Burke, the Sons' harmonies blended, and he could step out and do a solo as well as Lee Kitchens.

By July 1989 the group decided it was time to do a recording session. Burke recalled, "I just footed the bill on the cassette. I got Ben Speer to produce it because Ben remembered how the Sons sounded." A great musician and gospel music arranger, Ben Speer would have seemed the perfect choice to produce any gospel music group—except perhaps the Sons of Song.

The son of G. T. "Dad" Speer—one of the first James D. Vaughn music teachers—Ben Speer clung to a rigid and dogmatic musical philosophy that had been inculcated by his father from the time Ben and his brothers and sisters were in the cradle. A profile of older brother Brock Speer in the *Singing News* stated: "Dad Speer was a perfectionist and there was no artistic interpretation! We had to do it right because that's the way I was brought up . . ." Artistic interpretation was the essence and hallmark of the Sons of Song sound. They had never sung a song as it appeared on a sheet of music; in fact, they often boasted that they never sang a song the same way twice. Now, however, they were coupled with a producer who had had it drilled into his head at a young age that you sang it just as you saw it on the page, and you opened your mouth so that the audience could understand the words. Needless to say, these differing approaches to music— orthodox versus unorthodox—led to a clash at the recording session.

One of the most distinctive group-singing tricks utilized by the Sons of Song was an old doo-wop vocal technique. In describing it, Jean Bradford noted, "Instead of landing on a note point blank, they would slur up to it and hang on to it in harmony." A musical maverick like Ralph Carmichael might think such a technique creative. However, during the session, the dogmatic Ben Speer found it offensive and told the group to cut it out.

"Why?" asked Calvin. "Because it sounds like the Ink Spots," Speer replied. What was wrong with that? Calvin wondered to himself. However, although Speer may have had some rigid views on the proper way to sing gospel music, he was also perceptive and musically sophisticated. He knew he couldn't keep the Sons of Song from being themselves, and the finished product revealed that he capitulated to their pop and rock stylings.

The album was recorded at StarGem Studio, a popular state-of-the-art Nashville recording facility favored by the country music crowd. Speer assembled six fine session players, including super-sideman steel guitar player Sonny Garrish. Gary Primm expertly handled the keyboard work, freeing Bob Robinson to concentrate on vocals. Bobby All, who played on the Sons' *Encore* session, provided tasteful acoustic guitar work. The superb musicianship was at the opposite end of the spectrum from the instrumental amateurishness on *Great Songs My Way*.

Ben Speer provided the instrumental arrangements while remaining true to the original Sons' vocal arrangments. Speer stopped just short of overproducing the session; the bass guitar should have been backed out a little more in the mixdown, but the final result was the finest recorded product to come from the Sons since the early 1960s. As expected, the Sons sang all the old hits again but with a precision that resulted from skill and experience.

Calvin and Robinson sounded better than ever, effortlessly singing tunes they had performed hundreds of times in the past. Burke had fine solos on "Hide Thou Me" and "Lonesome Road." For Burke to even attempt "Lonesome Road" was nothing less than an act of courage, as this was Don Butler's signature song—the number that showcased his jazz-influenced style. Burke did a fine job, his deep, booming baritone tracking Butler's stylings.

Burke had to drop out of the Sons not long after the recording session. He was a busy, successful businessman with too many irons in the fire to tour full-time with the group. By that point, another baritone candidate had entered the picture. Gospel gadabout Roy Pauley had mentioned to Calvin that he'd love to sing with the group if they had an opening for a baritone. Pauley, a columnist with the *Singing News*, had a full-time ministry with his wife, but was excited about joining up with the legendary group. Calvin and Bob Robinson were likewise excited about the possibilities of having Pauley join them. Pauley—tall, roguishly handsome, and personable—*looked* like a member of the Sons of Song, and his baritone voice blended well with the other two. Pauley's voice lacked the depth of Butler's, Kitchens's, and Burke's—the previous baritones—but he sang good harmony and was competent as a soloist. The three agreed to give it a try. They began by recording a video at a popular Georgia Christian nightclub, the Joyful Noise.

Calvin's friend Billy Warren, a videographer and recording studio owner, taped the video. Considering the lack of rehearsal, their performance was decent. The tunes on *Joyful Noise*, as it was entitled, included many of the Sons' standards. Everyone was excited during the taping. Pauley was pleased to be a member of such a legendary group, and Calvin and Robinson were glad to have a baritone with stage presence again, something missing from the Sons since the early 1960s and Don Butler. As Warren taped their performance he, too, was elated about the trio's possibilities. He kept saying to himself, "We got us a Sons of Song again." Calvin, always energetic on stage, was unusually animated throughout the video. Plans were made to tour. Pauley would give the group the oompf that had been missing since Butler's departure three decades earlier. It was going to be just like old times.

Then Robinson astounded everyone by abruptly moving to California to pursue church work. With Robinson gone, the Sons of Song were history. As Robinson himself once said, "If it didn't have me and Calvin, it wasn't the Sons of Song." It was back to square one for Calvin. He had taken some emotional jabs over the years, but Robinson's departure floored him. Another dream up in smoke. To add to Calvin's woes, shortly thereafter Wally Fowler died while on a fishing trip with his family. Calvin, Robinson, and Burke had done a tour with Fowler in the 1990s, who was then booking a lot of the older groups from the heyday of southern gospel music.

Calvin was now in his sixties, and a career in gospel music seemed out of the question. It was time to throw in the towel. But he still enjoyed singing in front of a group of people, so in late 1993 he became music director at the

Lookout Mountain United Methodist Church, joining Joyce, who was the organist. Wes Newton was also featured as a soloist and additionally served as boys' counselor on youth retreats. The job paid no money and no one came up after church and asked for an autograph, but Calvin was now singing music for all the right reasons.

Surrendering his dreams had been painful, but he realized that he wasn't alone. In fact, by the 1990s most of the southern gospel singers his age were also out to pasture. Some, like Hovie Lister, stewed in bitterness. It seemed the times had passed Lister by. Many of the young people in southern gospel music had never heard of him, and he was upset about being forgotten by an industry that he had helped create. As leader of the Statesmen, he had done some things in the 1950s and 1960s that he shouldn't have done, but he wasn't a bad person. His main shortcoming had always been that he had pursued the American dream—fame and fortune—a bit too zealously. Other senior citizen gospel singers also sat around and thought about the good old days. The old-timers of southern gospel music were simply no longer in demand and had nowhere to sing. But all of that was about to change, in a most serendipitous way.

32. The Holy Accident

I will arise and go to my father, and say unto him, Father, I have sinned against Heaven, and before thee.

—*Luke 15:18*

By the 1990s Bill Gaither had achieved fame and fortune as a gospel music songwriter and performer. Countless Gaither compositions, cowritten with his wife, Gloria, had been chart toppers, and many were prominent in church hymnals. In addition, Gaither had won the Dove Award—gospel music's highest honor—numerous times and had also been voted into the Gospel Music Hall of Fame. Over the years he had gotten involved in producing, publishing, and recording. His astute business instincts, coupled with a strong work ethic and musical talent, had made him both wealthy and powerful in the gospel music industry. Yet despite commercial success and material wealth, he and Gloria were deeply committed Christians who seemed to embody and personify the very best traits of the religion, particularly compassion and tolerance.

Gaither grew up listening to gospel music on an Indiana farm not far from Indianapolis. As a teenager he talked his parents into taking the family down to Nashville for an all-night singing. He was soon playing and singing with various local groups. After college he formed the Gaither Trio with his wife and his brother, Danny, who sang lead. Bill and Gloria Gaither had met while teaching high school, later married, and were high school English teachers until their success in singing what they called "inspirational" music required them to give up teaching. Their proficiency with words and language is apparent in their lyrics. A Gaither song is almost always richly textured and superbly crafted; their compositions are usually a collaboration involving Bill's music and ideas and Gloria's lyrics. Gloria Gaither never considered herself a singer and finally persuaded Bill to let her stop performing. Gaither then formed a new group, the Gaither Vocal Band, which, until recently, featured not only talented vocals but also the witty shenanigans of one of the funniest Christian comedians—Mark Lowry, who was the group's baritone. A happy person, Gaither loves laughter, and there is always a lot of it around him, often at his expense, particularly when Lowry is around.

In 1991 Bill Gaither assembled a group of gospel music old-timers in Nashville to record an album. He realized that many of those who had forged and defined gospel music in the mid-twentieth century didn't have many years left, and he wanted to get them together as a sort of last hurrah. To that end, he assembled the legends of gospel music—Jake Hess, James Blackwood, Vestal and Happy Goodman, J. D. Sumner—and others, including Larry Gatlin, in what he described as an attempt to capture and preserve the roots of gospel music. Gaither succeeded on a scale he never imagined. After the group had finished their work on the album, he had an employee videotape them as they gathered around the studio piano and sang old gospel standards. In taping the group, Gaither merely wanted to come away with a keepsake of the occasion; he didn't intend for the tape to be viewed by anyone other than himself and perhaps a few gospel music historians.

Gloria Gaither once remarked that—planning and goal-setting notwithstanding—the lives of most Christians are nothing less than a "holy accident." In hindsight, the videotaping of the group of aging gospel music singers who had assembled at Woodland studios in 1991 seems just that—a holy accident. By making a visual record of the session, Bill Gaither unwittingly changed the course of southern gospel music, and by extension the stalled career of Calvin Newton.

People associated with a popular religious television program learned of the videotape and persuaded a reluctant Gaither to let them air it. Gaither didn't consider the video to be of professional quality, but he nonetheless permitted it to be broadcast. The viewer response was overwhelming. Many wrote laudatory letters about how excited and pleased they were to see the gospel legends singing again on television.

Both a visionary and an entrepreneur, Gaither realized there was a market for a music product of this nature. He subsequently began churning out similar videos of gray-haired greats sitting in a semicircle singing, accompanied by their younger gospel contemporaries. Future efforts were much more polished and sophisticated than the first amateur taping in 1991. The actual videotape sessions were preceded by audio soundtracks recorded by various backup singers in a Nashville recording studio, then played back as the group selected to perform on the video sang along with it, a mild deceit that enhances the overall sound, making it fuller and richer.

The Gaither videos revitalized southern gospel music. Many dormant or abandoned careers were resuscitated through the relatively new medium and the adroit marketing strategies of the formidable Gaither business organization. Calvin saw the first video and realized what an appearance on a Gaither video would mean for his career. With tears streaming down his face, as he watched with friends and family in Birmingham, he said, "I should be there." When he got home, he sat down and wrote a heartfelt letter to Gaither, with the poignant line "Bill, nobody ever asks me to sing anymore." Joyce polished his remarks and mailed the letter to the Gaither organization in Indiana. He had no idea what Bill Gaither's response would be. Calvin was still shunned by many in southern gospel music, some of whom were now appearing on the Gaither videos. However, the response wasn't long in coming; in fact, he received an immediate reply, telling him to come to Alexandria, Indiana, for the next video and to expect to sing and be loved.

Bill Gaither recalled, "I told him, 'Hey, this is not a closed shop. You are more than welcome to come up and be a part of it.' The first time he came up he didn't sing any solos; he basically just sat and sang with everybody else and just soaked up the spirit. The next time he came up I had him testify and sing." Gaither's attitude towards Calvin was completely different from that of the powers-that-be who had ruled the southern gospel music kingdom during its heyday. Whereas they slammed the door of opportunity shut on Calvin, Bill Gaither opened it wide. Moreover, Gaither seemed to relish the role of the forgiving patriarch, welcoming home the various prodigal sons who had wasted their substance on riotous living.

Through the Gaither videos the world heard not only Calvin's heartfelt testimony about his rise and fall but also other sorrowful stories from those with legendary last names who had succumbed to various worldly temptations. Mylon LeFevre, Jimmy and Ron Blackwood, and Donny Sumner all confessed in tearful candor to bouts with drugs and other personal problems. Ron Blackwood had, like Calvin, served time in a federal prison. Donny Sumner got hooked on cocaine in Las Vegas in the 1970s when the group he sang with—the Stamps—were backing Elvis Presley. Jimmy Blackwood got involved in drugs when he left gospel music to play in a rock group. In his testimony he tells of having to call his parents, James and Mim Blackwood, who came to bail him out of jail, and, despite their unhappiness with the situation, told him first thing, "We love you, son."

Gaither explained his attitude towards gospel singers like Calvin, LeFevre, Sumner, and the Blackwoods in his book *Homecoming*: "As for the way singers have conducted themselves on the road over the years, I have to say there were inconsistencies, as there probably are today. These are people of clay and people who have failed, but they are also people who have asked forgiveness, and God has restored them. In my opinion, our videos are in many cases monuments to the grace of God, restoration, and reconciliation."

He added that "if a sin is under the blood and in the past, I'm not going to hold it against a person any more than God would hold it against them."

The atmosphere of gospel music changed dramatically under Bill Gaither's influence. Instead of the backstabbing and personal agendas at the expense of others, there was a spirit of love, fellowship, and camaraderie. The stars of southern gospel music were now in the twilight of life and delighted at the opportunity to have a forum to showcase their talents. Everyone seemed eager to put behind them the bitterness and acrimony that had pervaded the industry during its heyday.

Calvin appeared on Gaither videos the first year but was never allowed to sing a solo. "I was just a hummer," Calvin recalled good-naturedly. The next video was *All Day Singin'*. As the taping began, others stepped forward to sing solos as Calvin dutifully waited his turn. When it appeared that he once more was going to be passed over, Calvin later admitted, during a break he got off from the others and "boo-hooed like a baby." But near the end, his turn came—Gaither gave him the mike. However, before he sang, he had a piece he wanted to say. Because it amounted at least in part to a mea culpa and was highly personal, Calvin asked Gaither to turn off the cameras before he began. Thinking that Gaither had complied with his request, Calvin poured his heart out, with every word and gesture captured on videotape. His sincere, spontaneous utterances revealed a lifetime that had seemed to alternate between joy and sorrow, success and failure, agony and ecstasy.

At the end of his emotional statement the spellbound audience of gospel singers erupted in forgiving applause. In addition, his old arch nemesis, Hovie Lister, came over and hugged Calvin in a warm, loving embrace, a truly touching moment in which decades of bitterness and hostility evaporated in an instant. From that time on, the two were close friends; in fact, Hovie even helped secure bookings for Calvin, a 180-degree turn for the leader of the greatest gospel quartet ever.

Calvin then blew everyone away with his masterful performance of the old standard "Hide Thou Me." He has appeared on almost all Gaither videos since then and has had featured solos on several, including the opening solo on *Sing Your Blues Away*. Calvin's association with Bill Gaither and his appearance on the Gaither videos conferred upon him a legitimacy that he had lacked for decades. Suddenly, Calvin was marketable. He seized the opportunity by developing a ministry that limited itself to church appearances. Calvin would sing and give his testimony, detailing the decades of wasted years and how he had turned his life around. He would be candid, admitting that he had spent time in prison, sometimes, with a twinkle in his eye, characterizing his incarceration as "free room and board."

Calvin knew how to book appearances; he had done that for the Sons of Song back in the 1950s and 1960s. He used his appearances on Gaither videos as a calling card when he contacted a church about appearing there. The pastor was usually receptive when Calvin mentioned that he sang with Bill Gaither and could be seen on the videos. Occasionally, the preacher would respond that he had seen him. After years of struggling to book appearances, now he could almost choose when, where, and how often.

Calvin enlisted his long-time talented friend Jean Bradford to accompany him on piano, and his son, Wes, also performed, backing his dad and then doing a couple of solos, including his great version of "I Bowed on My Knees and Cried Holy." Wes also set up the sound equipment and sold tapes after the concert. Calvin had no set price; he sang for what is called "love offerings," based on donations by members of the church or an amount tendered by the church itself. The love offerings were sometimes modest but usually quite lucrative, with some dates paying more than he would have asked. Calvin was doing much better than he had done during the 1950s as a star.

One weekend in the mid-1990s, Calvin sang at a small rural church near Rome, Georgia. The pastor there mentioned to a friend of his that Calvin Newton of the Sons of Song had sung at his church. He did so because his friend was a huge fan of gospel music. The friend's name was Parnick Jennings. Parnick subsequently contacted Calvin, who came down to Rome to meet him. A wonderful relationship ensued.

Parnick Jennings was born and grew up in Rome, Georgia, where his dad owned a funeral home. His parents were religious, but Parnick stated that he wasn't saved until he received the call while attending church services in Brooklyn, New York, during his army days. Although he got a degree in journalism from the University of Tennessee, Parnick realized upon graduation that he wanted to work with his dad at the funeral home. Accordingly, he spent his adult life comforting the bereaved. He expanded his dad's business into a highly successful operation that eventually included his own son, Parnick, Jr. Parnick loved gospel music, and he decided to put his journalism degree to work by hosting a gospel music radio show in Rome during the 1950s; it became an area staple over the years. During the 1990s he began hosting a gospel music television show that was sponsored by his funeral home and that featured old black-and-white footage of the popular gospel groups during the fifties. He also began to produce old-timers' gospel music shows at the Rome City Auditorium.

When he met Calvin at the small rural church near Rome, the two struck up an immediate friendship. Parnick was inspired by Calvin's amazing story of sin, expiation, and redemption. In addition, he was captivated by Calvin's enormous talent and warm, charming personality. Calvin, in turn, was taken by Parnick's gentle, considerate, loving disposition. Although Calvin was a few years older, he quickly perceived Parnick as the older brother he had never had. Parnick became interested in Calvin's career, and began bringing Calvin into the Rome area to sing with the other gospel old-timers at the city auditorium. Many of the gospel stars of the 1950s, including members of the Homeland Harmony Quartet and the Statesmen, the LeFevres, and Jake Hess, lived near Rome or within easy driving distance.

It became apparent to Calvin that he was at a disadvantage at many of the singings because he was not in a group. Those in the audience wanted to hear the quartets sing their old popular songs in gospel harmony. Consequently, Calvin formed what he called the New Sons of Song, which was composed of him, Statesmen Quartet tenor Wallace Nelms, and former Blackwood Brothers bass singer Ken Turner. Nelms spent hours studying and learning to imitate the quivering, tearful vibrato sound of Bob Robinson. Enormously talented in his own right, both as a vocalist and a pianist, Nelms can render a good imitation of Robinson's voice. Turner, however, made no attempt to sound like Don Butler or Lee Kitchens. In addition, he usually insisted on doing his goofy air trombone skit that he had always performed when he was with the Blackwood Brothers. The three appeared together whenever Parnick invited them to one of his singings, but that was about it.

Nelms continued to sing with the Statesmen, too, and rarely had any type of scheduling conflict, since both groups rarely sang. If they appeared on the same show, Nelms simply did double duty. Calvin and Nelms also teamed up a few times with Big John Hall, a former Blackwood Brothers bass singer. Hall is an excellent bass singer, but neither he nor Turner fit the bill for the baritone/bass part. Calvin continued to sing on the weekends at churches with Wes and Jean Bradford, but Jean soon tired of the traveling. In keeping with the times, Calvin replaced her with a soundtrack.

By 1997, Calvin and Parnick were close friends. Parnick noticed that, despite Calvin's success in securing regular church bookings on the weekend, he still drove to his concerts in an old van that had mileage well into six figures. During the depression, Parnick's father had allowed people to barter eggs, vegetables, and other items to pay off funeral expenses when the family had no money. Having grown up witnessing such charity, Parnick also wanted to help others, particularly those who lacked material wealth. He asked Calvin what he could do to help boost Calvin's career.

Calvin mentioned that he didn't have any recent recordings to sell; in fact, the last time he had been in a recording studio was back in the late 1980s with Charlie Burke and Bob Robinson. He needed to get back in the studio so he would have some current CDs to sell as he toured. He could also market them by mail. However, a recording session sufficient for a compact disc would take three days. In a state-of-the-art studio, with a producer, session musicians, and background vocalists, the costs could easily run between fifteen and twenty thousand dollars. Like most, Calvin didn't have that type of money, and having a history of bankruptcy, he couldn't get a loan to finance such an undertaking. Parnick, on the other hand, was a man of means, and could easily assume the costs. The two struck a partnership: Parnick would pay for the recording session, thus becoming the executive producer, and would be repaid out of future CD sales.

Calvin was absolutely ecstatic at the prospect of making a new CD. Parnick insisted that it be first class, and the two decided on Bill Gaither's new ultramodern studio in Alexandria, Indiana. Arrangements were made and Calvin began selecting material and rehearsing his solos at home each day. In December 1997, Calvin and Parnick, now business partners, drove to Gaither Studios in Alexandria, Indiana, to record the compact disc to be entitled *Home Sweet Home*. Bill Gaither was supportive of Calvin's project and generously allowed Calvin to use prerecorded vocal and instrumental tracks on several of the tunes, which resulted in lower studio costs. Also, Gaither subsequently listed the CD in his product catalogs, which were mass-mailed to thousands, giving it tremendous exposure to gospel music fans all over the world.

An interesting footnote to the CD is that all of Calvin's vocal tracks were actually practice sessions. A recording session is often done in layers. The musicians put down a rhythm track; then the singer comes in and does the vocal part. After the rhythm and vocal tracks are put down, the producer will sometimes add other tracks, a process known as "sweetening." In this instance, Calvin sang vocal tracks for the session players to help them put down their instrumental tracks. Wearing headphones, the session players could hear Calvin singing, which facilitated their playing on cue. The track with Calvin's voice would be erased or simply not used, and Calvin would record his tracks the following day as he listened to the instrumental tracks. Unfortunately, Calvin sang himself hoarse on the first day and was unable to sing on the second. To inspire the musicians, Calvin had put everything he had into the first day's session. Even a strong, trained voice can become fatigued, particularly when the singer is trying to achieve the best possible sound.

Just as a football player can't perform with a muscle pull, neither can a singer go into a recording studio with a hoarse voice. With the studio time already booked, canceling would have been an absolute disaster. Parnick Jennings had already invested thousands of dollars. Calvin, wringing his hands, was beside himself with worry. Was this yet another catastrophe in a lifetime of horrible misfortune? It certainly appeared that way. Parnick gently counseled Calvin to trust in the Lord; everything would be all right.

Roger Byrd, the producer, also told Calvin not to panic. Possessed with a good sense of humor, Byrd called Calvin "Wild Man," having heard of Calvin's onstage and offstage shenanigans. Bryd suggested they review the accommodation vocal tracks that Calvin had recorded the day before to help the musicians get their parts right, and it turned out that they were just fine. The accommodation vocal tracks would become the final vocal tracks. Calvin breathed a sigh of relief while Parnick thanked the Lord.

Home Sweet Home is Calvin's best effort in a recording studio. Much of the credit for this outstanding CD has to go to Byrd, whose fine producing skills manifest themselves in the arrangements, choice of instrumentation, use of background vocalists, and excellent mix. Technically, the CD is as good as anything Calvin had ever done, equaling or surpassing the fine session Ben Speer produced for the Sons of Song in Nashville in 1989.

The tunes Calvin and Byrd selected for the CD were a diverse mix of public domain standards and newer songs. Calvin reprised "Sweetest

Mother" and "Wasted Years," songs he had recorded with the Oak Ridge Quartet and the Sons of Song. Also included were two Gaither standards, "Thanks to Calvary" and "A Sinner Saved by Grace," and Calvin's interpretation of these numbers was passionate and emotional. Jack Toney's lighthearted novelty song "Holy Roller" is a tune that seems to have been written specifically for Calvin. ("Holy Roller" was one of the main epithets that southern Illinois schoolchildren taunted Calvin with when he was growing up.) However, this song is upbeat (the Holy Roller is rolling to the Pearly Gates), and Byrd had the backup vocalists jazz it up with an Andrews Sisters sound on the chorus.

Both Calvin and Parnick were extremely pleased with the CD. It was a quality product, and sales were brisk. Parnick decided that the logical follow-up would be a video recording, which was made at the Rome, Georgia, city auditorium on June 11, 1999. Parnick enlisted the Rome Area Wide Choir to provide vocal accompaniment, and Calvin got Wallace Nelm to produce the venture. Calvin's grown children, Wes and Jackie, sang, as did Calvin, Ken Turner, and Wallace Nelms, singing together as the Sons of Song. With the support of Gaither and Parnick Jennings, plus his own maturity and commitment, things were beginning to fall into place for Calvin, and the best was yet to come.

33. Redemption

Bring forth the best robe, and put it on him; and put a ring on his hand, and shoes on his feet.

—Luke 15:22

In 1999 promoter Charlie Waller temporarily moved his Grand Ole Gospel Reunion to Birmingham, Alabama, from Greenville, South Carolina, where it had been held for the past several years. The yearly event featured southern gospel music old-timers—the stars of the 1940s, 1950s, and 1960s. Attendees would see and hear the Statesmen, Palmetto State, the Weatherfords, the Johnson Sisters, the Rebels, the Florida Boys, and many others as well, including Calvin, who sometimes would team up with Lee Kitchens and Jimi Hall for a Sons of Song number.

It was music by old-timers for old-timers. Senior citizens by the thousands had flocked to it faithfully since its inception in 1988. Someone pointed out that when Bill Gaither started bringing all the old gospel greats together to sing, Charlie Waller had already been doing it for several years.

The GOGR, as it was called, had been such a success in Greenville that hotel and restaurant accommodations had become inadequate. Waller sought an alternate site, and it wasn't happenstance that he chose Birmingham. Alabama's largest city has always been a gospel music hotbed, particularly in the 1950s when the city auditorium there would overflow its six-thousand-seat capacity once every month when Wally Fowler's all-night singing rolled around.

Birmingham in August is one of the hottest spots in North America, with temperatures frequently hovering near one hundred by early afternoon. However, it is the high double-digit humidity that makes outdoor activities unpleasant, foolish, or dangerous. August 1999 was worse than usual, and, to make things even more untenable, a long drought had pushed the temperatures upward where they remained for weeks.

Calvin and his son, Wes, got a taste of the Alabama heat when an overworked alternator broke down on their van as they came down Interstate 59 from Lookout Mountain. Noticing the glowing red dash light, Calvin quickly sought an exit. With the vehicle stopped, Wes flipped the hood and then jumped back as he surveyed the motor: it was on fire. "We got this guy to tow us to his garage, and he fixed the alternator, but we had to stand out in the sun for four hours. The guy didn't have an air-conditioned office and it turned out that was the hottest day of the year," Calvin recalled.

So accustomed was Calvin to bad luck and misfortune that by the time he got to Birmingham he was wondering what else would happen. As it turned out, quite a bit would, and all good. But first, Calvin had become lightheaded from the prolonged hours in the heat, and when he couldn't stop sweating he went to his hotel room and rested for about an hour and a half. He felt fine after that, so he freshened up and went downstairs to meet and glad-hand friends and gospel music colleagues. Most sixty-nine-year-olds wouldn't bounce back that quickly.

But Calvin Newton was not like most sixty-nine-year-olds. At the 1999 Grand Ole Gospel Reunion, he neither looked nor acted like a man a few weeks away from his seventieth birthday. In fact, he could have easily passed for someone in his mid-fifties. As he made his way down to the lobby of the spacious hotel where the performers and attendees were staying, there was a sparkle in his eye, a spring in his gait, and a quickness in his voice. He moved nimbly, smiling frequently and easily at the countless numbers who knew him, radiating personal warmth and charm. He joked with the men and flirted innocently with the women, recalling some minor incident that happened forty or fifty years ago. He didn't work the room like a brassy politician with an agenda, but like a grateful relative at a reunion, eager to see family. He seemed to possess confidence and humility in equal portions.

The Grand Ole Gospel Reunion is three days of almost nonstop gospel music singing and related activities, including a "This Is Your Life" program, midnight breakfasts, morning and afternoon songfests with much impromptu and improvised singing, and big four-hour concerts on Thursday, Friday, and Saturday nights. Calvin had been appearing at GOGR for years, but was never featured like the Statesmen or Florida Boys. The most Charlie Waller had ever allowed Calvin to sing was a couple of songs at the concerts, a virtual cameo role compared to many of the others.

In 1999 Waller had scheduled him onstage after midnight on Saturday, in essence tossing Calvin a crumb, while allowing the Statesmen, Lily Fern Weatherford, and the Florida Boys a lot more exposure during the early evening hours. Calvin accepted his minor assignment with equanimity. He and Wes could set up a record table and sell some cassettes and videos, including Wes's new CD.

Late Saturday night as the event was drawing to a close, Calvin was backstage chatting with a friend when Waller told him not to go anywhere because he was going to ask him and a couple of others to form an impromptu group and sing a couple of tunes onstage. No problem, Calvin replied, but he'd need to go back to the record stand to tell Wes. "Calvin, I don't trust you. You stay right where you are," Waller replied. Calvin was puzzled and upset by Waller's remark. He silently wondered, What does Charlie mean, he doesn't trust me? Heck, I'm nearly seventy years old. What does he think I'm gonna do?

Obediently, he waited backstage as Waller excused himself to go make some announcements. The first one was to name the newest winners of the Living Legend Award. Calvin had no idea who they would be, but at least he had a good vantage point from which to see the presentation. Waller dispensed with formalities, stating without fanfare that this year's inductees were Calvin Newton and Jerry Redd. Calvin was flabbergasted. Waller, who often comes across as brusque, never gave any indication that he held Calvin in such esteem or worthy of such a prestigious award. As he accepted the brass-and-mahogany plaque, Calvin felt both humbled and proud. He had always considered Jerry Redd the finest first tenor ever in southern gospel music. Calvin had sung with Redd briefly with the

Abernathy All-Stars in the 1960s. In turn, Redd had always considered Calvin the finest stylist in gospel music, which is quite a compliment considering that most people say Jake Hess. "Nobody can interpret a song the way Calvin can," Redd explained.

The Living Legend Award was actually the second prestigious award for Calvin during the late 1990s. In October 1998 Calvin, as a former member of the Blackwood Brothers, was inducted into the Gospel Music Hall of Fame. The Gospel Music Association inducts both individuals and groups, and when groups are inducted, all of the former members are included. Calvin received his Hall of Fame certificate in the mail from James Blackwood, along with a short congratulatory note.

Although Calvin had felt honored when he was inducted into the Gospel Music Hall of Fame as a member of the Blackwood Brothers Quartet, he felt both honor and sheer delight when he learned he would be inducted again, this time as a member of the Oak Ridge Quartet. He had only been with the Blackwoods for about seven months and was never mentioned in the various Blackwood Brothers' books that were published over the years, an omission tantamount to revisionist history. In addition, he wasn't invited to James Blackwood's home in 1995 when Bill and Gloria Gaither made a videotape there entitled *The Blackwood Brothers Family Reunion*. His feelings were hurt, but he knew that he had never really fit in with the serious, straitlaced Blackwoods. If James Blackwood didn't want to acknowledge that he had been with the group, it wasn't the end of the world.

However, the Oaks were one big happy family. All the former members felt especially proud when the current group made a difficult but highly successful transition to country music in the mid-1970s. Throughout the 1980s the dynamic quartet filled large venues and churned out hit after hit as one of country music's most dominant acts. The current group of Oaks likewise felt warmth and admiration for their predecessors, who had laid the groundwork that they followed to superstardom.

The Oaks appealed to country music fans primarily because of their tight gospel harmonies and their high-energy stage act, which had originated with Calvin and Bob Weber jumping over pianos or off stages, doing hilarious impersonations of other groups, and performing other crowd-pleasing antics. As writer Walter Carter stated, when Calvin joined the group they went from exciting to outrageous. Throughout their existence the Oaks always dared to be different.

Craig Havighurst of the *Nashville Tennessean* informed readers on the following day, October 31, 2000, that "[a]bout 12 members from various incarnations of the Oak Ridge, including 80-year-old Lon Deacon Freeman, were on hand to celebrate the induction of a group that began in 1945 as a traditional southern gospel quartet and evolved in the 1970s as a leading country act."

Smiles, laughter, joking and recalling the good times were the order of the day. Someone remembered when William Lee Golden ran the Oaks' tour bus into the back of the Speer Family bus, causing Brock Speer to collapse in a dead faint in Willie Wynn's arms. Golden's mishap prompted the story about the time when Willie hit a mule in Mississippi early one morning while driving at a rapid clip, knocking the poor animal through the front windshield of the bus, its huge carcass landing in a spot where Smitty Gatlin had been standing only moments earlier. Of course none of the Oaks drove faster than Calvin, especially when they were racing to arrive on time for their shuttle dates, singing in as many as three different places in one night.

It was a night for gaiety, so no one mentioned the group having to disband in the 1950s because they couldn't get bookings, even though they were one of the top five groups in gospel music. Nor did they talk about the early 1970s when the Oaks were ostracized by many in gospel music for letting their hair grow to shoulder length and dressing flamboyantly. They may have been the black sheep of gospel music, but they had fun and they had lots of fans.

The audience was treated to a rendition of the Oaks' big gospel hit "Jesus Is Coming Soon," sung onstage by all twelve of the inductees. Willie Wynn, Calvin, and Joe Bonsall sang first tenor; Deacon Freeman, Jim Hamill, and Duane Allen were the second tenors; Gary McSpadden and William Lee Golden were superb as baritones. Ron Page, Noel Fox, and Richard Sterban sang the low notes, while Tommy Fairchild played flawless piano.

Calvin had been asked to take some photographs, so he purchased a disposable camera and had Joyce take pictures of him with the current group of Oaks. He also wanted a picture of those who were sitting at the table with him and Joyce, so he called out to man seated nearby, "Hey, sonny, would you mind taking our pictures?" The man—dapper, debonair, and urbane—smiled graciously and said he would be delighted. Taking his time, he took several photos, making suggestions about posing, even displaying a streak of perfectionism. Calvin thanked the man, who once again smiled and said it was his pleasure.

As soon as the stranger was out of earshot, Gary McSpadden whispered, "Calvin, are you crazy? Do you know who that is—that's Tony Brown!" Brown—at the time, president of the huge MCA record label in Nashville—has been regarded as the most powerful person in country music for the past few years, Music Row's rainmaker, or hit maker. In the 1970s, he was Elvis Presley's piano player. After that, Brown played keyboards in Emmylou Harris's renowned Hot Band. Earlier, he had played piano for a short period with the Oaks as well as with J. D. Sumner's Stamps Quartet. Yet those accomplishments were nothing compared to his success as a record producer. Country music superstars George Strait, Vince Gill, Reba McEntire, Tracy Byrd, Patty Loveless, Wynonna Judd, and Trisha Yearwood have all relied on Brown to produce them, as have rising stars Chely Wright and Rebecca Lynn Howard.

Calvin's face flushed crimson with embarrassment at having turned a music mogul into a flunky. He immediately sought out Brown and apologized. Nonsense, replied Brown, dismissing Calvin's social blunder with a wave of the hand. Brown told Calvin he had grown up listening to him, and he admired and respected Calvin enormously. At the conclusion of their chat, Calvin asked Brown if he would let Joyce take a picture of the two of them. Absolutely, responded Brown.

A few days later, Calvin received the following note on MCA stationary:

It was an honor to see you at the Hall of Fame event. You have no idea how much your talent inspired me when I was starting out. I was blown away to get to see you again.

> You're the coolest.
> Tony B

That evening in the silence of his motel room as he held the impressive gold medallion he had been given hours earlier, Calvin reflected on the prestigious awards that had come his way in such a short period. Three terrific honors in three years: twice voted into the Gospel Music Hall of Fame and also designated a Living Legend by the Grand Ole Gospel Reunion and the irascible Charlie Waller. The seemingly endless drought was over, and the world had finally recognized him and his enormous talent. As Joyce slumbered nearby, he looked up heavenward, smiled, and said quietly, "Thanks."

34. Wasted Years . . . Why?

As a young man he seemed to have been disproportionately blessed. He had looks, charm, talent, and athletic ability. He also had that magical and magnetic trait called charisma, which over the years attracted women desiring romance and men who wanted friendship. Thelma Cook, wife of former Oak Ridge Quartet baritone Carlos Cook, said that during the 1950s women flocked to him like flies to honey. Countless others paraphrased Thelma Cook's observation. Indeed, the most common remark uttered by those interviewed for this book—both men and women—was that Calvin was a "ladies' man."

Yet if he was a ladies' man, he was also a man's man. Men admired him and cherished their relationships with him. More than one interviewee spoke of his physical prowess, including anecdotes of Calvin making short order of someone in a fistfight. Ron Blackwood mentioned that Calvin was the only man who consistently beat his dad—R. W. Blackwood—in arm wrestling. Unaware that others had said the same thing, several men confided, "Calvin and I were like brothers," to emphasize the closeness of their bond. He has a Rolodex full of names of people who speak of him with love and admiration. He maintains ties with the myriad number of friends he has acquired over a lifetime, even those going back to his childhood, six decades ago.

Calvin is unselfish, having loaned money to and done countless favors for friends and associates. In recent times he has booked many gospel groups for no fee. In the 1970s when a relative of Billy Warren's died, Warren wished aloud that Calvin could sing at the funeral. Penniless, Calvin hitchhiked to the funeral in a suit to grant his good friend's wish. When Hovie Lister complimented Calvin on a shirt he was wearing in 1999, Calvin went to three different shopping malls looking for one like it to buy for his old antagonist but new best pal.

There is probably no one more devoted to his family than Wesley Calvin Newton. Married now for over thirty-nine years, he and Joyce remain affectionate and loving. Performing at the First Baptist Church in Pulaski, Tennessee, in 1998, he told the audience about having gone to Ireland the past spring, saying that the next year would be much better because "Joycie" would be going, too.

In the past five years he has worked hard to develop his son's singing career, often intentionally saying and doing things onstage to allow Wes to overshadow him. With Wes standing beside him, he will relate some story about how Wes stole the show in Ireland or St. Louis or wherever they have performed recently. At the Grand Ole Gospel Reunion in Birmingham, he took Wes on stage with him and let Wes sing during the portion of the program when he himself was scheduled to sing. Promoter Charlie Waller was miffed until Wes hit some notes that had the audience standing on their feet, applauding for an encore. Calvin stood by beaming.

When his daughter married and his younger sister contracted lung cancer, Calvin purchased two mobile homes and put them on each side of his house so both could be close by and to help them out financially. Recently, Calvin heard from a younger cousin who was suffering from depression and was down on his luck. Calvin insisted the cousin move nearby so he and Joyce could look after him until things got better.

His high-spirited and often outrageous social skills have always captivated audiences. The normally reserved Don Butler once remarked, "When Calvin went on stage, nobody on this earth that has been birthed could handle an audience as master of ceremonies better than him." Carlos Cook, who was actually displaced as emcee of the Oak Ridge Quartet by Calvin, stated that Calvin could hold an audience in the palm of his hand.

Forty years after having heard Calvin's opening monologue at Haleyville High School, I quoted it back to him word for word.

There is an innocence about him that is truly amazing, considering his age and his life experiences, which include two terms in maximum-security prisons with murderers, rapists, child molesters, and Mafia figures. Bill Gaither recalled that when Calvin came backstage to meet him at a Chattanooga concert in the early 1990s, "He was still the wide-eyed boy that I remember him as—there was that brightness in his eyes." Calvin indeed has a lot of little boy in him. On one Gaither video in particular, seated with the other singers, his demeanor and behavior seem like that of an overly deferential child, almost desperately seeking attention and approval.

It would seem he had all of the ingredients for a successful, happy life—good looks, winsome charm, staggering talent, and championship athletic ability, plus a tender heart that caused him to look out for and be protective of family, friends, needy people, and animals. What happened? Given his capabilities, he should be an icon by now, right alongside Jake Hess, James Blackwood, Hovie Lister, and J. D. Sumner. The reason he isn't has to do with his self-destructive tendencies. Over the years, others may have shot him down, but he supplied the ammunition, more than once.

Why did he sabotage his life and others with wild hedonism and criminal activity? How could one person's identity change over a period of time from great gospel music singer to career criminal "well-known in law enforcement circles"?

One characteristic stands out above all others, and it is the key to understanding him: he is a paradox.

Kris Kristofferson once described Johnny Cash in song as "a walking contradiction—partly fact, partly fiction." Calvin can be equally contradictory. During his younger days he might have given you the shirt off his back, but the shirt might have been one he had stolen out of a car. As his female boxing manager once remarked, he sang like an angel but fought like a demon, something rarely said about anyone. And while he may have an innocence about him, he also possesses the wariness and cunning of an ex-con. He can be trusting but suspicious, sunny yet cynical, and both sincere and dissembling.

The personal warmth and charm can occasionally give way to furious emotional outbursts. A few years ago in a public setting, Calvin exploded in anger when Jimi Hall asked him when he was going to pay him for some work Hall had done for Calvin in a recording studio. After he disputed Hall's claim, telling him he didn't owe him anything, Calvin added, "I'll mop up the floor with you." Hall was more embarrassed than frightened by the tirade, feeling that onlookers perceived the two as a couple of ridiculous old codgers about to duke it out. Calvin realized immediately that he had acted inappropriately and regretted having caused the scene. As soon as he got home, he profusely apologized in a letter to Hall, saying that he was sorry he lost his temper and that he certainly didn't mean what he had said in a moment of anger. He added that he honestly didn't recall owing Hall the money, but that could have been due to a slight stroke he had suffered recently which had caused a memory loss. In addition to saying he was sorry, Calvin included a check for the amount allegedly owed. Hall was not mollified, later stating, "He hasn't changed a bit."

In the 1950s, when he was single, Calvin began having an affair with the wife of one of his best friends. Within days, however, Calvin and the man's wife became so guilt-ridden and shamed by what they were doing that they tearfully admitted the affair to the man. Each begged for forgiveness and received it from the stunned, hurt husband. The man remained married to his wife and with the passage of time Calvin resumed his friendship with the reconciled couple, staying in touch and periodically visiting with them over the years. The story reveals that while Calvin struggled with a good side and a bad side, in this instance, as in many, the good side won out.

When Calvin was doing a remodeling job on a house in the early 1980s he saw a boy nearby throwing rocks at a dog. Calvin told him to stop; the boy told Calvin that the dog was his and he would throw rocks at it any time he pleased. The next day Calvin was back with a pack of wienies that he used to entice the dog to jump in his panel truck. He took the dog away and gave it a new home. The dog is now old and infirm, but has lived a full and happy life since being rescued as a puppy. Calvin saved the dog by stealing it from its owner.

Calvin's male ancestors on his father's side were equally paradoxical, often spending six days a week raising hell, then all day Sunday praying it didn't come crashing down on them. Calvin's paternal grandfather, Ed Newton, spent his youth fighting with knives and his adulthood helping his preacher sons, even buying a huge tent for one to preach in. Calvin's dad and uncles were hellions early on but eventually became men of the cloth. Yet later, Calvin's dad soured on the church's restrictive rules, which he felt had possibly harmed his children's development. Consequently, he wrote a fiery polemic entitled "Our Apologies to the U.S.A." and submitted it for publication to the church newspaper, *The Evangel*. Soon thereafter, Leonard Newton quit the ministry, began smoking and drinking again, and years later had an affair with his wife's nurse, marrying the woman shortly after his wife died.

In an effort to better understand Calvin's contradictory conduct, one can begin by reviewing some of the more common criminological and psychological theories. Many professionals feel that heredity is the key to understanding how we behave. Others maintain that a person's environment—especially socialization through family, church, school, and friends—accounts for behavior. Unfortunately, the two are usually hopelessly intertwined, and this is particularly true with Calvin.

Calvin grew up in a harshly restrictive fundamentalist home with parents who forbade their children to engage in worldly activities such as going to the movies or participating in school athletics. The Newton girls couldn't wear makeup or jewelry. The message was clear: Christianity was serious business and not much fun. The consequences were especially severe— either toe the line or burn in Hell. Anyone coming of age under such conditions could easily feel oppressed, overwhelmed, guilty, and inadequate.

Like many in the depression era, Calvin's parents were extremely authoritarian, placing a high value on obedience and conformity and tending to favor punitive and forceful disciplinary measures. Calvin's older sister, Nora, a psychologist, stated that Calvin had so many limits put on his behavior as a child that when he attained adulthood he simply didn't know how to handle all the freedom he had acquired.

His parents rarely revealed affection for their children. "I knew my dad must have loved me because he worked hard to put food on the table, but he never told me," said Calvin. His mother and father were both good people and good parents, yet his need for love and affection from them was simply not met. Country music executive Buddy Killen observed, "When I moved to Nashville and witnessed firsthand the incredible self-destruction of some entertainers, I noticed a common background among them: almost without exception, they had love-deficient pasts . . . They were adults who, through no fault of their own, had seen their self-worth battered during their formative years."

Calvin's dad, Leonard Newton, worked hard to provide for his family on a coal miner's and then a preacher's wage, but there simply wasn't enough for frills or extras, and Calvin never forgot his somewhat austere upbringing. On a classification questionnaire at Atlanta Federal Prison, he was asked if his father provided for the family. In big, bold letters, Calvin printed, "Barely." Intellectually, Calvin realizes that his dad did the best he could. Emotionally, he feels that there should have been more.

Calvin's parents raised their son in accordance with the strict tenets of the Church of God, not realizing it would lead the headstrong young man to eventually rebel against all forms of authority. Yet obedience and conformity were not only mandated by the Church of God; they were also societal norms. Until the tumultuous 1960s, every facet of American society was imbued with the notion that you did what you were told by authority figures, and you did so without question. Calvin's free spirit rankled against such restrictions.

The cruel taunts of school-aged children who looked down on the Church of God bore deeply into Calvin's psyche, scarring it with hurt, humiliation, and rage. Calvin fought frequently as a young boy because he suffered the multiple juvenile social stigmas of being poor, a "Holy Roller," a preacher's son, and the new kid on the block because of how frequently his family moved. He came out of his youth feeling fear, anger, shame, and a strong sense of inferiority.

Reflecting on his life, Calvin says, "Basically, my *biggest* problem was I didn't like myself." Countless empirical studies show a strong correlation between low self-esteem and criminal behavior; in fact, low self-esteem is perhaps the most common trait shared by lawbreakers. In addition, he has also always been a quintessential risk taker. In Calvin's case, there is a relationship between his low self-esteem and his risk-taking behavior, borne out by his statement that "I was constantly trying to prove myself due to my feelings of inadequacy." Riding for miles on top of speeding automobiles, jumping off stages, and wading out into the ocean on a cold winter day were all part of his efforts to impress someone, which he felt was necessary in order to get approval and acceptance.

Recent studies by psychologists have led them to conclude that risk takers have distinctive "type T" personalities. Prominent scientists, athletes, and artists are said to be type T sorts whose risk taking has led them to important discoveries, amazing physical feats, and masterly creations. Einstein and Galileo are considered to have been type T personalities. However, psychologists warn there is a negative type T, also—those who are drawn to delinquency, crime, drug use, and a variety of other destructive behaviors. Calvin might very well fall into this category, given that crime and drug abuse are both risk-taking activities.

Bill Gaither, who has a master's degree in guidance counseling, stated, "He was quite an extraordinary talent, and a very explosive talent. I think sometimes with explosive personalities and charismatic kind of people like that, sometimes comes the other side, too." Gaither's observation is consistent with type T negative personality theory.

Calvin's abuse of amphetamines and other stimulants might seem puzzling, considering that he has always been an active, energetic sort. He was attracted to stimulants mainly because they heightened his self-esteem. With pills he liked himself, and had more energy, too. This led to more animated and outrageous stage performances, which delighted audiences and subsequently mandated pills before every concert. Bill Gaither has observed that Calvin is a perfectionist. Calvin believed that anything less than perfection from him was unacceptable to others, and the amphetamines deceived him into thinking he was coming close to achieving that.

In his autobiography, *I Almost Missed the Sunset*, the perceptive Gaither speculated on why people such as Calvin engage in self-destructive behavior. "One of the biggest causes of drug and alcohol abuse may be that we men feel intimidated, short-changed, and threatened in our society.

Some feel they have not received a fair shake, which can cause depression. That depression can lead to substance abuse and crime. Then, some who feel they cannot live honestly at an economic level they feel they deserve will do so dishonestly."

Support for Gaither's explanation is provided by Don Butler, who stated, "Calvin always wanted to live like the others who were successful, and he wasn't able to do so. He always lived above his means. He found the quickest way to do that as he saw it in his own mind was just to steal things and sell them and make money."

It is easy to construe crime as a type of rebellion, and Don Butler thinks Calvin's criminal acts were such manifestations. "Rebellion and frustration. Calvin had a long history of frustration within gospel music. He didn't feel like he was getting his due when he was with the Oak Ridge although he was the star. He rebelled against his upbringing and all the traditional things of the church. He had that anger and he had to have an outlet for it."

Calvin has not committed any crimes in over twenty-five years. We know that age is inversely correlated with criminal activity: that is, generally speaking, the older one gets, the less crime he or she commits. This process is referred to as desistance, or "aging out," and apparently applies to Calvin. He has obviously matured, and his remarks about being broken by the Atlanta federal prison lead one to conclude that he has also been deterred from future criminal acts. In fact, he is now a law-and-order person, complaining about criminals being coddled in prison and laws not being harsh or severe enough—perhaps this is another aspect of his paradoxical personality. There are no easy answers to the questions posed by Calvin's puzzling life. An acquaintance said, "He did those things because that's just the way he was; he was just being Calvin Newton." It is an explanation that may come as close as any to illuminating his inconsistent behavior.

35. Sunset

Standing at the top of the mountain he lives on, Calvin looks off into the distance for a long moment and then turns and says, "You know something? Every day is like Christmas to me now. I mean that; I've never been as happy in my life as I am right now. I'm happy because I'm surrounded by people who love me, and that is what life is all about.

"The most important person in my life is my wife, Joyce. I've never known anyone like her. She stood by me when anyone else would have said 'enough.' She never once thought about leaving me. She stood by me; she protected me, she fought for me, and she never gave up on me." He laughs and then says, "I'm not gonna kid you, in the beginning, she chased me—she meant to have me. Well, I'm glad she got me 'cause I would be dead now if it weren't for her."

"But just as I owe Joyce for having kept me alive, I owe Bill Gaither for having given me my career back. How can you repay someone who does something like that? I mean, I was an exile, an outcast, a pariah in gospel music for over thirty years. That man restored me, and made me whole, and I'll never forget that and I'll never be able to pay him back, but I'll be eternally grateful. I know some people have said that God sent me into their lives to help them. Well, God sent Bill Gaither into my life to help me, just as he did Parnick Jennings, too."

He stops and picks a wildflower, smells it, and then continues, "Would you believe that, even at my age, I have heroes? My son, Wes, is a hero. I thought about him when I was in prison, and he was just a little boy, but the man of the house. He must have felt so overwhelmed, but he never

313

complained. Now, he is a grown man, and a more gentle, loving soul you'll never find. Despite all the trouble I got into, he never stopped loving me, not for a single second. Now, he's not only my son, he's my best friend. We spend a lot of time together, and we enjoy every bit of it.

"Jake Hess is a hero of mine. Me and Jake go back over fifty years. We nearly starved to death together up in Greenville, South Carolina, but we were young and tough then. Jake's had health problems in the last few years but he's still performing. He's supported me a lot over the years and I'll remember that—always."

He lays the flower down tenderly and then looks off into the distance with sad, unfocused eyes. "So many of the guys I started out singing with are dead now. Hovie and James both passed away this past year. The Lord knows I butted heads with both in the distant past but any unpleasantness was decades ago and is now forgiven and forgotten. I loved both of them dearly and miss them enormously. There'll never be another two like them. I miss Wally Fowler, too. He gave the Sons of Song our first big break and then helped us again, many times, booking us and helping us get materials and recording contracts. Wally's never gotten his due, for sure."

As we turn to head back to his house he says, "The good Lord gave me the ability to sing. I often feel guilty when I hear of others who took singing lessons for years and still only sound average. I never had a lesson in my life. What talent I have is God given. I've received letters from all over the world from people who told me they were led to Christ after hearing me sing. I got several after my testimony on Bill Gaither's *All Day Singin'* video. You have no idea how gratifying that is, and I think that's the reason I was put on this earth—to minister to people through song. I'll keep doing it as long as the Lord will let me.

"I began singing gospel music professionally over fifty years ago with Melody Masters Quartet. They were the forerunner of the Statesmen and when I was with them we sang harmonies you wouldn't believe. We would all gather round an old Schure microphone to sing. Afterwards, we would sell songbooks out of the trunk of someone's car. Then we would drive all night for our next concert. Now, you have cordless mikes, digital recording, and Internet marketing. If you need to travel any distance, you fly."

"Southern gospel used to be cutthroat, and I'm glad it's no longer that way. Bill Gaither changed everything, and for the better. It was hard to make a living singing gospel music in the old days because most fans were poor and many didn't have the money to buy records or go to concerts. Now, people have a lot of disposable income, but they have so many different things to spend it on. There's all types of entertainment: cable television with sixty or seventy channels, theaters with twenty different movies to choose from, shopping malls with clothing stores, nice restaurants, and video games for kids.

"I had a great career singing gospel music, even if it was abbreviated. I sang with the Blackwood Brothers when they were the most popular group in the world. But I had more fun singing with the Oak Ridge Quartet than any other group. That group—well—we didn't have a clue; I mean, not a clue! The name of the game was have fun." He breaks out into a big grin as he recalls those days with the Oaks.

We continue our walk, admiring nature's beauty. He's silent for a moment, and it is obvious he is collecting his thoughts. Then he slowly begins, searching for the right words. "The Sons of Song . . . we were something special—no doubt. I've often wondered what would have happened if we hadn't had the wreck. All three of us had problems, but so does everyone else. I know this: for a brief, shining moment—a little more than a year—no one could touch us. We were the best. We sounded the best, we looked the best, and wherever we sang we always got the most applause, no matter who else sang with us. I don't mean to brag, but there's never been a group like the Sons of Song."

Overhead, he notices a commercial jet miles above. To the eye it is only a tiny, bright, metallic object in the distance. He studies it for a few moments as his little dog, Bimby, chases a butterfly. He then furrows his brow and says, "The tragedy of 9/11 caused most Americans to reflect on what our priorities are and should be. If any good came out of those catastrophic events, I think it was this: it caused us to turn back to our basic values of God, family, country, and freedom. Gospel music articulates those values, so when people ask me about the future of southern gospel music, I tell them that it's more relevant now than it ever has been. It's part of our culture, particularly in the South. So, I say to anyone pondering the future of gospel music—I'm pretty sure it'll be with us for a long time, if not the duration."

We walk a piece in silence; then, he stops suddenly and says, "I know a lot of people don't know what to make of me, because I did a lot of crazy, foolish things in my life. I just hope everyone remembers this: I paid for my crimes. I spent over three years behind bars—three years! More than a thousand days of my life I was locked up. Believe me, I was punished severely for what I did. I paid my debt to society—with interest."

"I've also paid for my sins. The Lord chastened me, but then through the power of his almighty grace, he forgave me. Every time I sing now, I sing to his glory."

As Joyce pulls her car into the driveway, arriving home from work, he continues to talk, holding forth about life, love, happiness, friendship, and lessons learned the hard way. While he once coveted money, jewelry, expensive automobiles, and other worldly possessions, it is obvious that he now takes pleasure in small things: flowers by the roadside, the companionship of a tiny dog, a handmade Christmas card from a friend, and watching *Judge Judy* on television with his wife. He realizes that people are more important than things. He never hated others, but now no longer hates himself. He was once his own worst enemy, but not anymore. Instead, he now acts like a person who watches out for himself—going for daily four-mile walks, resisting the occasional urge for a cigarette, and politely declining a second piece of cake.

At long last, he has obtained serenity, contentment, and peace of mind. After a lifetime of marching to the beat of a different drummer, he is now in step with the world—"politically correct," he calls it. He is still Calvin Newton, but he is older and wiser, kinder and gentler. The anger and unhappiness that once threatened to consume him have given way to maturity and wisdom. To borrow a phrase from the great African-American poet Langston Hughes, his soul has grown deep like the rivers.

While others his age sit on park benches, putter in flower gardens, or frolic with grandchildren, he travels thousands of miles a year, performing in churches and civic auditoriums, just as he did a half-century ago.

He and his two grown children, Wes and Jackie, have formed a trio—the Newton Gang—and are wowing audiences everywhere. Like the Sons of Song, it is a group featuring three soloists that come together to sing flawless harmony. Having recently lost thirty pounds through rigid dieting, he is close to what he weighed when he boxed as a middleweight. In his seventies, he is living life to the fullest, fueled by an indomitable spirit that never gave up.

Discography/Videography

Audio Recordings

1948—Blackwood Brothers

Calvin Newton, first tenor; James Blackwood, second tenor; R. W. Blackwood, baritone; Bill Lyles, bass; Hilton Griswold, piano.

All recordings are 78 rpm.

White Church	1142	Just a Little Talk with Jesus	Lord, Build Me a Cabin in Glory
White Church	1143	What a Friend We Have in Jesus	Riding the Range for Jesus
White Church	1144	Just a Closer Walk with Thee	When God Dips His Love*

*Calvin did not sing on this number; the first tenor part was sung by Cat Freeman.

1953 to 1956—Wally Fowler and the Oak Ridge Quartet

Note: Although the record label presents the group as Wally Fowler and the Oak Ridge Quartet, Fowler actually sang on only two songs that were recorded by the group from 1953 to 1956: "I Have But One Goal," and "In My Father's House." Calvin Newton did not sing on either of those two songs, according to Oak Ridge Quartet pianist Bobby Whitfield.

All of the Oak Ridge Quartet recordings between 1953 and 1956 were made in Nashville, Tennessee, either at the Castle or at Owen Bradley's recording studio, except for "Go Out to the Program," which was recorded at a radio station.

1953

Gospeltone	1058	In the Sweet Forever	I Have But One Goal
Gospeltone	1060	Crying in the Chapel	I Believe
Gospeltone	1062	This Heart of Mine	Someone to Care

Quartet members: Joe Allred, first tenor; Calvin Newton, second tenor and lead; Carlos Cook, baritone; Bob Weber, bass; Livy Freeman, pianist.
Session musicians: Grady Martin, guitar; Ernie Newton, bass.

1954

Dot	45-1200	I Wanna Go There	In My Father's House
Oak Ridge	45-1070	When He Reached Down His Hand	Life Is a Ball Game*
Dot	1201	Walk in the Light	Supper-Time

*Solo by Joe Allred

Quartet members: Same as 1953, except for Bobby Whitfield on piano.
Session musicians: Grady Martin, guitar; Ernie Newton, bass; Marvin Hughes, organ.

1955–56

Oak Ridge	45-1064	Go Out to the Program, part one, part two

Note: There were no session musicians on "Go Out to the Program," which was arranged by Calvin Newton.

Oak Ridge	45-1072	When They Ring Those Golden Bells	Rain, Rain, Rain
Wally Fowler	1066	I Wanna Be More Like Jesus	You'll Never Walk Alone

Quartet members: Same as 1954.
Session musicians: Chet Atkins, guitar; Owen Bradley, organ.

Oak Ridge	45-1074	He	I'm Gonna Live the Life I Sing About
Oak Ridge	45-1076	Tearing Down the Kingdom of This World	I Am a Pilgrim

Note: "Tearing Down the Kingdom" was arranged by Calvin Newton.

Quartet members: Cat Freeman, first tenor; Calvin Newton, second tenor and lead; Les Roberson, baritone; Bob Weber, bass.
Session musicians: Chet Atkins, guitar; Owen Bradley, organ.

1958 to 1972: Sons of Song Albums

Sacred LP	7-9053	*South's Most Colorful Singers*	1958

Side One: If You Know the Lord; Sometimes I Cry; He'll Make a Way; My Jesus Knows; Open Up Those Pearly Gates; Heavenly Love
Side Two: Something Within; What a Friend; Since Jesus Came into My Heart; I Asked the Lord; Roamin' River

Sacred LPS	6010	*Riverboat Jubilee*	1960

Side One: Old Camp Meeting Time; Lonesome Road; Heaven's Jubilee; When They Ring Those Golden Bells; O Rock of Ages; Somewhere a Voice Is Calling
Side Two: Lord, I Want to Go to Heaven; He's Everywhere; Amazing Grace; Sorry, I Never Knew You; Not by Bread Alone; Do You Know Jesus

All songs on Sacred Label were recorded at Radio Recorders Studio, Hollywood, California, and were produced by Ralph Carmichael and Earle Williams.

Session musicians on both Sacred sessions were: Bobby Hammack, piano; Lloyd Lennom, bass; Bobby Gibbons, guitar; Les Barnett, organ.

Sons of Song personnel: Calvin Newton, Bob Robinson, Don Butler.

Songs of Faith   105   *Wasted Years*   1961
Side One: Wasted Years; Highway to Heaven; Had It Not Been for You; I've Got Love; How Far Is Heaven; Psalms [*sic*] of Victory
Side Two: Thank You for Taking Me Home; If I Had My Life to Live Over; The Old Gospel Ship; My Little Boy Blue; I'm On My Way

Note: *Wasted Years*—SOF105—was reissued three times: on Big Gospel label as BG-SLP 112; on Gospel World Records as GW 105, entitled *I'm on My Way*; and on Zest as ZLP-1000, entitled *Songs of Inspiration*, with one additional song.

Session musicians: Not listed.
Sons of Song personnel: Calvin Newton, Bob Robinson, Lee Kitchens.

Songs of Faith   104   *Unto Him*   1962
Side One: Unto Him; Pass Me Not Oh Gentle Savior; Spiritual Medley; Have You Seen My Daddy Here; Sweetest Mother; Into the Light
Side Two: Anytime, Anywhere; Jesus Knows All about You; This Man; I'll Never Be Forsaken; American Medley; Songs of the Cross
Session musicians: Not listed.
Sons of Song personnel: Calvin Newton, Bob Robinson, Don Butler.

Songs of Faith   111   *Something Old, Something New*   1963
Side One: In the Garden; Way Up Yonder; Rock of Ages; I'm Building a Bridge; Whispering Hope; My Prayer Forever
Side Two: Precious Memories; Jesus, Use Me; Never Grow Old; Distant Hills; Take My Hand Precious Lord
This album featured a section of violins and arrangements on six numbers by Bill Justis.
Session musicians: Not listed.
Sons of Song personnel: Calvin Newton, Bob Robinson, Don Butler.

Songs of Faith   130   *Gospel Time*   1965
Side One: Home Is Where I Long to Be; My Questions Will Be Answered Someday; That's When I Call the Lord; Ashamed; I'm Just Beginning; Precious Is My Lord
Side Two: Sound the Alarm; I'll Read the Bible; Calvary; If You're Without Him; Daniel Prayed; I Walked Alone
Session musicians: Bill Purcell and Jerry Smith, piano; Wayne Moss, lead guitar; Fred Carter and Harold Bradley, guitar; Pete Drake, steel guitar; Fred Murphy, accordion; Lightnin' Chance and Joe Zinkan, bass.
Sons of Song personnel: Calvin Newton, Bob Robinson, Lee Kitchens.

Albums 104, 105, and 111 were recorded at Sam Phillips Studio, Nashville, Tennessee, and were produced by Bill Beasley.

Album 130 was recorded at Columbia Recording Studio, and was produced by Cecil Scaife.

White Church   12-1791   *The Sons of Song Sing 12 Lee Roy Abernathy Songs*   1971
Side One: You Can't Put a Price on Your Soul; Hard Labor; My God Goes with Me; Beautiful Streets of Gold; He's Such a Comfort to Me; All About Jesus
Side Two: Lord, I'm Ready Now to Go; I'm Building a Bridge; I'm Gonna Roll Along; The Big Boss; Connect Me with My Lord; Mom and Dad
Recorded at Lee Roy Abernathy's home studio in Canton, Georgia in 1962.
Produced by Lee Roy Abernathy.

Note: The album WC 12-1791 was reissued in 1996 as a cassette entitled *Calvin Newton Presents the Original Sons of Song.*

1957 to 1962—Single Releases with the Sons of Song
Decatur, Georgia

Fox	2143	Old Gospel Ship	He Knows Just How Much You Can Bear

Hollywood, California

Sacred	575	Something Within	Roamin' River
Sacred	576	Open Up Those Pearly Gates	If You Know the Lord
Sacred	579	Lonesome Road	Do You Know Jesus
Sacred	580	Amazing Grace	Somewhere a Voice Is Calling
Sacred	581	Not by Bread Alone	He's Everywhere
Sacred	582	When They Ring Those Golden Bells	O When I Meet You

Nashville, Tennessee

Zest	13	Wasted Years	I've Got Love
Songs of Faith	8020	If You Know the Lord	Open Up Those Pearly Gates
Songs of Faith	8029	Anytime, Anywhere	Into the Light
Songs of Faith	8036	In the Garden	Precious Memories

1959—Single Release as "Cal Newton"
Atlanta, Georgia
Produced by Bill Lowry and Cotton Carrier.

Scottie	240	Just As You Are	Every Feeling I Have

Recordings from 1980 to Present
1980—Cal Newton Family
Crystal Manufacturing   *Collector's Edition*
Side One: Jesus Loves Me; Momma, Can't You Hear the Music; I Wanta Go There; I Know a Man Who Can

Side Two: Lord, I Need You Again Today; We're Not Home Yet; I've Not Always Walked; He Keeps On Working My Problems Out for Me; Bride of Christ
Recorded at the Sound Room, Fort Oglethorpe, Georgia.
Produced by Lari Goss.
Studio musicians: Lari, Ronnie, and James Goss.
Cal Newton Family: Cal, Wes, and Jackie Newton; Jean and Carolyn Bradford.

1980—Sons of Song
Trail Records   TSRC 2160   *Encore*
Side One: Wasted Years; Sorry, I Never Knew You; My Jesus Knows; Spiritual Medley
Side Two: Walking Up the King's Highway; Sometimes I Cry; The Cross Medley; Jesus, Use Me; Pass Me Not O Gentle Savior
Studio: Tri-State Recording, Kingsport, Tennessee.
Executive producer: Tilford Salyer.
Studio musicians: Bobby All, bass; Russell Mauldin, drums. Bob Robinson played piano.
Sons of Song personnel: Calvin Newton, Bob Robinson, Lee Kitchens.

Cassettes

1984—Cal Newton
Crystal Manufacturing   *Cal Newton: Great Songs My Way*
Side One: His Last Prayer; Golden Bells; Amazing Grace; Precious Lord, Take My Hand
Side Two: Hide Thou Me; Just in Time; Till He Comes; What a Day That Will Be
Recorded at Voice of the South Studios, Atlanta, Georgia.
Produced by Billy Warren.
Session musicians: Not listed.

1989—Sons of Song
Ambur Records and Homeland Records   *Wasted Years*
Side One: Wasted Years; Old Camp Meeting; Hide Thou Me; Lonesome Road; Palms of Victory
Side Two: Mamma, Can't You Hear the Music; Going Home; Heaven's Jubilee; Sometimes I Cry; More of You
Recorded at Stargem Studios, Nashville, Tennessee.
Executive producer: Charles Burke.
Producer: Ben Speer.
Session musicians: Robin Mew, bass guitar; Bobby All, acoustic guitar; Mike Severs, electric guitar; Gary Primm, keyboards; Jerry Kroon, drums; Sonny Garrish, steel guitar.
Sons of Song personnel: Calvin Newton, Bob Robinson, Charles Burke.

1997—*Calvin Newton Presents the Complete Library of the Original Songs of Song*
Crystal Manufacturing

Volume One
Side One—If You Know the Lord; Sometimes I Cry; He'll Make a Way; My Jesus Knows; Open Up Those Pearly Gates; Heavenly Love; Something Within; What a Friend; Since Jesus Came into My Heart

Side Two—I Asked the Lord; Roamin' River; Old Camp Meeting Time; Lonesome Road; When They Ring Those Golden Bells; O Rock of Ages; Not by Bread Alone

Volume Two
Side One—Heaven's Jubilee; Somewhere a Voice Is Calling; Lord, I Want to Go to Heaven; He's Everywhere; Amazing Grace; Sorry, I Never Knew You; Do You Know Jesus; Precious Memories
Side Two—Jesus Use Me; Never Grow Old; Distant Hills; Take My Hand Precious Lord; In the Garden; Way Up Yonder; My Prayer Together

Volume Three
Side One—Wasted Years; Highway to Heaven; Had It Not Been for You; I've Got Love; How Far Is Heaven; Palms of Victory; Thank You for Taking Me Home; If I Had My Life to Live Over
Side Two—The Old Gospel Ship; My Little Boy Blue; I'm on My Way; A Soul Is Saved; I'm Building a Bridge; Whispering Hope; Heaven's Jubilee

Volume Four
Side One—Unto Him; Pass Me Not Oh Gentle Savior; Spiritual Medley; Have You Seen My Daddy Here; Sweetest Mother; Into the Light; Anytime, Anywhere; Jesus Knows All About You
Side Two—This Man; I'll Never Be Forsaken; American Medley; Songs of the Cross; You Can't Put a Price On Your Soul; Hard Labor; My God Goes with Me; All About Jesus; Lord, I'm Ready Now to Go

Volume Five—"The only live concert ever recorded by the original Sons of Song. This is the way it was, folks."
Side One—Introduction; Jesus Use Me; Something Within; Open Up Those Pearly Gates; Calvary; I Don't Know Why (Sometimes I Cry); Heaven's Jubilee; Lonesome Road
Side Two—Highway to Heaven; Sorry, I Never Knew You; Wasted Years; Pass Me Not; Old Gospel Ship; Amazing Grace

Note: Although advertised as the original Sons of Song, the group is actually composed of Calvin Newton, Bob Robinson, and Lee Kitchens. The sound quality is extremely poor, which mars the re-creation of what appears to have been an outstanding concert. Of interest is that Lee Kitchens served as the emcee. Calvin stated that when his behavior became erratic in the mid-1960s, promoters insisted that someone else be the emcee.

Neither Calvin nor Kitchens can recall where the recording was made. Their best guess is either St. Louis or Atlanta, sometime around 1965.

Compact Disc
1998—*Calvin Newton*
No label   PB2550   *Home Sweet Home*
My Home Sweet Home; The Old Account Was Settled Long Ago; Sweetest Mother; Sin Ain't Nothin' but the Blues; When the Savior Reached Down for Me; I Go to the Rock; Thanks to Calvary; Holy Roller; At the Altar; Wasted Years; Sinner Saved by Grace; Leave It There

Recorded at Gaither Studios, Alexandria, Indiana.
Executive producer: Parnick Jennings.
Producer: Roger Byrd.
Session musicians: Dane Clark, drums; Steve Dokken, bass; Sandy Williams, guitar; Mike Close, keyboards; Chris Leiber, synthesizer.
Background vocals: Marsh Hall, Craig Patty, Cozette Myers, Shelly Harris.

Videos

1991—Sons of Song
Cal Newton Presents . . . Sons of Song—"Joyful Noise"
Follow Me; Little Boy Blue; Jesus, Use Me; Since Jesus Came into My Heart; Something Within Me; Pearly Gates; Old Gospel Ship; Sorry, I Never Knew You; Pass Me Not; He Reached Down His Hand
Recorded at Joyful Noise Supper Club, Atlanta, Georgia.
Videographer and producer: Billy Warren.
Personnel: Calvin Newton, Bob Robinson, Roy Pauley.

1999—Sons of Song
Vintage Video: The Gospel Music Hall of Fame Video Library Series
Executive producer: Wally Fowler.
Released individually as volumes 8, 20, and 21 and collectively with all three as Limited Collector's Edition. These videos are black-and-white footage of the Sons of Song's appearances on Wally Fowler's television show in the early 1960s.

Volume 8—Wasted Years; Highway to Heaven; Amazing Grace; The Old Gospel Ship; Something Within; Lonesome Road; How Far Is Heaven; God Is Everywhere; Had It Not Been for You; Heaven's Love

Volume 20—Heavenly Love; Had It Not Been for You; Follow Me; Take My Hand, Precious Lord; Since Jesus Came into My Heart; This Little Light of Mine; In My New Home; Unto Him; This Man; He Will Meet You There; Spiritual Medley; Anytime, Anywhere; Pass Me Not Oh Gentle Savior; Into the Light; Do You Know Jesus; Heaven's Jubilee

Volume 21—Oh When I Meet You Up in Heaven; I Know the Lord Will Make a Way; Lord, I Want to Go to Heaven; Sorry, I Never Knew You; My Prayer Forever; I've Got Love; When They Ring Those Golden Bells; One Night When Things Went Right for Me; You Can't Put a Price On Your Soul; If I Had My Life to Live Over; Ole Camp Meeting Day; My God Goes with Me

1999—Calvin Newton
Calvin Newton & Friends Live: In Concert
I Sing Because; Thanks to Calvary; Joy Comes in the Morning; Holy Roller; I Know a Man Who Can; The Longer I Serve Him; Does Jesus Care; Wasted Years; One Day at a Time; Highway to Heaven; He's Everywhere; Jesus Use Me; Hide Thou Me; I Bowed On My Knees and Cried Holy (Wes Newton solo); I Believe in You; Amazing Grace (Jackie Newton solo)

Recorded at Rome, Georgia, city auditorium on June 11, 1999.

Executive producer: Parnick Jennings.

Producer: Wallace Nelm.

Also appearing: Rome Area Wide Choir, Wes Newton, Jackie Sue Newton, and Calvin Newton, Wallace Nelm, and Ken Turner as the Sons of Song.

Note: Calvin Newton has also appeared on numerous Bill Gaither videos.

The author is deeply indebted to those listed below for providing information about and recordings of the various groups Calvin Newton recorded with over the years:

Blackwood Brothers—Hilton Griswold and Ed Gosa

Oak Ridge Quartet—Bobby Whitfield

Sons of Song—Don Butler, Calvin Newton, Johnny Carter, and especially gospel music historian John Crenshaw, Jr.

Sources

Books

Angle, Paul M. *Bloody Williamson: A Chapter in American Lawlessness.* Chicago: University of Illinois Press, 1952.

Bak, Richard. *Joe Louis: The Great Black Hope.* Dallas: Taylor Publishing, 1996.

Barnes, Margaret Anne. *The Tragedy and the Triumph of Phenix City, Alabama.* Macon: Mercer University Press, 1998.

Bronson, Fred. *The Billboard Book of Number One Hits.* New York: Billboard Books, 1992.

Bufwack, Mary, and Robert K. Oermann. *Finding Her Voice: The Saga of Women in Country Music.* New York: Crown Publishers, 1993.

Carmichael, Ralph. *He's Everything to Me.* Waco, TX: Word Publishing, 1986.

Carter, Walter, and Ellis Widner. *The Oak Ridge Boys: Our Story.* Chicago: Contemporary Books, 1987.

Colson, Charles W. *Born Again.* USA: Chosen Books, 1976.

———. *Life Sentence.* USA: Chosen Books, 1979.

Conn, Charles W. *Like a Mighty Army: A History of the Church of God.* Cleveland, TN: Pathway Press, 1996.

DeNeal, Gary. *A Knight of Another Sort: Prohibition Days and Charlie Birger.* USA: Shawnee Press, 1998.

Dennis, Allen. *James Blackwood Memories.* USA: Quail Ridge Press, 1997.

Escott, Colin, and Martin Hawkins. *Good Rockin' Tonight: Sun Records and the Birth of Rock 'n' Roll.* New York: St. Martins Press, 1990.

———. *Sun Records: The Brief History of the Legendary Record Label.* New York: Quick Fox, 1980.

Feiden, Doug. *The Ten Million Dollar Getaway: The Inside Story of the Lufthansa Heist.* New York: Jove Publications, 1980.

Fishbein, Diana H., and Susan E. Pease. *The Dynamics of Drug Abuse.* Boston: Allyn and Bacon, 1996.

Fisher, Eddie, and David Fisher. *Been There, Done That.* New York: St. Martin's Press, 1999.

Gaither, Bill. *I Almost Missed the Sunset.* Nashville: Thomas Nelson Publishers, 1992.

Gaither, Bill, and Jerry Jenkins. *Homecoming: The Story of Southern Gospel Music Through the Eyes of Its Best-Loved Performers.* Grand Rapids: Zondervan Publishing, 1997.

Garofalo, Reebee. *Rockin' Out: Popular Music in the USA*. Boston: Allyn and Bacon, 1997.

Goff, James R., Jr. *Close Harmony: A History of Southern Gospel*. Chapel Hill: University of North Carolina Press, 2002.

Guralnick, Peter. *Last Train to Memphis: The Rise of Elvis Presley*. Boston: Little, Brown and Company, 1994.

Hess, Jake, with Richard Hyatt. *Nothin' But Fine: The Music and the Gospel According to Jake Hess*. Columbus: Buckland Press, 1996.

Hull, Kenneth C. *Lily May: A Legend in Our Time*. USA: Kenneth Hull, 1985.

Jorgensen, Ernst J. *Elvis Presley—A Life in Music: The Complete Recording Sessions*. New York: St. Martin's Press, 1998.

Killen, Buddy, with Tom Carter. *By the Seat of My Pants*. New York: Simon & Schuster, 1993.

Kingsbury, Paul, ed. *The Encyclopedia of Country Music*. New York: Oxford University Press, 1998.

Larkin, Colin, ed. *The Guinness Encyclopedia of Popular Music*. Middlesex, England: Guinness Publishing, 1992.

Lesher, Stephan. *George Wallace: American Populist*. New York: Addison-Wesley, 1994.

Louis, Joe, Art Rust, Jr., and Edna Rust. *Joe Louis: My Life*. New York: Harcourt Brace Jovanovich, 1978.

Moore, Scotty, with James Dickerson. *That's Alright, Elvis*. New York: Schirmer Books, 1997.

Newton, John. *Out of the Depths: The Autobiography of John Newton*. London: C. J. Francombe & Sons, Ltd., 1925.

O'Brien, Darcy. *Murder in Little Egypt*. New York: William Morrow, 1990.

Oerman, Robert K. *A Century of Country: An Illustrated History of Country Music*. New York: TV Books, 1999.

Perkins, Carl, with David McGee. *Go, Cat, Go!* New York: Hyperion Press, 1996.

Racine, Kree J. *Above All: The Fascinating and True Story of the Lives of the Blackwood Brothers Quartet*. Memphis: Jarodoce Publications, 1967.

Rambo, Buck, and Bob Terrell. *The Legacy of Buck and Dottie Rambo*. Nashville: Star Publishing, 1992.

Roland, Tom. *The Billboard Book of Number One Country Hits*. New York: Billboard Books, 1991.

Russell, Herbert K. *A Southern Illinois Album*. USA: Shawnee Books, 1990.

Stamper, Pete. *It All Happened in Renfro Valley*. Lexington: University Press of Kentucky, 1999.

Swift, Catherine. *John Newton*. Minneapolis: Bethany House Publishers, 1991.

Taylor, David L. *Happy Rhythm: A Biography of Hovie Lister & The Statesmen Quartet*. Lexington, IN: TaylorMade WRITE, 1994.

Terrell, Bob. *The Chuck Wagon Gang: A Legend Lives On*. USA: Bob Terrell, 1990.

———. *The Life and Times of J. D. Sumner*. Nashville: J. D. Sumner, 1994.

———. *The Music Men: The Story of Professional Gospel Quartet Singing*. Asheville, NC: Bob Terrell, 1990.

Terrell, Bob, and J. D. Sumner. *Elvis: His Love for Gospel Music and J. D. Sumner*. Nashville: WCI Publishing, 1991.

Warner, Jay. *Just Walkin' in the Rain*. Los Angeles: Renaissance Books, 2001.

Watkins, T. H. *The Great Depression: America in the 1930s*. New York: Little, Brown, 1993.

Weatherford, Lily Fern, and Gail Shadwell. *With All My Heart: A Life in Gospel Music*. Carrollton, TX: Alliance Press, 1999.

Whiteside, Jonny. *Cry: The Johnnie Ray Story*. New York: Barricade Books, 1992.

Woodroof, Horace. *Stone Wall College*. Nashville: Aurora Publishers, 1970.

Wolfe, Charles K. *Classic Country: Legends of Country Music*. New York: Routledge, 2001.

——. *In Close Harmony: The Story of the Louvin Brothers*. Jackson: University Press of Mississippi, 1996.

——. *Kentucky Country: Folk and Country Music of Kentucky*. Lexington: University Press of Kentucky, 1982.

——. *Mahalia Jackson*. New York: Chelsea House Publishers, 1990.

Wolff, Daniel. *You Send Me: The Life and Times of Sam Cooke*. New York: Quill, 1995.

Booklets

Scott, W. *A History and Information Booklet of USP Atlanta*, 1998.

Brushy Mountain State Prison Tour Guide Visitor Booklet

Periodicals

Birmingham News

Breckinridge (Kentucky) News

Chattanooga Times

Columbus (Georgia) Enquirer

Fort Lauderdale Sun Sentinel

Good News (newsletter for the Gospel Music Association)

Gospel Singing World

Gospel Voice

Haleyville (Alabama) Advertiser

Jubilee, The Newsletter of Prison Fellowship

Life

Nashville Banner

Owensboro (Kentucky) Daily Messenger

Saturday Evening Post

Singing News

Sons of Song Fan Newsletter

Time

Robertson County (Tennessee) Times

Winston Salem (North Carolina) Journal

Public Records

Charlotte, North Carolina, Police Department
Federal Bureau of Prison Documents Obtained under the Freedom of Information Act
Robertson County, Tennessee, Criminal Court Clerk's Office
Tennessee Department of Correction Prison Documents
United States Senate Subcommittee Report. *Staff Study of the United States Penitentiary, Atlanta, Georgia.* Permanent Subcommittee on Investigations of the Committee on Governmental Affairs, United States Senate. January 1980.

Videos

Bill and Gloria Gaither present *All Day Singin' and Dinner on the Ground with Their Homecoming Friends.* Gaither Video Series. Alexandria, IN: Gaither Music Company, 1995.

Bill and Gloria Gaither present *The Blackwood Brothers Family Reunion.* Gaither Video Series. Alexandria, IN: Gaither Music Company, 1995.

Bill and Gloria Gaither present *Hovie Lister and the Sensational Statesmen—An American Classic.* Gaither Video Series. Alexandria, IN: Gaither Music Company, 1994.

Bill and Gloria Gaither present *O Happy Day Old-Time Southern Singing Convention.* Gaither Video Series. Alexandria, IN: Gaither Music Company, 1994.

Gaither Gospel Series Hall of Honor, Volume II. *The Gatlin Brothers Come Home.* Alexandria, IN: Spring House Music Group, 1997.

The History of Southern Gospel Music, Volumes 1 and 2. Valley Village, CA: Greystone Communications, 1997.

Index